WHERE HAVE YOU GONE, HARRY TRUMAN?

Also by Stanley A. Weiss

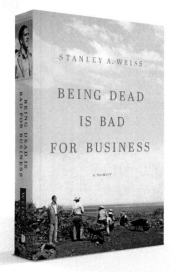

Most of us spend our lives
talking ourselves out of things.
But what could you accomplish if
you never held yourself back?

What if, despite your fears,
you went for broke every time?

You might live a life as extraordinary
as the one Stanley Weiss has lived
for nearly a century.

A skinny Jewish kid from Philadelphia training to fight and likely die in the US invasion of Japan in 1945, Stanley Weiss came home to the death of his loving but weak father, who left his mother penniless. Vowing on the spot not to let his insecurities limit him as they had his father, Weiss pledged that his mother would never have to worry.

Inspired by a Humphrey Bogart movie, Weiss moved to a foreign country to hunt for treasure—where Rule Number One was "Don't Die." Along the way, his zest for living has taken him from the company of legendary artists and poets in Mexico, to writers and beatniks in 1960s San Francisco and Hollywood; from drunken nights with a notorious spy to friendships with three of the men who played James Bond; from glamorous parties in Gstaad and Phuket to power politics in London and Washington, DC. A story of growth, tenacious focus, and good humor, it stretches from the days of "Don't Die" to Weiss's response when asked why business executives were interested in preventing nuclear war: "Being dead is bad for business."

For those who believe the world is shaped by ordinary people who push themselves to do extraordinary things, Stanley Weiss's story will inspire and surprise while reminding us all that being dead is bad for business—and being boring is bad for life.

"Rumbustious, warm and disarmingly candid . . .
This is an astonishing life, recounted with humor and wit."

—*The Wall Street Journal*

WHERE HAVE YOU GONE, HARRY TRUMAN?

SELECTED WORKS

STANLEY A. WEISS

AUSTIN   NEW YORK

Published by Disruption Books
Austin, TX, and New York, NY
www.disruptionbooks.com

Distributed by Disruption Books

For ordering information or special discounts for bulk purchases, please contact Disruption Books at info@disruptionbooks.com.

The article "Consumers, Environmentalists Would Benefit from NAFTA" is reprinted by permission of *The Christian Science Monitor*.
The article "Because of NAFTA, Eyes of The World Are on Chiapas and Mexico Cares" is reprinted by permission of the *Houston Chronicle*.
The article "When Closed Means Open: How the Pentagon is Backing Off its Pork-Barrel Pledge" is reprinted with permission of *The Washington Post*.

Cover design, text design, and composition by Kimberly Lance

Print ISBN: 978-1-63331-019-3
eBook ISBN: 978-1-63331-020-1

First Edition

Contents

INTRODUCTION

Bravery Where I See It

I WAS PRETTY SURE THE ROOM WAS BUGGED.

I was in Moscow in the summer of 1961 with my business partner, Ara Oztemel, to close a deal to buy chrome from the Soviet Union and import it into the United States. It was a remarkable deal, coming at the height of the Cold War. Shortly before my visit, Soviet premier Nikita Khrushchev had, in President John F. Kennedy's own words, "beat the hell out of" Kennedy at their only summit meeting in Vienna. Construction on the Berlin Wall was about to begin, and the Cuban Missile Crisis was still a year away.

But for now, my biggest problem was whether my hotel room was bugged. "God, I wish I had more soap," I had mused aloud into the empty room. Not a minute later, a hotel attendant had arrived at my door—with more soap.

That chrome deal was an early preview of what I would come to preach in my columns later on—that economic ties can thrive where politics and ideology divide. No matter what insults were being traded on the international stage, business could play a helpful role in building international relationships and bringing a practical perspective to policy. This realization would lead me, 20 years later, to start Business Executives for National Security (BENS) and begin writing opinion pieces on everything from nuclear proliferation to politics in countries from Mexico to Indonesia.

But it would take years to get there.

By any measure, I've lived my life to the fullest. Selling everything and going for broke to follow my girlfriend to Paris. Befriending British diplomat Guy Burgess on the way back, only to discover later that he was a member of the Cambridge Five spy ring. Moving to Mexico in search of gold as an impulsive young college student on the G.I. Bill in the early 1950s, inspired by the movie *The Treasure of the Sierra Madre*. Following trails of ants, scuffing my hands and knees, and wiggling into narrow mine shafts as I built my successful business in minerals from the ground up—literally.

I've gotten to know Bond, James Bond, three times over, in the person of Sean Connery, Roger Moore, and Pierce Brosnan. I spent a long night drinking with Richard Burton as his girlfriend, actress Elizabeth Taylor, waited back in his hacienda. I watched the counterculture movement explode before my eyes in 1960s San Francisco and was there when police dogs attacked anti-war protesters in Chicago's Grant Park at the Democratic National Convention in 1968. I produced a cult Western classic, *The Hired Hand*, starring a young Peter Fonda. I became close friends with two intellectual giants who were also close friends and agreed about nothing—William F. Buckley and John Kenneth Galbraith.

"If you can't take a risk, you can't make a gain," the man in the white hat says in *The Treasure of the Sierra Madre*. By the time I celebrated my 50th birthday, I'd taken plenty of risks and made plenty of gains. I'd played the angles, and then I'd played it straight. I'd built a business. I'd become a successful man. Not bad for a Jewish kid from south Philadelphia who dropped out of college.

But I felt something was missing. I wanted to feel like my life was worth something more. I wanted to give back to my country.

My struggle for a worthy purpose took me to Harvard, where in 1977 I became—at the urging of Galbraith—the Business Fellow at the Center for International Studies. Much of that year at Harvard was spent listening to conversations among a number of Harvard and MIT experts. I called them the Nuclear Theologians, and the gist of what they had to say was, "We have only 32,000 nukes, and the Soviets have 34,000. We're in deep trouble." I thought that was insane. I thought the right question was, how do we prevent even one nuclear weapon from falling on us or one of our allies?

That's why, after a few more endeavors (like starting an ill-fated political party that helped teach me what I *didn't* want ruling over me) I founded BENS—not as a think tank, but as a "do tank." We were a group of business executives using our successful business practices to propose solutions on some of the most pressing national security issues.

Why did a group of business executives care about the nuclear danger? Well, as I once told *Today Show* co-host Jane Pauley, and as I've repeated frequently since—including in the title of my 2017 memoir—being dead is bad for business.

To make an impact, I needed to get our name and our positions into the policy debate. That's when I started writing op-eds and columns, and that's where this anthology begins. As the Reagan administration's tough talk and big defense expenditures drove the confrontation with the Soviet Union to its height, I pressed the case for never using a single nuclear weapon again and for spending prudently on the military. Back then, of course, presidential tough talk was "Tear down this wall"—not the other way around.

You'll also see how I argued on behalf of BENS for smarter defense spending as the end of the Cold War brought talk of a "peace dividend" and as the Gulf War made flashy new weapons like the Patriot missile popular. Perhaps our biggest influence, though, was in closing unnecessary US military bases and working with Senator Sam Nunn and Senator Richard Lugar to create a joint US-Soviet nuclear risk control center, helping to prevent an accidental nuclear war.

As BENS took off, delegations of BENS members undertook fact-finding missions to countries around the world. Visiting India in 1997, BENS members met with Indian officials at the highest levels. I came away convinced we were neglecting an important partner. In this anthology, you will see some of the columns I wrote, urging a new beginning between the United States and India. When President Clinton finally met with the Indian prime minister, *The Calcutta Telegraph* gave us credit: "Why did the United States President, Bill Clinton, undoubtedly one of the busiest heads of state, seek a meeting with the Indian prime minister, I. K. Gujral, in New York? The answer is a four-letter word: BENS—Business Executives for National Security."

Through my work with BENS, and through my travels in Southeast Asia with my wife, Lisa, I deepened my expertise and developed an extensive network of contacts that gave me insight into parts of the world Americans barely knew. On each trip, I try to meet with and interview a cross-section of the country's elite, many of whom have become friends over the years: businessmen and -women, members of parliament, foreign service officers, leading editors and journalists, retired generals, ambassadors—even presidents. Whether because of foresight or sheer dumb luck, I've managed to be present at the creation as the United States gradually started to recognize the importance of the East and engage the very countries I was writing about. I've touted the strategic importance of countries like Indonesia and Myanmar, long before American policymakers came to the same conclusions. I've explained how history, culture, and decisions made long ago influence the international challenges we face today. I've even had a front-row seat as country after country in Southeast Asia evolved away from dictatorship or autocracy toward democracy—and maybe back again!

As you'll see, there are a few defining principles throughout my columns over the years.

First: good economics makes good politics. Trade ties can build indispensable relationships, even between enemies. And as we saw in Mexico, true democracy and political reforms followed the new economic forces and increased scrutiny that NAFTA brought to Mexico. The power of economics also magnifies the role businesses can play in advancing international relations.

Second: most of the great challenges we face today, including the vast majority of our most frustrating political headaches, were caused by colonial powers arbitrarily creating nations with no regard for ethnic or religious backgrounds, history, or traditions. Many of these decisions occurred in the aftermath of World War I, while some occurred in the waning days of World War II. As we see in the Middle East, forcing people to live in situations they see as illegitimate only breeds instability and conflict—and we shouldn't be afraid to revisit lines on a map if we can move the world toward greater self-determination.

But finally, the key principle you'll see in my columns over the years is the vital importance of credible US leadership around the world. I don't love the legacy of colonialism, but I do believe the United States is, to quote Bill Clinton, the "indispensable nation." I try not to be a knee-jerk interventionist, but I do consider myself an internationalist: I believe the world is better off for US leadership—economic, strategic, and moral leadership. Often, that might take the form of the United States encouraging dialogue, or trade, or leveraging our investments to achieve some outcome. I have rarely advocated an overtly militaristic response to a crisis. At its best, I believe America has stood up for important principles in the world, and taken a tough stand when necessary.

A few years before I went to Mexico to reinvent myself, a US president went to Mexico to reinvent a relationship. Harry Truman's state visit, like all such visits, was highly scripted. But it would be defined by an impromptu gesture.

Truman decided, on a whim, to go to Chapultepec Castle. US forces had stormed the fortress in 1847 during the Mexican-American War. Rather than surrender, six teenage cadets stabbed themselves or jumped to their deaths.

Truman emerged from his car, walked solemnly toward a stone monument to *Los Ninos Heroes,* and—as Mexican soldiers standing at attention wept openly—laid a wreath. "Brave men don't belong to any one country," Truman told reporters, "I respect bravery wherever I see it."

To me, Truman exemplifies US leadership at its most credible. He was honorable in his dealings, even if it meant acknowledging hard truths about our past or treating our former enemies with dignity. He was straightforward, but he wasn't imprudent. He didn't dumb things down, but he spoke to people as adults. When he said he'd do something, he did it.

If people didn't respect his honor, they took his threats seriously. When *Washington Post* music editor Paul Hume criticized Margaret Truman's singing, Truman warned Hume that he'd need "a new nose and a lot of beefsteak for black eyes" if Truman ever met him. Several years earlier, at the conclusion of World War II, Truman had promised to use overwhelming military force if the Soviets continued to occupy northern Iran. The Soviets backed down.

As I write, Russia has occupied eastern Ukraine. Syria has descended into chaos and catastrophe. Our new US president tweets one thing today and something entirely different tomorrow. He has rejected the Trans-Pacific Partnership free trade agreement we worked hard to negotiate with our Asian partners, and he has called NATO and other basic alliance commitments into question.

We will pay a huge price across the globe for the absence of credible and consistent US leadership. If our partners can't count on the United States, they have no choice but to turn toward others who may not share our values. If we want to shape the world we live in, we must lead.

In my struggle for greater purpose, I've asked a lot of questions. Some I answer in these columns; others I leave for time and smarter minds to answer. But as I continue to reflect on the world today and the state of US leadership, I always come back to one lingering question.

Where have you gone, Harry Truman?

THE BENS YEARS:
FIXING THE PENTAGON

Going for Broke

Inc. Magazine, March 1983

AMERICAN WEAPONS, NOT RUSSIAN, WILL BE THE DEATH OF US YET, AND part of the reason is the unblinking support of the business community.

Suppose you were asked to approve a plan to expand your business that

- was based on 20-year-old assessments of need;
- called for pursuing dozens of redundant options simultaneously;
- offered your suppliers no incentives to reduce their prices to you; and
- lacked a clear management strategy.

Sounds like an invitation to fiscal disaster, doesn't it?

Suppose you were also asked to approve a set of government policies that, according to substantial evidence, would hurt investment, slow the growth of jobs, increase the pressure for higher taxes, and cost more than any government program in history? Would it help if you learned that many informed observers thought the policies wouldn't work anyway?

Unfortunately, you are already being asked to endorse such a plan and to endorse government policies that will probably produce those disastrous effects.

It is all part of the biggest spending spree in history, undertaken by the Pentagon. Present plans call for military outlays of more than $1.6 trillion over the next five years. Much of it will be spent on dubious projects or wasted altogether, unless businesspeople speak out soon.

For too long, the business attitude toward military spending has been one of unquestioning support. Many of us are veterans; we have seen our country's way of life threatened before, and we are apprehensive of the current Soviet threat. We want to be patriotic Americans. Besides, many executives believe that military spending, needed or not, is probably good for business. If, however, we applied our basic business instincts, and our experience, to the issue, we would probably change our minds. A number of us have begun to look at defense with a business eye, and what we see is shocking.

Believe it or not, there hasn't been a top-to-bottom assessment of our military spending as it relates to national security needs in more than 20 years.

That means that every time a new crisis arises, a new mission is added to our military establishment, with little sense of how each mission fits into our overall priorities. This unchecked growth of defense programs has reached a point that now calls for us to be capable of fighting, simultaneously, several big wars on several continents and oceans—a strategy so demanding that the Defense Resources Board told the Joint Chiefs of Staff last year that its budget was $750 billion too small for all the missions it proposed to accomplish.

Even within each defense mission, there is a lack of discipline in developing and procuring weapons. Take, for example, the need for a weapon to defend Western Europe against a new generation of Soviet tanks. A recent analysis in the *Washington Post* described nearly 20 different weapons now planned, under development, or being stockpiled to meet just that one threat. Some, like the neutron bomb, are highly controversial. Others, like the Copperhead artillery shell and the Maverick missile, have failed to meet their performance goals. Still others have escalated dramatically in cost.

Altogether, we are pouring billions into this mission. Any seasoned business executive would choose one or a few of the most promising options. The Pentagon simply plows ahead with every weapon system the defense-contracting community can dream up. The US Army alone has more than 300 weapons projects under development. How can we expect the average soldier to be trained in, or even be familiar with, so much high-tech weaponry? Everyone is now aware of the saga of the MX missile, for which no fewer than 30 different basing modes have been rejected at some point, including the well-publicized "dense pack" scheme.

Part of the reason there are so many redundant and even incompatible weapons under development is the Pentagon's preference for "cost-plus" contracts. These guaranteed-profit deals are an almost irresistible lure to military contractors. Under a cost-plus contract, the Air Force reportedly bought aluminum ladders that cost $1,676 each through a "sole source" contract, while almost identical ladders, competitively bid, cost $576, and similar civilian "off-the-shelf" models cost $160. Under cost-plus contracts, according to other reports, two aircraft parts rose in price from $16 and $77 to $3,034 and $1,017, respectively, in one year. Meanwhile, over at the helicopter division of a major defense contractor, two production teams work in separate buildings on similar helicopters—one military and one civilian.

The duplication is necessary, say company officials, in order that the two design teams not "contaminate each other."

Small wonder that the *Wall Street Journal* labeled the Pentagon an "enormously inefficient nationalized industry." As *Business Week* noted, the Pentagon has had a blank check and a murky set of priorities for so long that it has begun to develop its own industrial base.

The problem with unnecessarily transferring large sectors of industry out of the civilian economy and into the Pentagon's industrial base is that it wastes so many resources. Take investment. One reason for our stagnating productivity (output per man-hour) has been the lack of modern plant and equipment. As Simon Ramo, a science advisor to President Reagan and a founder of TRW Inc., notes in *America's Technology Slip*, more than half of all federal research and development funds are devoted to military uses, and more than half of all our scientists and engineers are engaged in defense-related research.

Indeed, the areas in which the United States competes well with other nations are increasingly those concerned with "military tech." Yet even those areas may not serve us well in the future, as the military pursues state-of-the-art advances that are less useful for civilian applications than advances that improve economy and reliability. While the Japanese develop cheaper, more reliable computer chips with greater storage capacity, the US military seeks the development of much higher-speed, much costlier chips. More than 70 percent of the latest generation of computer chips sold in the United States were built in Japan. Once, we dominated the market.

It is in fields like this—information processing and civilian aerospace—that military demands are most likely to push up costs by straining capacity. That could not only ignite a new round of inflation, but it could also choke off the worldwide competitive viability of the very industries that many economists look to for the growth stimulus for the '80s. According to an analysis that appeared recently in the *New York Times*, the currently projected levels of military acquisitions will create inflation, production bottlenecks, and excess capacity in a number of industries, notably microcomputers, industrial plating, machine tools, aerospace, glass, and industrial ceramics.

Unprecedented levels of military spending also distort job creation. A recent study by Employment Research Associates (using the Bureau of

Labor Statistics Input-Output Model of the US economy) found that spending for weapons actually costs more jobs than it creates. Retailing and basic industries such as steel and automobiles tend to be especially hard hit.

It isn't just a matter of cleaning up what President Reagan's budget director David Stockman called the $30 billion "swamp" of waste in military procurement, although that certainly needs to be done. It is more a matter of addressing the main goal of all military spending—ensuring our national security.

What, exactly, is national security? The more we think about it, the more we realize that it must be based on factors like the strength of our economy and the morale of our people, just as much as it is based on the quantity of our arms. Some years ago Dwight D. Eisenhower expressed this thought well: "No matter how much we spend for arms, there is no safety in arms alone. Our security is the total product of our economic, intellectual, moral, and military strengths."

Has the heavy defense spending of the last 10 years made us more secure? Has it actually been good for business?

How much is our security enhanced by the last $1 billion or S10 billion spent on weapons in any given year? The difference between an increase of more than 9 percent a year in spending, as President Reagan has called for, and 3 percent as Senator Ernest Hollings (D-South Carolina) and others have called for, amounts to more than $250 billion by 1987. How much of a federal budget deficit is too much? And how much crowding out of private investment can we tolerate? Congress is weighing these options now.

Business executives could be a great help in resolving this debate ·by developing practical alternatives to economically destructive policies and by articulating a business perspective on military spending practices. This is the reason that a number of us have formed an association we call Business Executives for National Security Inc.

We want to contribute our business experience in assessing risks, in weighing costs and benefits, and in identifying commonsense plans of action. The dividend on our investment will be a return to general business prosperity.

Eisenhower's remarks on military spending, quoted above, continued for a few more lines. Now is a good time for us to heed his further wisdom:

Let me elaborate on this one great truth. It happens that defense is a field in which I have had varied experiences over a lifetime, and if I have learned one thing, it is that there is no way in which a country can satisfy the craving for absolute security—but it can easily bankrupt itself, morally and economically, in attempting to reach that goal through arms alone. The Military Establishment, not productive in itself, must necessarily feed on the energy, productivity, and brainpower of the country, and if it takes too much, our total strength declines.

Yo-ho-ho and a Bundle of Bucks?

Daily News, January 26, 1984
(with Stanley Fine)

WHEN THE US NAVY LAST YEAR ANNOUNCED ITS DECISION, AMID GREAT hoopla, to site a battleship group at the Stapleton piers on Staten Island, Senator Alphonse D'Amato [R-New York] set the welcoming tone: "Jobs, jobs, jobs." Mayor Edward Koch of New York was enthusiastic: "In terms of dollars," Koch told reporters, "it's terrific. It means jobs."

How many jobs? "Thousands," seemed to be the consensus, but in tracking down those numbers the past few months, what we found astonished us. As a case study of the hype surrounding the economic benefits of defense spending, the battleship siting episode is a gem. It also aptly illustrates how popular half-truths about military spending fueling the economy can create a climate of zeal in which military strategy considerations are almost forgotten.

The search for a port for the *Iowa*'s Surface Action Group was triggered by a Navy decision to avoid the possibility of a Pearl Harbor type mistake of concentrating too many ships in a single port. The Navy set up a study team to weigh the complex and important military implications of various sites. Despite this auspicious beginning, the scent of barreled pork soon filled the air.

The competition to berth the Surface Action Group came to resemble nothing so much as the habitual municipal struggles to attract Shriners' conventions and high-tech enterprises.

Now let us consider the actual economic impact of the base. Senator D'Amato's office said he "stands by" the $500 million/9,000 jobs estimates previously given and referred to a "standard 2.5 multiplier" to explain the numbers. Further inquiries were directed to the Federal Reserve Board. But the Fed and subsequently the Commerce and Labor Departments all reported that no general multiplier exists for the economic impact of military spending. All said that any military project has a unique impact which must be uniquely measured.

A spokeswoman in Secretary of the Navy John Lehman's office predicted that 3,600 Defense personnel would be employed at the base, receiving $20,000 average salaries, for an annual payroll of $72 million. She put the number of permanent outside civilian jobs at 300–400 and temporary construction jobs at 1,500–2,000. The official report of the Navy study team leading up to the Staten Island selection estimated base construction costs at $103 million over four years.

Sorting all this out, one discovers:

The 3,600 military personnel already working in DOD will be transferred to the Staten Island base—no comfort to any New Yorkers unless they join the Navy and get assigned to the base.

The 3,100 Navy men assigned to the ships spend 50 of every 90 days at sea, and much of their payroll will be spent aboard ship or in other ports.

The other 500 Defense personnel are likely to remain on the base itself, spending for amenities in commissaries where neither sales, property, or franchise taxes can be levied.

The 1,500–2,000 temporary construction workers could receive about 18 months' employment from construction work. New permanent local jobs: 300–400. If 400 earn an average of $20,000 each, the annual payroll would be $8 million.

The probably inflated $500 million/9,000 jobs figure reveals more than sloppy calculations. Pentagon and local officials will be tempted to play fast and loose with impact figures as long as Congress encourages it. And Congress will encourage such actions by treating national defense like just another "pork barrel" program for political patronage purposes in congressional districts.

Are warships supposed to defend our country or promote public sector employment? Are military base-siting decisions supposed to implement a coherent strategy or to reward successful political brokers? The whole tawdry spectacle of the base chase and the political grandstanding which accompanied the site selection announcement demonstrate the extent to which national defense is being "sold" not on the basis of strategy but on the basis of jobs and payroll.

It is time for Congress and the Pentagon to candidly tell the American people that military spending is a necessary *common sacrifice* which could never function effectively as an economic development program even if we wished it to be one. Certainly military bases create some jobs. But then so does *any* kind of private or public sector spending. Indeed, reputable studies have concluded that military spending creates *fewer* jobs than a wide range of other spending options.

The Complex Meaning
of Ike's Famous Talk

The Wall Street Journal, January 17, 1986

TWENTY-FIVE YEARS AGO TODAY A BELOVED AMERICAN PRESIDENT, preparing to return to private life, delivered the most remarkable political speech of his career.

When Dwight D. Eisenhower sat down before the television cameras on January 17, 1961, to offer his parting thoughts after two terms in office, the nation had every reason to expect a straightforward summary of Ike's eight years in the White House—and perhaps some policy suggestions for the future.

But from the opening reference to his half-century of public service, Eisenhower's farewell address aimed for a much wider vision.

The speech's most startling passage, and its best remembered today, was a blunt assessment of the danger of a large standing army coexisting with a permanent arms industry. Coming as it did from the only career military officer to serve as president in this century, Ike's warning about the "military-industrial complex" created shock waves that were felt at his news conference on the morning following the speech and have not ceased since.

Unfortunately; the military-industrial complex phrase "is nearly always quoted out of the context of the speech." Eisenhower was neither condemning nor praising the military-industrial complex. Rather, he was making a much deeper point.

The essence of the speech, to which Ike returned again and again, was the need for balance—"balance between the clearly necessary and the comfortably desirable," "balance between cost and hoped-for advantage," and, perhaps most important of all, "balance between the actions of the moment and the national welfare of the future."

Political balance is threatened, Ike said in his address, when interests or factions in the country wield unchecked power—either as the result of growth over time or as the result of specific crises.

Two such factions concerned Eisenhower enough that he mentioned them explicitly in the speech. One faction was created by an alliance between elements of the federal government and the scientific community. Science could become corrupted by a dependence on federal funding, Ike warned, and, conversely, "public policy could itself become the captive of a scientific-technological elite."

The other faction that worried him was the military-industrial complex. The United States had been "compelled to create" a huge national-defense establishment, Ike said, because it could no longer risk an emergency improvisation in defense and because it would face a "hostile" and "ruthless" ideology for an "indefinite duration."

But here, as with the bond between science and government, Eisenhower saw the possible pitfalls: "The potential for the disastrous rise of misplaced power exists and will persist."

Ike didn't advocate the destruction of the military-industrial complex, any more than he advocated the dissolution of the federal government's relations with the scientific community. Instead, he characteristically urged his fellow citizens to keep the parts of the whole in proportion: "Only an alert and knowledgeable citizenry can compel the proper meshing of the huge industrial and military machinery of defense with our peaceful methods and goals so that security and liberty may prosper together."

The task of democratic leadership, Eisenhower said, was to ensure that democracy's boisterous, contending factions served the nation, but never directed it.

The astonishingly prophetic quality of the speech is clear today each time a special interest prevails upon Congress or the president to yield to what Ike called "the temptation to feel that some spectacular or costly action could become the miraculous solution to all current difficulties."

A Good Dose of Free Enterprise Can Fix Pentagon Procurement

Electronic Engineering Times, November 28, 1988

BOTH PRESIDENTIAL CANDIDATES PROMISED TO IMPROVE DEFENSE acquisition, determined to prevent any more scandals like the one that rocked the Pentagon earlier this year.

As a business executive, I would like to recommend that President-elect George H. W. Bush consider more than just quick political fixes. For meaningful improvement, he should take some lessons from the world of free enterprise to clean up the business of defense.

One caveat: the Department of Defense does not operate in a free-enterprise environment. That does not mean, however, that we cannot translate most of the basic practical and proven methods of non-defense business into measures that would make our nation more secure.

In order to succeed, any enterprise needs two things: a clear goal and a workable plan. In business, the goal can be any number of things, from building a better mousetrap to increasing market share. In defense there is only one goal: obtaining the best defense for the lowest cost.

In business, the plan is formulated by the top managers and the representatives of the stockholders. In defense, it is vital that the top managers, namely the president, the secretary of defense, the senior military officers, and the representatives of the people (the congressional leaders) contribute to the plan.

Business defines success in terms of the bottom line: profits or losses. In defense, the bottom line is avoiding conflict—and if that is not possible, winning in battle.

What business rules apply?

To win, we need guns that shoot straight, ships that sail true, airplanes that fly right, and well-trained soldiers, sailors, and pilots with high morale. If we score high in each of these columns, our bottom line will add up: the best defense for the lowest cost. To implement the plan and to reach our goal, there are four good models from business to apply:

- **Buy competitively.** Today, less than 8 percent of our defense dollars is awarded in a genuinely competitive way: widely advertised, with sealed bids opened simultaneously.

  That number could be more than 50 percent, excluding new or major weapons systems. And even these could be purchased more competitively.

- **Build prototypes.** Successful businesses know that however good an idea looks on paper, the real test is in the prototype.

  The Pentagon has used prototype buying in the past. The F-10, one of our best fighter planes, was purchased after extensive prototype tests encouraged by David Packard, then the deputy secretary of defense.

  Unfortunately, in the majority of cases, the Pentagon does not "fly before we buy," but rather purchases "paper airplanes"—brochure descriptions and inflated promises. Prototype buying works. We should spend more money up front for a better payoff in the long run.

- **Test operationally.** As a responsible business does with its products, we should test our weapons and equipment before we buy, produce, and deploy them. The Department of Defense now has an office of testing and evaluation, but it is understaffed, underfunded, and under-supported. If we test weapons in their developmental stage and under realistic combat conditions, we can discover and correct the inevitable "bugs" before flawed equipment ends up in the hands of our troops.

  And we should let the people who actually used or will use this or similar equipment help test it. Successful companies field-test new products—the Pentagon should, too.

- **Adopt personnel policies that promote and retain our best people.** Right now, procurement officers have few incentives to work hard for good acquisition. Since procurement is not a glamour specialty, procurement officers too often fall victim to the military's "up-or-out" rule. We should consider creating an independent procurement corps. And we should provide more attractive career paths so we can offer good people better incentives to do their best work and to stay on the team.

With annual expenditures for procurement exceeding $150 billion, all Americans are shareholders in the business of our nation's defense.

And as shareholders, we bear a certain responsibility.

As President Dwight D. Eisenhower said in his farewell address in 1961, "Only an alert and knowledgeable citizenry can compel the proper meshing of the huge industrial and military machinery of defense with our peaceful methods and goals so that security and liberty may prosper together."

Base Closing Can Benefit Local Economy

The Baltimore Sun, January 3, 1989

WHEN THE LIST OF 145 US MILITARY BASES PROPOSED FOR CLOSING OR realignment was released last Thursday by a Pentagon commission, affected communities and some of their congressional representatives predictably began protesting.

But communities can and do recover from base closings. An analysis of the 100 bases closed between 1961 and 1977 conducted by the Office of Economic Adjustment shows that there was a 50 percent increase, on average, in civilian employment *after* the military left.

Former military installations have been successfully converted into 42 municipal airports, 12 four-year colleges, 32 vocational schools and junior colleges, 14 high schools, and 75 office and industrial parks.

The secret is to start early, start fast, and not give up. Although it's natural for a community to grieve when it loses a major employer, it is critical that it move quickly to develop a diverse business base to replace the military presence. Instead of fighting the inevitable, successful communities develop a shared vision of their future, and then they work hard to implement it. Here are some examples:

- When the Air Force closed down the Kincheloe Air Force Base in 1971, Chippewa County, Michigan, lost its largest employer. The population dropped 30 percent virtually overnight; unemployment soared and bank deposits withered. Today, the Chippewa County Industrial Park thrives where the base once stood. It employs 2,400 local residents, nearly four times as many people as the base did. Unemployment is down to 5.8 percent—the lowest ever. Savings to the taxpayer from closing Kincheloe have amounted to $100 million annually—$1 billion since 1977.
- The former Dow Air Force Base in Maine has become Bangor International Airport, a stopover and fueling point for international flights. The barracks, mess hall, and gym became a community college. There

are now 2,500 civilian jobs at the old base, with a payroll of $40 million.
- Salina, Kansas, converted the former Schilling Air Force Base into an active airport and industrial park, providing 4,000 new jobs to replace the ones that were lost when the base closed.
- Boston turned the decrepit Charlestown Navy Yard into a thriving center of medical research, waterfront, and condominium development. The Brooklyn Navy Yard was transformed into an industrial park—within five minutes of City Hall. Quonset Naval Base in North Kingstown, Rhode Island, is now home to 80 companies, ranging from computer designers and car importers to the Electric Boat division of General Dynamics.

By drawing on such basic American values as cooperation, hard work, and inventiveness, these communities have shown that we as a country can begin to make the tough decisions that have so long been politically deadlocked.

There is also a lesson here for politicians. They can best serve their local interests by serving the national interest. Instead of protesting the closings, they should draw their constituents together, helping them create a vision for their community and then working with them to bring it to fruition.

For a Heftier Peace Dividend, Replay the 1922 Air Corps vs. Navy Bombing Showdown at Sea

The New York Times, July 3, 1990

MIKE TYSON VERSUS BUSTER DOUGLAS? MOVE OVER. HERE'S AN EVEN better heavyweight bout.

It's a rematch between two even better-known brawlers. With a potential purse of more than $100 billion, you'd think these two would be screaming to square off. But since their first and only bout in 1922, these titans have done everything possible to avoid stepping into the same ring. Might they both fear they have glass jaws?

And who are these reluctant rivals?

The Navy and the Air Force.

To keep the dollars flowing smoothly, both services traditionally claim that their prize weapons are invulnerable to attack. And they rarely question each other's claims. But back in 1922, General Billy Mitchell of the Army Air Corps (now the Air Force) tested the Navy's boast that its battleships were unsinkable. He KO'd a heavily favored Navy battleship with a bomb dropped from a plane.

In what had to be one of the greatest fixes of all lime, the judges ruled the match a draw. And for the last 40 years, the Navy and the Air Force have enjoyed nearly equal purses.

Despite some strong words and an occasional shove, the two have not squared off since their original bout. Now, with both sides backing new contenders to project US power abroad in the year 2000, a rematch is in order.

The Air Force's B-2 stealth bomber is an untested comer that silently brags, "You can't hit what you can't see." The Navy's money is on its aircraft carriers, protected by the Aegis radar system and its eye-in-the-sky satellites. Navy brass, like Muhammad Ali, claim, "They can run, but they can't hide."

The Navy claims its ships can spot the Air Force's stealthy planes. (This has not prevented it from building its own small stealth aircraft, the A-12

Avenger II.) "No way," says the Air Force. But the first time the Air Force used its stealth F-117A fighter in combat, in Panama, the bombs missed their targets. Will they hit ships at sea? Who's telling the truth?

Let's resolve this dispute the old-fashioned way, with a reprise of the bomber-versus-battleship match. Give the promoters a chance for the Navy's Aegis and associated satellites to detect and engage the Air Force's stealth bomber before it can slip in close enough to drop a bomb. Whichever system loses retires from the fight game. And the real winner, of course, will be the taxpayer.

Consider the stakes. The Air Force wants to spend $61 billion more to build more B-2s—and further billions for F-117As. The Navy wants $30 billion for a fleet of Aegis destroyers plus $52 billion for the A-12. If the ship wins the contest, taxpayers can reap a $113 billion windfall. Why spend money on three undetectable planes that can be detected? Even if the planes win, the payout is a respectable $30 billion.

That's a payday even a fight promoter like Don King would envy.

General Colin Powell: Into the Breach

Newark Star Ledger, July 15, 1990

IN AN UNPRECEDENTED MOVE, GENERAL COLIN L. POWELL OF THE JOINT
Chiefs of Staff has publicly called for a thorough re-assessment of America's
defense establishment. The call to take charge and move out on this project
comes not a minute too soon.

To date the Pentagon has not responded with sufficient verve to the
kaleidoscopic changes around the world and shifting priorities at home.
Recently Senator Sam Nunn [D-Georgia], chairman of the Senate Armed
Services Committee, identified what he termed "blanks" in the administration's FY 1991 defense budget and five-year defense plan. In a word, his
observations dealt with the "what" and "how" of our national security policy: What threats (old and new) does the United States face? What is the best
strategy for dealing with them? How much money will it cost?

How big should our forces be? What weapons will they need?

Unless the blanks are filled, the combined effect of "peace dividend"
fever, pork barreling, and service parochialism promises to make a shambles
of our military establishment.

Now, like the proverbial cavalry, General Powell has arrived. In calling
for a fundamental review, he recognizes explicitly that the world and the
military threats we face are different, and the amount of money we will allocate to defense will be significantly lower in the years to come. His proposal,
if carried out, would go a long way toward filling in the gaps that Senator
Nunn has identified. And that means that the future military establishment
will be dramatically different from what exists today.

Identifying how it will be different will be a contentious and painful
process. The scope of the adjustment is hinted at when General Powell
points to what must be examined anew: military doctrine, training, mod-
ernization rates, housing, personnel levels. The old rules of engagement
must be rewritten.

The review has the potential to set off a tremendous turf battle among
the services. Powerful advocates will argue their particular competence to

handle the emerging military requirements—and the "necessity" of maintaining their share of the defense budget. As General Powell put it: "It will be a difficult task to rationalize the competing demands."

No kidding. Although we are 40 years removed from the last major roles and missions debate, the bruises are still felt. And while many voices over the years have been raised for another such review (usually by retired chairmen of the JCS), the pain of doing it outweighed the cost of not doing it.

But the recent events changed that calculation and General Powell has dramatically opened up the front. Now is the time for his boss, Secretary of Defense Richard Cheney, to follow up with reinforcements.

Under the Goldwater-Nichols Defense Reorganization Act of 1986, the secretary can direct the chairman of the Joint Chiefs of Staff to conduct just the kind of review General Powell proposes. This approach has four distinct advantages:

- It would combine four separate service viewpoints into a unified military plan.
- It would provide military advice on how to cope with an uncertain budget and changing threats.
- It would provide military options, at different budget levels, for dealing with military needs.
- It would provide Congress and the American people the basis for a constructive debate on the future of our national defense.

Time is short. Congress is expecting the peace dividend tree to bear fruit (the tree, of course, being in someone else's state or district). The Pentagon will have to produce a budget and a five-year defense plan in only eight months. By all indications legislators expect the new defense blueprint to incorporate large spending reductions. Pleading for patience, General Powell has warned Capitol Hill that "you're going to break this force if you ask us to do it too quickly." But DOD may face a similar fate if it doesn't quicken its gait.

Postpone Judgment on Defense Systems

Dallas Times Herald, February 7, 1991

THE EARLY SUCCESS OF AMERICA'S HIGH-TECH WEAPONRY IN THE PERSIAN Gulf may be used to resuscitate defense projects thought to be dead or dying. When Congress begins to take up the defense budget in a few weeks, many members will find it tempting to accept early military assessments and base judgments on the next generation of weapons on the performance of the last. This would be a tragic mistake.

There is understandable awe in watching a Patriot missile arc through the sky and destroy an incoming Scud missile. Or in watching two "brilliant" bombs fly through the front door of a fortified bunker like homing pigeons.

President George H.W. Bush and many on Capitol Hill think they have already learned lessons from this war. High-tech works and defense systems count. Strategic Defense Initiative (SDI) proponents see the success of the Patriot as validation that a successful ballistic missile defense can be mounted. The president's new defense budget calls for $4.6 billion—$1.7 billion more than was spent last year—for "Star Wars" research.

Similarly, support for the B-2 stealth bomber, which the House voted to kill last year, is rising with the apparent successes of the $106 million per copy F-117 stealth fighter. After $27.6 billion, only two of the planes are flying. Yet the president's 1992 budget calls for building four new B-2s, and his preliminary 1993 budget calls for building an additional seven.

At best these judgments are premature. At worst, dangerous illusions based on inappropriate models. The Patriot, for instance, began its life in the 1960s as a problem-plagued surface-to-air missile and was adapted for its current use as an afterthought less than five years ago. It has little in common with the exotic weaponry envisioned by the Strategic Defense Initiative Organization and its supporters. Similarly, the F-117 stealth fighter has nothing in common with the B-2 bomber except some of the radar absorbing materials in its frame.

We shouldn't rush to judgment. We especially should not let the experiences of the first weeks of battle, encouraging as they are, determine the shape of future defense budgets. First, our evidence of the overall effectiveness of our high-tech weaponry is still largely anecdotal.

Second, it remains to be seen how great a role these weapons will play in the eventual outcome of the war. It is still likely that ousting Iraqi forces from Kuwait will have to be done the old-fashioned way: in grinding ground combat.

Third, it is unclear that Iraq provides a model for the most likely "next threat." Our current arsenal was built to counter a Soviet thrust in Europe.

For all of these reasons, it is imperative that we undertake a careful and deliberate review of the missions, performance, cost, and overall utility of our high-tech weapons, *after the fighting is over.*

We can, however, begin to start laying the groundwork for the review today.

Who Cares About National Security

Defense Week, September 5, 1995

IN THE 1980s, THERE WAS A CARTOON THAT BEST SUMMED UP THE BATTLES over Pentagon spending. It depicted a general pointing to a map and telling then–Secretary of Defense Caspar Weinberger, "At last! A weapons system absolutely impervious to attack—it has components manufactured in all 435 congressional districts!"

Even at the height of the Cold War, defense spending often had a lot more to do with generating local jobs and votes than promoting national security.

The problem may be even worse today. With declining defense budgets and looming—if less clear—threats, our country can ill afford to siphon off defense dollars for domestic purposes.

Yet even President Clinton thundered recently against closing unnecessary military bases that would free up $19 billion for more urgent defense priorities. The commander-in-chief termed the recommendations of the independent base closing commission an "outrage" that ignored the economic impact on local communities. When he finally accepted the commission's list of recommended base closings, the president did so with all the enthusiasm of someone having to gulp down a dose of cod liver oil.

When it comes to putting local concerns above national security, Clinton is hardly alone. The House of Representatives, now controlled by Republicans, decided to scrap a new Seawolf nuclear submarine the Navy says it wants, and instead buy 20 additional B-2 stealth bombers the Air Force doesn't want. Moreover, according to a recent General Accounting Office report, the $2.2 billion B-2 has met only 12 percent of its flight objectives for stealth, and 7 percent for survivability.

What these two positions have in common is domestic politics. Many of the bases on the closing list that President Clinton railed against are located in California, a state crucial to his re-election hopes. Similarly, final assembly of the B-2 bomber takes place at a plant in Southern California. There has to be a better way of deciding how to allocate defense spending other than jobs and politics. Particularly now.

Consider today's national security threats:

- **Terrorism.** In the wake of the homegrown bombing in Oklahoma City, this threat has zoomed to the top of the list. Someday, a terrorist incident—domestic or foreign—could involve nuclear, biological, or chemical weapons, with incalculable consequences.

  Combating these dangers requires more resources devoted to intelligence gathering. In terms of hardware, it means making sure US forces are capable of carrying out a surgical strike anywhere in the world. In terms of organization and training, it means a closer collaboration between America's law enforcement agencies and its military forces.

- **Regional war.** The war between the Serbs and the Moslems in Croatia isn't about to break out on the streets of Washington. But the civil war is tearing the fabric of the NATO alliance and weakening the effectiveness of the United Nations, both of which have served as instruments to advance American security interests. If the failure in ex-Yugoslavia is primarily a political failure of nerve and of commitment on the part of the West, it also represents a failure of military options. In the future, the United States must have choices beyond deploying massive numbers of ground troops, as in Iraq, or undertaking an ineffective and risky bombing campaign in Bosnia.

- **Drugs.** There is no more serious direct threat to American security interests than drugs. Drug dealers have infiltrated and destabilized a number of countries in the Western Hemisphere and now threaten Mexico. The impact of illegal drugs on the fabric of American society is well known. House Speaker Newt Gingrich (R-Georgia) asserted that anyone who is responsible for shipping narcotics into the country should be put to death. Surely some additional defense dollars should go toward controlling the importation of illegal narcotics and helping our neighbors more effectively attack the drug cartels.

- **Information warfare.** Forget the Ebola virus; a computer virus could wipe out Wall Street. Our centralized, high-technology society is highly vulnerable to new threats, and our response so far has mostly taken the form of looking the other way.

Instead of focusing on these security threats, Congress and the White House often look to defense spending to promote short-term domestic goals. For instance, self-described Republican defense hawks played a key role in adding $550 million to next year's military construction budget for dozens of projects—such as dining facilities and fitness centers—that the Pentagon did not request. Not surprisingly, eight out of every 10 dollars devoted for new military construction projects is going to home states of members of Congress who sit on the House National Security Committee.

For every politician like Republican House Budget Chairman John Kasich of Ohio, who wants to withhold funding for additional B-2s, or Minnesota Democratic Representative David Minge, co-chairman of the congressional "pork busters" coalition and who fought a losing battle against military construction add-ons, there is a politician like Republican Representative Jerry Lewis of California. Lewis is trying to get the Army to spend $10 million to expand the airfield at its Fort Irwin, California, training center on the theory that the Army needs a better airfield from which to move troops and equipment. Sounds like a good idea—until you discover that the Air Force is already making nearby Edwards Air Force Base available to the Army.

The Pentagon's piggybank has always been used to fund local pork-barrel projects and maintain local jobs. In the old days, there was more than enough money go around. But those days are over. Despite the proposed congressional increases, the defense budget will still be down 40 percent since the fall of the Berlin Wall—a decrease that could be particularly damaging if too many of the remaining dollars are spent as a military welfare program.

Politicians of both parties have campaigned on the theme of change. But when it comes to our nation's security, the more things change, the more they stay the same. Today, the cartoon general might look at a map detailing defense spending in each congressional district and lament: "No wonder we can't provide for the common defense. We're too busy using defense dollars to promote congressional welfare."

When Closed Means Open:
How the Pentagon Is Backing Off
Its Pork-Barrel Pledge

The Washington Post, March 12, 1995

THIS YEAR WAS SUPPOSED TO BE THE "MOTHER OF ALL BASE CLOSINGS." BUT something happened on the way to the battle.

Originally designed as a clever, and necessary, way around the problem of trying to close unneeded military installations long kept open by pork-barrel politics, the successful seven-year base-closing program is in danger of going out with a whimper instead of a bang.

And it's too bad. The decision to scale back the Pentagon's list for the fourth and final round of base closings is penny wise and dollar foolish. Investing today in the upfront costs of closing obsolete military facilities will yield taxpayer dividends tomorrow four times as great.

So what happened? Why is a plan that once aimed at closing an additional 100 major military bases now targeting only a third that many?

The answer is not a profile in courage. Ultimately, the Pentagon decided that closing that many bases would be too difficult and too costly in the near term.

Political calculation—by both the White House and Congress—also played a role. California, home to the largest number of military installations and the richest store of electoral votes, was a major focus of past base closures. This time, it was hardly nicked. Similarly, South Carolina lost installations in prior years but is now slated to gain. It is home to the chairmen of both congressional committees that control the Department of Defense budget. Neither lawmaker has been a fan of the base-closing process from the beginning.

Call it coincidence, call it fairness, call it wasteful. As a result, the size of the military's overhead will continue to be seriously out of whack. Since Cold War peak levels, the defense budget has decreased by more than 40 percent; the size of the military force has been reduced by a third and procurement cut by two-thirds. But even after three rounds of base closings, the Pentagon's "infrastructure"—bases, depots, shipyards, and laboratories—has gone down by less than 20 percent.

The impetus for the base closings started building more than a decade ago, when the Pentagon found itself with a military base structure that far outstripped the size of its forces. By the mid-1980s, the country had 3 million men and women under arms, but enough bases to support 12 million troops. Some bases were built for the Indian Wars; one had a moat.

Yet every time the Pentagon tried to shut down an obsolete base, it ran into the informal quid pro quo on Capitol Hill—I won't vote to close your base if you don't vote to close mine. The result: not a single major base was shut down until 1990. As the Cold War drew to an end and the military became smaller, the problem only grew. Fewer troops should have meant fewer bases.

Obviously, some way was needed to take the politics out of the base-closing process. If Congress was not going to be part of the solution, at least it should cease being part of the problem. Working with Texas Representative Dick Armey of Texas, now the House majority leader, Business Executives for National Security, a group of private industry leaders concerned about a strong, affordable defense, helped push through legislation that created the Base Closure and Realignment Commission. Composed of private citizens, the commission's task was to identify bases that could be closed without regard to politics.

Here's how it works. The commission examines the Pentagon-generated list of possible base closures and recommends those it feels should be shut down or consolidated. No bartering, no gamesmanship. The theory is that as long as the closings are spread equally around the country and Congress has to vote up or down on the entire package, the base closures would sail through.

Indeed, they have. The first commission in 1988 resulted in agreement to shut down 12 major facilities, ranging from Cameron Station in Alexandria, Virginia, to the Presidio in San Francisco. The Pentagon estimates this first round is already saving the taxpayers some $750 million annually. In 1991 and 1993, an additional 55 major bases and many smaller ones made the list. When the hundreds of installations are closed or restructured, the Defense Department believes the savings will grow to more than $4 billion a year.

This last and final round, announced by Defense Secretary William Perry earlier this month, calls for closing 33 major bases and scores of smaller ones for additional savings of $1.8 billion annually.

But getting congressional approval to close bases has proven far easier than actually carrying out the plan. Communities, addicted to the military's presence, mount high-profile, sophisticated public relations campaigns to save the installations. They lobby their representatives and advocates in the military and the White House. Time and energy that should be put into finding new commercial uses for bases go instead into new schemes to keep alive sites that were supposed to close completely.

The fear of losing jobs helps drive this destructive cycle. What is discouraging is not just the return of politics as usual but that the community fears are largely misplaced. A Defense Department study of almost 100 bases shut down during the 1960s and 1970s showed that when the bases were converted for civilian use, more jobs were created than were lost in affected communities. Former military facilities were transformed into 14 high schools, 32 vocational schools and junior colleges, 12 four-year colleges, 42 municipal airports, and 75 office and industrial parks. It wasn't easy. It took planning, persistence, and work. But the payoff was a more stable, prosperous local economy.

When England Air Force Base appeared on the list, the town of Alexandria, Louisiana, through foresight and planning, figured out a way to replace the lost jobs and income. The one-time fighter base now houses a civilian airport and industrial park with 15 occupants, generating far more employment and revenue for the community than the base ever did. Packard Bell is producing computers at the Sacramento Air Depot, which is shutting down two years ahead of schedule. And in the past 18 months, since Chanute Air Force Base in Rantoul, Illinois, was closed, some 20 companies have located or expanded on three square miles. Devising ways to reuse military bases is time better spent than working to prevent their closure.

Unfortunately, the communities rarely get much help from the federal government. Current law stipulates that the Pentagon and other federal agencies get first call on what to do with the bases scheduled for closing. If the federal government passes, the bases are offered to local governments or nonprofit agencies. Only as a last resort are closed military facilities offered for sale to private interests. No wonder base closings have been fought, at least initially, by nearly every community.

As the base-closing process enters its last and most important round, the administration and Congress should rethink this policy to allow local communities, not Washington, to have first call on bases scheduled to be closed. And, as Defense Secretary Perry wisely suggested, there should be still another round of base closings.

Ensuring that bases are indeed closed does more than save money. At issue is the nation's security: Will defense dollars go for guns or pork? Military readiness or obsolete bases? The national interest or local self-interested?

An Indefensible Military Budget

The New York Times, February 7, 2002
(with William A. Owens)

CONGRESS CHEERED PRESIDENT BUSH'S PLEDGE, IN THE STATE OF THE Union address, to spend "whatever it costs to defend our country." But here's the secret: Mr. Bush already has most of the money he seeks. And absent real reform, most of the additional money Congress ultimately approves—the president has requested a quarter of a trillion dollars more over the next five years—will never reach our fighting men and women in the field.

That's because the real challenge is not spending more or less on defense. It's spending better.

Most, if not all, of the resources necessary to finance a 21st-century military are already available. But they're wasted on mid-20th-century business practices. An astounding 70 percent of the defense budget is spent on overhead and infrastructure (the bureaucratic "tail"). Only 30 percent directly reaches our combat forces in the field (the "tooth"). No community would tolerate seven out of every 10 police officers sitting at their desks pushing paper. The nation should not tolerate such a ratio in the military.

Just how backward is the business of defense? It can take the military up to three weeks to replace parts—something the private sector can do in two days. Of the Pentagon's $7 billion travel budget, $2 billion is spent on administrative overhead.

These were just a few of the painful findings in a report issued last year by the Tail-to-Tooth Commission, sponsored by Business Executives for National Security, an organization of business leaders that takes no position on the size of the defense budget. The commission—composed of corporate chief executives and former members of Congress, defense secretaries and military leaders—reviewed the findings of 18 major studies over the last 15 years on military expenditures and offered a step-by-step road map of how to reform the military so that it runs more like a business.

For example, the military should be freed from nonmilitary missions like family housing; the private sector can do it faster, better, and cheaper. The

Defense Department's byzantine acquisitions system and the archaic defense accounting system, which can lose track of billions of taxpayer dollars, need to be updated, and excess military bases that sap billions of defense dollars should be closed.

These vital reforms may now be forgotten in the fog of war. Throwing money at the Pentagon is certainly one way to buy more defense, but in the long term it will not help improve our security. New money for the armed forces may well become an excuse to maintain inefficient old habits.

Yet reform is more important than ever. President Bush came into office promising hard choices at the Pentagon. Cutting the bloated bureaucracy and reinvesting the savings to transform the military was one of Defense Secretary Donald Rumsfeld's priorities. The day before September 11, he declared that "every dollar squandered on waste is one denied to the war fighter." He pledged to "wage an all-out campaign to shift Pentagon's resources from bureaucracy to the battlefield, from tail to the tooth."

But real reform had already succumbed to a confluence of forces resistant to change—vested interests, organizational complexity, and institutional inertia. The necessities of waging an all-out campaign against Al Qaeda and the rush of new military spending now threaten to sink the reform boat.

The fact is that a more agile military needs an equally agile support team. We will never get the faster, lighter, and more lethal military we want— no matter how much we spend—if it's tied to a slow, heavy supply chain. Streamlining would not only save billions; it would help build a leaner, more effective military to fight the war on terrorism.

An easy-money approach avoids hard decisions and risks undermining the confidence of the American people just as public trust in government has soared during this war.

We should not forget the public backlash against defense contractor scandals and $700 toilet seats during the military buildup in the 1980s. Support for military budget increases will evaporate if the Pentagon devours billions in new funding but fails to shed the fat.

We and all Americans can agree with the president that we must spend whatever it costs to defend our nation. But no amount will be enough if we cannot spend our military dollars more efficiently.

WEAPONS OF
MASS DESTRUCTION

Chemical Weapons:
A Valuable Treaty to Ratify

International Herald Tribune, September 11, 1996

THE UNITED STATES SENATE IS ABOUT TO VOTE ON WHETHER TO RATIFY A treaty that would help combat terrorism: the Chemical Weapons Convention. The agreement outlaws production, purchase, storage, and use of chemical weapons and the agents that produce them anywhere in the world.

The convention is strongly supported by every member of America's Joint Chiefs of Staff, the secretary of defense, the director of the CIA, and the United States chemical industry.

The convention will become international law whatever the Senate does. As of today, 160 countries have signed it, including the United States, and 61 have ratified it. It enters into force within 180 days of its ratification by the 65th nation.

US ratification should be no contest. But it is opposed by a small band of senators who have never met an international agreement they liked or trusted. In a word, they believe that any person, country, or institution not made in the USA is, well, un-American. The leader of the band is Jesse Helms, Republican of North Carolina.

There is also a group of senators from both parties with respectable concerns about the treaty's effect on America's security, freedom of action, and industry. But those fears and reservations are unwarranted.

America is now required by US law to destroy virtually its entire chemical arsenal by 2004. The convention would put other nations on the same footing.

Today the United States has to act unilaterally to isolate outlaw nations. Its recently enacted Iran-Libya Sanctions Act has produced resentment among its allies, with little or no effect on the target countries.

With the Chemical Weapons Convention in place, companies in China providing Iran with facilities suited for making deadly chemicals would face severe sanctions by the entire industrialized world.

Russia, with the world's largest stockpile (40,000 tons of chemical weapons, vulnerable to theft), would be subject to international scrutiny, allowing inspectors to take inventory and secure those weapons.

If Libya continued building its underground chemical weapons facility, the United States would still be free to take whatever measures it felt were necessary to prevent the plant from going into production.

No arms control agreement is 100 percent verifiable. And there is no easy way to deal with outlaw states, or government-sponsored terrorists. But the convention would supplement national intelligence and provide America with otherwise unavailable means to detect chemical weapons activities.

It creates a paper trail to trace the production and sale of sensitive chemicals. It contains tough enforcement measures, including short-notice challenge inspections and economic sanctions against treaty violators. It is the first arms control agreement with very sharp teeth.

Critics of the treaty claim that American chemical corporations and thousands of small companies not involved in any way with chemical weapons production would be burdened with a mountain of new paperwork, and that hordes of foreign inspectors would be poking their un-American noses into US plants and shoplifting trade secrets. Nonsense.

Of 25,000 US companies, only 200 are ever likely to be liable to on-site inspections. In an industry subject to continuing inspections by the Environmental Protection Agency and the Occupational Safety and Health Administration, and which fills out more forms than almost any other sector, the addition of a simple one-page report on chemical weapons compliance each year can hardly be considered a major paperwork burden.

The American chemical industry has spent more than 15 years working on the Chemical Weapons Convention. It concluded that the benefits far outweigh the costs, and that real costs would come from not ratifying the agreement.

The convention is unique. It has folded into one treaty an arms control agreement that bans an entire class of weapons with a non-proliferation regime that forbids trade with any nation in noncompliance.

Avoiding a Russian Arms Disaster

The Washington Times, November 6, 2005

(with Ted Turner)

HURRICANE KATRINA DROVE HOME THE STAGGERING DEVASTATION THAT disasters—natural or man-made—can inflict. Meanwhile, July's attacks on the London Underground reminded us that terrorists can still strike major world cities. Now imagine the two joined together: terrorists, armed with weapons of mass destruction, unleashing Katrina-scale chaos and death in the heart of a US city.

Such attacks are hardly unthinkable. Roughly half of Russia's weapons-grade nuclear materials are poorly protected. In the small Russian town of Shchuch'ye, nearly 2 million shells of VX and sarin nerve gas—each lethal enough to kill 85,000 people—lay stacked in chicken coop–like structures. The September 11 commission said Al Qaeda has pursued getting and using these weapons as a "religious obligation" for more than a decade.

Fortunately, unlike with hurricanes, much can be done to prevent this nightmare from becoming real. One of our first and best lines of defense is the Cooperative Threat Reduction (CTR) program, created by former US Senator Sam Nunn, Georgia Democrat, and Senator Richard Lugar, Indiana Republican. Since 1992, the program has eliminated thousands of Russian nuclear warheads, missiles, submarines, and bombers.

But in recent years, a set of burdensome congressional restrictions has marred the program and led to a series of disruptive stop-and-start cycles. Key projects vital to America's security have ground to a halt for months on end because, for example, Russian human-rights obligations were not met or the paperwork to waive them was not completed.

Congress now has the chance to end such dangerous disruptions once and for all. Mr. Lugar, decrying those misplaced priorities, introduced language to repeal all the restrictions, which the Senate embraced by an overwhelming, bipartisan 78–19 vote in July. But until the full Congress approves it, CTR's vital efforts remain in danger, from both a national security and a business perspective.

DANGER OF DELAY

Current restrictions carry real costs on the ground. In mid-2002, all new CTR projects—including security upgrades at 10 nuclear weapons storage sites—stalled for four months because the conditions could not be certified. Destruction of the Shchuch'ye stockpile was delayed some 15 months from 2001 to 2003 for similar red-tape reasons.

Such stoppages not only prolong threats to America, but they also endanger the hundreds of millions of taxpayer dollars already invested in Shchuch'ye and other projects. So long as the conditions remain, these dangerous disruptions are inevitable.

WASTED RESOURCES

In a yearly drama, defense staffers and intelligence analysts must spend thousands of hours assessing Russian compliance with CTR restrictions— even when it is immediately clear Russia cannot meet them. Nor can the president simply waive the conditions without first submitting to this annual exercise in foregone conclusions.

Abetting such delays or allowing concerns like human rights, however important, to threaten human existence massively is the height of folly. We not only agree with Mr. Lugar that, during a war on terror, these artificial barriers "are destructive to our national security"; we see them undermining one of the best investments our country can make.

CTR simply is good security on the cheap. At an annual cost of as little as one-tenth of 1 percent (0.001) of the Pentagon budget, the program has deactivated and helped guard 6,760 Russian nuclear warheads. It has upgraded security to the Shchuch'ye depot and similar sites. It also helped remove all nuclear weapons from Ukraine, Belarus, and Kazakhstan.

Today, CTR continues upgrading security and aiding accounting of nuclear weapons transportation and storage. It also works to destroy biological weapons production facilities and lock down pathogen collections in Russia and the former Soviet republics.

CTR's largest current project, eliminating the Shchuch'ye stockpile, will rid us of all 2 million of those weapons—and cost each American roughly the same as a large latte.

Nor is this money "foreign aid": More than 80 percent of CTR funds go to five US prime contractors that dismantle and destroy these weapons.

The risk of a Katrina-scale terrorist attack with Russian weapons is too critical to tolerate any delays to these crucial efforts. Congress must act and free us to meet what President George W. Bush calls "the greatest threat before humanity today."

United States, Russia Can Build on "Cold Peace"

Asia Times, October 24, 2007

TO WATCH SENIOR AMERICAN AND RUSSIAN OFFICIALS IN MOSCOW recently, it's clear that US-Russian ties—once seen as a budding strategic partnership—now exhibit all the frustrations and finger-pointing of a dysfunctional relationship.

After keeping his guests—Secretary of State Condoleezza Rice and Defense Secretary Robert Gates—waiting for some 40 minutes, Russian President Vladimir Putin railed against Washington for "forcing" its policies on Eastern Europe and sarcastically suggested that a planned US missile defense system was feasible "somewhere on the moon."

Despite Gates's reassurance that the 10-interceptor system would have "no impact" on Russia's massive nuclear arsenal, Russian Foreign Minister Sergei Lavrov warned that Moscow would "neutralize this threat," evoking previous Russian threats to target its nuclear weapons against system sites in Poland and the Czech Republic.

Moscow's recent decision to resume Cold War–style bombing patrols is "something that belongs in another era," said Rice, who called for "countervailing institutions" to balance the autocratic Russian president.

While Rice accused Iran of "lying" about its nuclear ambitions, Lavrov warned against "unilateral" (read "American") actions against Tehran, which Putin this month became the first Kremlin leader to visit since Josef Stalin in 1943.

But Russia and the United States have too much at stake to let their big chill harden into a new cold war. Yet as they grow apart with different priorities—including Putin's new scheme to retain power as prime minister—a genuine reconciliation is unlikely anytime soon. How, then, to make the best of this cold peace?

Going forward, Moscow and Washington should remember that, in many ways, they are made for each other. As the two largest nuclear powers—both

victims of Islamic jihadis—there is no substitute for US-Russia cooperation in reducing nuclear arsenals, preventing the spread of weapons of mass
destruction, and combating terrorism.

Washington won't succeed in curtailing nuclear programs in North
Korea and Iran without Moscow. Russia won't truly succeed in diversifying
its oil and gas-dependent economy, or gain membership in the World Trade
Organization, without American investment and assistance.

For its part, Washington might win back some Russian hearts with a little
empathy for their post-Cold War trauma. After all, how would Americans
react if, having lost the Cold War, their country disintegrated, the Warsaw
Pact expanded to Mexico, and Russia proposed installing a missile defense
system in Cuba?

"In the Russian mind, their country was flat on its back after the Cold
War, and the United States walked all over them," says Brent Scowcroft, the
national security advisor to President George H. W. Bush. "The facts are
almost irrelevant. That's how Russians feel."

To avoid fueling Russian paranoia, the North Atlantic Treaty Organization
should proceed slowly—if at all—with eventual membership for former Soviet
states like Ukraine and Georgia. To show Moscow that the United States wel-
comes a real economic partnership, Congress should finally repeal a Cold War
relic—the Jackson-Vanik amendment, originally designed to promote Russian
Jewish emigration, but which continues to block normal trade relations.

For its part, Moscow must resolve its post-communist identity crisis and
accept its 21st-century post-superpower status rather than cling to illusions
of a 19th-century empire. This includes recognizing that zero-sum security
thinking—including intimidation of smaller neighbors from the Baltics to
Georgia—ultimately leaves Russia more isolated and less secure.

Moreover, Moscow should realize that its long-term security lies with
the West, not the East. Despite deepening military and trade ties with China,
Russia—with its plummeting population—could find its empty Far East and
Siberian border regions with China vulnerable to enduring territorial claims
by Beijing.

Fortunately, a foundation of trust—however fragile—exists on which to
rebuild a relationship based on mutual interests. A former US aid official in
Russia highlights a range of ongoing US-Russian partnerships tackling common threats, from HIV/AIDS to money laundering to human trafficking.

Most significantly, Washington and Moscow recently marked 15 years of the Cooperative Threat Reduction program—championed by US Senator Richard Lugar and former senator Sam Nunn—that has destroyed or deactivated more than 10,000 Soviet-era nuclear missiles and warheads. "But even more important than the weapons we've destroyed," Nunn tells me, "is the trust that has been built between Russians and Americans—trust that can be the foundation for cooperation in other areas."

For much the same reason, there's hope in the American proposal unveiled in Moscow for a "joint regional missile defense architecture" that includes Russia and, perhaps, Russian and American military personnel at one another's missile sites. The resulting transparency and information-sharing could hasten the greatest trust-building steps of all: removing American and Russian nuclear missiles from hair-trigger alert and further reductions in nuclear arsenals, including withdrawal of US nuclear forces from Europe.

Given the icy state of US-Russian relations, such progress may be hard to imagine. The roots of US-Russian friction will likely remain for years to come. Russians—flush with unprecedented oil and gas profits—will seek to restore their status as a great and global power. Americans—fearful of Moscow's authoritarianism at home and assertiveness abroad—will seek to constrain Russian ambitions.

In the meantime, to paraphrase Lavrov, these two uneasy partners don't have to experience a breakthrough in their relations. They just need to avoid a breakdown so that their mutual animosity doesn't trump their mutual interests.

START Treaty: What Republicans Can Learn from Reagan

The Daily Beast, December 20, 2010

AS PRESIDENT BARACK OBAMA BATTLES SENATE REPUBLICANS OVER ratification of the new US-Russia START Treaty on the Senate floor today, it's worth remembering that the phrase at the heart of this treaty—"arms reduction"—was born 23 years ago last week, in a high-profile summit between the United States and the Soviet Union in Washington, DC. Then, as now, to no one's surprise, the strongest voices of opposition came from communist-hating conservatives. But what was surprising was the unlikely target of conservatives' harshest criticism: Ronald Reagan.

In December 1987—less than six months after Reagan famously declared at the Brandenburg Gate, "Mr. Gorbachev, tear down this wall!"—Soviet general secretary Mikhail Gorbachev came to Washington to sign the Intermediate-Range Nuclear Forces (INF) Treaty. For the first time in history, the INF Treaty proposed the outright elimination of an entire class of missiles (and not just "arms control"): namely, nuclear and conventional ground-launched ballistic and cruise missiles with ranges between 300 and 3,400 miles. The United States had about 400 such missiles in Western Europe; the Soviets had four times as many across the Iron Curtain.

The treaty was too much for conservatives, who believed that the missiles were central to US relations with its Western European allies. The conservative stalwart *National Review* dedicated an entire issue to the INF Treaty, calling it "Reagan's Suicide Pact." Editor William F. Buckley sent Reagan the first copy, writing in an accompanying letter, "For the first time, I and my colleagues need to take very serious issue with you."

Henry Kissinger warned that the treaty undid "40 years of NATO." Conservative columnist George Will ridiculed "the cult of arms control," writing, "The Soviets want victories; we want treaties." Conservative Caucus chairman Howard Phillips fumed that Reagan had become "the speech reader-in-chief for the pro-appeasement triumvirate of (White House Chief of Staff) Howard Baker, Schultz, and (Defense Secretary) Frank Carlucci." Every Republican presidential candidate, save Vice President George Bush, opposed it. *New York Times* columnist William Safire seemed to sum it up best: "The Russians . . . now understand the way to handle Mr. Reagan: Never murder a man who is committing suicide."

That may remind you of some of the rhetoric coming from Senate Republicans today. Senator Jon Kyl, for example, complained that the administration "wasn't willing to stand up to the Russians." But there's a big difference. Republicans during the INF debate genuinely believed the treaty would weaken America's security. Senator Bob Dole, the Republican leader in the Senate, who was undecided on the treaty, put it bluntly: "I don't trust Gorbachev."

While the INF debate was a clash between two sets of principles, the new START debate seems to be a clash between principles and politics. Despite support from nearly every high-ranking US national security figure from the past three decades—from Kissinger to Brent Scowcroft to James Baker to Condoleezza Rice—Senate Republicans reportedly want to deny President Obama a political victory, despite Russian Prime Minister Vladimir Putin's threat that failure to ratify the treaty could kick off a new arms race. This not only threatens America's security; it sets a bad precedent: How will other nations take America seriously if it is so willing to sacrifice global agreements to petty domestic politics?

Eventually, many of the conservatives who opposed the INF treaty came around to support it. Nine days after the treaty was signed, Dole endorsed it. Five months later, the Senate ratified it. By the treaty's deadline of June 1, 1991, a total of 2,692 such weapons had been destroyed—846 by the United States and 1,846 by the Soviets. Gorbachev later wrote in his memoir, "The INF Treaty represented the first step on our way out of the Cold War . . . creating a security system that would be based on comprehensive cooperation instead of the threat of mutual destruction."

In years past, members of the current opposition to the new START Treaty have demonstrated a similar ability to rethink their positions. In the mid-1990s, Kyl, who leads the Republican opposition today, was also one of the leading opponents of the Chemical Weapons Convention—until a group of generals, led by Norman Schwarzkopf, whispered in his ear, "The boys need it."

Kyl changed his vote and the treaty passed.

It's unclear who is whispering in Kyl's ear today, or whether he'd be similarly willing to change his mind. But it may be worth passing along Reagan's words, delivered in a speech to the Center for Strategic and International Studies, 23 years ago this week: "Any successful foreign policy must be built not upon a Republican or Democratic consensus, but upon an American consensus . . . upon an agreement about our nation's aims in the world that is not sectional nor partisan, but rooted in the will and values of the American people themselves. That policy consensus is one that we must build for ourselves."

Don't Let the Crisis in Ukraine Damage Decades of Progress on Nuclear Cooperation

The World Post, March 18, 2015

(with Norton Schwartz)

THIS DECEMBER, THE WORLD WILL WITNESS THE 70ᵀᴴ ANNIVERSARY OF A publication best known for tracking the end of the world. Founded in 1945 by veterans of the Manhattan Project, which developed the atomic bomb, the *Bulletin of the Atomic Scientists* was launched in the wake of the devastating nuclear attacks on Hiroshima and Nagasaki, with the goal of informing the public about nuclear policy. But since 1947, it has been known largely for a metaphorical device it introduced in June of that year: the Doomsday Clock, which measures how close humanity is to extinction.

Launched at seven minutes to midnight, the clock hit two minutes after the first hydrogen bomb was tested in 1953; jumped back to 12 after the United States and the Soviet Union backed away from nuclear confrontation over Cuba in 1962; moved to three minutes at the height of Ronald Reagan-era US-Soviet tensions in 1984; and widened to 17 minutes in 1991, after the Berlin Wall fell and both sides began cutting their nuclear arsenals. While it has moved up and down ever since—based on new threats like climate change and other weapons of mass destruction—it never crossed five again.

That is, until January, when the Doomsday Clock moved back to three minutes to midnight, pushed, once again, by the danger of nuclear confrontation. With Israel threatening Iran over its nuclear program, Pakistan and North Korea building up stockpiles, China sinking billions into nuclear submarines and missile systems, and the White House seeking to modernize America's aging arsenal, the world, as *The Economist* put it, "is entering a new nuclear age." But make no mistake. Even with this burgeoning activity, the greatest threat today is being driven by an increasingly belligerent Russia, which is using its nuclear arsenal as a nationalist rallying cry while posing a dilemma for the United States: If Russia is no longer committed to arms reduction, should the United States continue to carry the flag for disarmament by itself?

It's hard to imagine, but when the Cold War ended in 1991, there were more than 52,000 nuclear warheads worldwide, about 97 percent of which were owned by the United States or the Soviets. That year, the US Senate, led by Sam Nunn and Richard Lugar, created the Cooperative Threat Reduction program, known as Nunn-Lugar. It provided training, technology, and US taxpayer dollars to dismantle and destroy nuclear and chemical weapons in Russia and the former Soviet states while preventing such materials from falling into the wrong hands.

The program has been highly successful, helping Russia and other former Soviet states deactivate more than 7,600 warheads while dismantling more than 2,600 vehicles that deliver nuclear weapons. *The Boston Globe* recently reported that from 2010 to 2012, the program "secretly removed enough highly enriched uranium from Ukraine to make nine nuclear bombs—some of it from parts of the country now wracked by violence and lawlessness."

It is the current crisis in Ukraine, brought on by Russian troops that first invaded the Ukrainian peninsula of Crimea and then ignited a border war in eastern Ukraine last year, that has seen nuclear tensions ratchet up, continuing a Russian position that hardened when Vladimir Putin won back the office of president in 2012. That same year, Moscow announced that it would not extend the Nunn-Lugar agreement, despite its overwhelming success. In 2013, the Kremlin decided to end Russian Defense Ministry involvement in the program entirely. In December 2014, clearly stung by Western sanctions imposed for its aggression in Ukraine, Russia announced the end of all remaining cooperation.

Far from reducing its stockpile, Russia has shifted to using its nuclear arsenal as a tool for intimidation. Close Putin ally Dmitry Kiselev, the head of Russia's main state news agency, who bragged last year that Russia was the only country that could turn America "to ash," told Russian viewers in February that while the Soviet Union "pledged to never use nuclear weapons first . . . Russia's current military does not." Political strategist Sergey Markov, reflecting a widely held Russian view, was quoted in the *Telegraph* as saying, "In Russia, we believe that Ukraine has been occupied by the United States . . . which is the first step in a war against Russia . . . Under these circumstances, the threat of nuclear confrontation is very real."

Meanwhile, Moscow has also begun to rebuild and modernize its arsenal, reportedly increasing its defense budget by more than 50 percent since 2007, a third of which has been spent on nuclear weapons. Its military now routinely carries out mock nuclear attacks on European capitals, and Russia recently staged nuclear exercises in the Arctic. For eight years, it has also reportedly been in violation of the Intermediate-Range Nuclear Forces Treaty—signed in 1987 by President Reagan and Soviet leader Mikhail Gorbachev—by developing cruise missiles with a range prohibited by the treaty. Such nuclear chest beating is finding an audience among Russia's young, who have bought T-shirts with slogans praising Russia's nuclear arsenal at a record clip. It's little wonder that anti-American invective has now reached Stalin-era levels in Russia, as the *Washington Post* reported this week.

Whether these nuclear taunts are real or are simply meant to placate hard-liners in Moscow, the question remains the same: What is Washington to do?

One path was illuminated last month by newly appointed Secretary of Defense Ash Carter, who suggested that America provide a strong response to Russia's violations of the INF Treaty, one that would clearly "make Russia less secure than they are today."

Some members of Congress have gone further, calling for the deployment of tactical nuclear gravity bombs and accompanying short-range aircraft at new sites in Eastern Europe. Others have called for the United States to abandon its arms-control efforts altogether and block implementation of a new Strategic Arms Treaty that the United States and Russia agreed to in 2011. Last December, Congress took a step in this direction by voting to defund US efforts to secure loose Russian nukes for the first time in a quarter century.

But this is foolhardy. The United States and Russia haven't worked hard for two decades to rid the world of nuclear weapons to abandon the effort at the first sign of difficulty. Carter is right to call attention to these violations and to stand firm in pressuring Russia to fulfill its obligations, but the United States needs to take a holistic approach to our arms-control agreements with Russia.

What should the United States do? Three things.

First, provide needed resources. Russia claims that it is planning to take over the responsibilities of the Nunn-Lugar program and increase related funding. But given the deteriorating economic situation in Russia, and the fact that there is still much to be done on the dismantling of weapons systems while securing nuclear materials, it is possible that there will be a window for US officials to restart cooperation by offering much-needed resources. The security of these weapons systems and materials is an issue that affects not only Russia but the United States and all other countries concerned about the potential for terrorist attacks.

Second, push to get relations back on track. US officials should stand ready to renew dialogue with any component of the Russian government that indicates willingness to work in this area. Specifically, the US Department of Energy should continue to pursue dialogue with Russian state atomic energy firm Rosatom, which, even though it tried to blame the United States for deteriorating relations in a January press release, has simultaneously expressed interest in eventually resuming cooperation.

Third, become an evangelist once again for nuclear diplomacy. The United States should become a loud voice in defense of the nuclear Non-Proliferation Treaty, which slows the development of nuclear weapons by discouraging enrichment of uranium, which is at the heart of the negotiations between Washington and Teheran over Iran's nuclear program today.

Nearly 70 years ago, one of the founding godfathers of the *Bulletin of the Atomic Scientists* wrote in a fundraising letter, "The unleashed power of the atom has changed everything save our modes of thinking, and thus we drift toward unparalleled catastrophe." His name was Albert Einstein. It's hard to believe that seven decades later, we are closer to midnight today than we were then. Here's hoping we get our "modes of thinking" back on track.

Hiroshima Saved My Life

The Huffington Post, May 26, 2016

AS PRESIDENT BARACK OBAMA PREPARES TOMORROW TO BECOME THE FIRST American president to visit Hiroshima since that fateful day 71 years ago, I've spent a lot of time thinking of friends long since gone. The atomic bombs that America dropped on Japan in August of 1945 took more than 200,000 lives. But they probably saved mine.

At the time, I was a young sergeant in the United States Army, being readied to participate in the full-scale invasion of Japan. The previous year, I had enlisted in the service just three weeks after my 17th birthday, a skinny Jewish kid from South Philadelphia eager to follow my big brother, Buddy, into war.

In the summer of '45, none of us knew how long the war in the Pacific would last. But the reports about the nearly three-month battle for the island of Okinawa were gruesome, with more than a hundred thousand Japanese killed, some by suicide. We didn't know at the time that America had suffered almost fifty thousand casualties, although we'd heard the number was massive. But we knew that the invasion of Japan would likely begin from this hard-fought island, and we all assumed that the Japanese homeland would be defended with equal ferocity. It was predicted that the mission would take the lives of more than a hundred thousand American G.I.s—including, most likely, me.

Then everything changed. One day in early August, I sat with a couple of guys in the barracks and puzzled over the local newspaper's story that an American plane had "dropped one bomb" on some Japanese city I couldn't pronounce and "destroyed" it. We understood how our B-29 long-range bombers had firebombed Tokyo with devastating results, taking 100,000 lives. But we were mystified to read that this so-called atomic bomb harnessed "the basic power of the universe" and loosed the "force from which the sun draws its power" upon a city called Hiroshima. What the hell did that mean? We scratched our heads about what the paper called this "greatest achievement of organized science in history."

I tried to make sense of the following stories about Einstein and $E=mc^2$, but had no more success than I'd had in my physics classes in school. What most mattered to us was whether this would shorten the war and whether we would still need to risk our lives invading Japan. When we learned about the second bomb three days later, we could see that the war was ending. Imagine our relief a week later, on August 15, when Japan surrendered.

Years later, revisionist historians argued that the Japanese would have surrendered without our using the bomb or invading their homeland. They believe we used the A-bomb not so much to save American troops lives but as a first step into the Cold War with the Soviets. Some of those same arguments have been advanced again in the run-up to President Obama's visit.

I became a close friend and associate in the 1970s with the pioneer and leading exponent of this revisionist view, Gar Alperovitz, a brilliant political economist and historian who earned his PhD at Cambridge, and was a founding Fellow of the Harvard Institute of Politics and a longtime professor at the University of Maryland at College Park.

Gar and I are only nine years apart in age, but we're of different generations, so we have understandably looked at this issue through different lenses. While I trained for the invasion, Gar was nine. He has studied the key documents of the time with all of his considerable scholarly skills. I never have.

Nonetheless, while Gar often cites some generals who believed that Japan's fall was imminent, I side with many of the other officers I knew then who believed the Samurai mind-set among the military who then controlled Japan would have never surrendered—because to surrender, in that culture, was the ultimate act of cowardice. I believe an invasion of Japan would have been a bloodbath for everyone. I believe Japanese emperor Hirohito ordered the military to surrender only because of the A-bombs that President Harry S. Truman decided to drop. I realize my beliefs are not based on academic findings. They are existential, a product of my direct experience and the feelings I had as my buddies and I waited in our barracks for our invasion orders.

But that doesn't mean that I don't look back on what happened in Japan seven decades ago with horror, because I do.

In fact, the threat of another Hiroshima disturbed me so much that years later, I got deeply involved in the anti-nuclear movement. I founded an organization in the mid-1970s called the Nuclear Information Resource Service, or NIRS, so citizens could learn about the dangers of nuclear reactors and take direct action locally. I co-founded a political party in the late '70s, called the Citizens Party, that ran an anti-nuke candidate against Ronald Reagan and Jimmy Carter in the 1980 presidential election.

In 1982, I founded a very different kind of organization called Business Executives for National Security, or BENS, which has focused on a wide range of defense and security issues ever since, including preventing the use of even one nuclear weapon while working to reduce the world's nuclear stockpiles.

I'm proud of that legacy, but it hasn't been enough. As America today overhauls its nuclear arsenal, Russian officials speak of their warheads as offensive weapons, and Pakistan quietly grows the world's third-largest nuclear arsenal with China's help, the Doomsday Clock stands at three minutes to midnight. That, in part, is why President Obama's visit is so important: to remember what happened yesterday so we can prevent what might happen tomorrow.

It does us no good to whitewash history, to change the narrative around Hiroshima, or to take decisions from 1945 out of the context in which they were made. For all the talk about whether Obama should apologize to Japan—with some even going so far as to suggest that Harry Truman should be considered a war criminal—I can guarantee one thing: nobody who lived through the Second World War, who fought in it, who lost family and friends to it, will look back on the end of the war with anything but gratitude and relief.

To this day, schoolchildren in Japan aren't taught the full story of what happened in the 1930s and '40s. They don't learn about the utter brutality of the Japanese war machine and the atrocities it committed across Asia that took more than 20 million lives and precipitated the fall of the atomic bombs. It's not hard to understand why. As human beings, it is only natural to want to push away the painful and unimaginable past, to avoid reliving the darkest moments of a proud nation's history.

But we shouldn't play along. We shouldn't let the story of that time be rewritten by those who seek today to position Japan in 1945 as a victim and not the aggressor it was. We shouldn't humor those who so easily want to forget, because many of us still remember. I remember.

I remember the stories from the so-called Rape of Nanking, when the

Japanese Imperial Army invaded the Chinese capital in 1937 and murdered up to 600,000 men, women, and children in the space of six weeks while sexually assaulting as many as 80,000 women first.

I remember the Palawan Island Massacre in the Philippines in 1944, when Japanese soldiers, wrongly believing an Allied invasion was imminent, herded 150 American POWs into an air-raid shelter and then burned almost all of them alive.

I remember the massacre of Manila in the winter of 1945 when Imperial troops, surrounded by Americans who stopped their artillery fire so the Japanese could surrender, chose instead to go on a civilian rampage, slaughtering more than 100,000 innocent civilians through beheadings, machine-gun sprays, and fire set to buildings with people inside.

It is hundreds of atrocities like these that America used to remember when we thought of Hiroshima, the tragically leveled city in the country that attacked us first—drawing far, far too many of our friends and neighbors into war in the South Pacific, who were never the same when they came home, or never came home at all.

Tomorrow, I hope the president celebrates the friendship that grew between America and Japan after the war, an example that all adversaries today can learn from. I hope he celebrates the living standards raised and the economies that grew through our partnership. I hope he uses the memory of 1945 to seek a new beginning in our efforts to rid the world of nuclear weapons once and for all.

But I hope he doesn't seek to rewrite the past or erase parts of our common history. In the end, telling the truth about the war is the highest tribute we can pay to the dead—and the living.

MEXICO

Consumers, Environmentalists Would Benefit from NAFTA

Christian Science Monitor, August 30, 1993

THE NORTH AMERICAN FREE TRADE AGREEMENT (NAFTA) IS LIKE THE heroine in *The Perils of Pauline*: Just when it appears to have escaped the clutches of its adversaries, it finds itself once again strapped to the train tracks with a locomotive coming 'round the bend.

The recently negotiated side agreements, designed to penalize governments that allow their companies to gain competitive advantage by flouting environmental and labor laws, should have ensured NAFTA's passage. They have not.

The latest threat to implementing the trade agreement with Mexico and Canada comes from the federal courts. A federal judge will decide whether to reverse a lower court ruling that said the Clinton administration must produce an environmental impact statement on the agreement before submitting it for congressional approval. Ironically, that ruling threatens to unravel an agreement that would bring immediate benefits to millions of hard-pressed United States consumers and dramatic long-term benefits to the Mexican-US border environment.

It is difficult to reconcile a pro-consumer stance with opposition to NAFTA. Reducing the already low barriers to trade between the United States and Mexico will cut the price of thousands of goods moving from south of the border, including food, clothes, and consumer electronics. That is why Consumers Union, the largest US consumer group, has been generally supportive of the accord.

The position of environmentalists that oppose NAFTA is even more difficult to understand. They contend that the agreement will drive large numbers of US firms south of the border to use Mexico as a pollution haven.

This is a "green herring." Any US firm that is looking for lax rules on pollution is already operating in Mexico—or Thailand, India, or China. The real issue is not the poor state of Mexico's environment today, but how best to help Mexico reduce its pollution tomorrow.

Mexico's environmental horror story is worst along the 2,000 mile US-Mexican border. Since 1965, unemployed men, women, and children who did not illegally cross into the United States to work have been "rented" to more than 2,000 foreign companies (mainly American). These are registered as "*maquildora* factories" or in-bound processing companies, with many tax and duty advantages. They are limited in their sales in Mexico, and they export almost entirely to the United States. Cheap labor provides the basis of the factory towns, industrial parks, and slums that make such a mess of the environment on both sides of the border.

NAFTA would help clean up this cesspool. It would encourage companies to move inland rather than concentrate along the United States border. In addition to reducing the pollution effects on the US side, this would help generate domestic political pressure in Mexico for more rigorous enforcement of environmental laws. It would also create an expanded market for US-manufactured pollution-control devices.

A clean environment has always followed, not preceded, economic prosperity. NAFTA will accelerate Mexico's development and thus its capability to pay for a healthier environment. After decades of US admonishments, Mexico is finally on the right track. If NAFTA's opponents succeed in derailing the accord, no one will lose more than hard-pressed US consumers and those concerned about the environment of North America—the very people that treaty opponents claim to represent.

Because of NAFTA, Eyes of the World Are on Chiapas—and Mexico Cares

Houston Chronicle, March 20, 1994

DICTATORSHIPS AREN'T WHAT THEY USED TO BE, AT LEAST IN MEXICO. Instead of quickly crushing the small band of peasant guerrillas known as the Zapatista National Revolutionary Army, the ruling Institutional Revolutionary Party has agreed on reforms that would do away with its 65-year-old hold on absolute power. It's as if China had sent flowers instead of tanks into the ranks of student protesters in Tiananmen Square, or the old Soviet leadership had invited Andrei Sakharov and other human rights activists to tea in the Kremlin instead of hounding them into exile and worse.

The difference between Mexico in 1994 and China in 1989 or the former Soviet Union in the 1970s is the North American Free Trade Agreement. This took effect on January 1, the same day the uprising in Mexico broke out. Long after the Zapatista rebellion in the southern state of Chiapas has been relegated to a historical footnote and rebel spokesman "*Subcomandante* Marcos" is remembered as just another pretty ski mask, New Year's Day 1994 will be celebrated as the day Mexico joined the first world.

Why is NAFTA so important? Because President Carlos Salinas de Gortari believes that NAFTA will do for Mexico in the 1990s and beyond what Franklin Roosevelt's New Deal did for America in the 1930s: create a prosperous and stable middle and working class to head off civil unrest.

His decision to follow the Asian model of development—free enterprise first, free elections later—has already paid enormous dividends. His government has encouraged foreign investment and trade, balanced the budget, cut annual inflation from 160 percent to 9.5 percent, created more jobs, and increased spending on health, education, and basic infrastructure. With NAFTA greatly expanding the nation's wealth, for the first time Mexicans will be debating how to divide a larger economic pie more equitably.

However, Mexico can no longer continue to be governed by the corruption, fraud, and violence that characterizes most third-world nations and expect the United States to remain a party to the controversial trade pact that barely passed Congress last year. That is why the PRI has agreed not only to local demands of Mexico's Indians in Chiapas, but also to an agenda for broad political reform, including guarantees that the presidential election in August will be internationally monitored to prevent a recurrence of the nationwide computer "breakdown" that ensured Salinas's victory in 1988.

Subcomandante Marcos and his Indian comrades were right to focus on the appalling poverty in rural Mexico and 500 years of oppression of Mexico's indigenous peoples. But they are wrong to fixate on land redistribution as the solution. President Salinas is criticized for providing inadequate support for rural peasants and for repealing the constitutional promise of land for all peasants who work it. But, as anyone who has lived and worked in the hills and villages of Mexico can attest, a few acres of overworked, overfertilized land produce, at best, a bare subsistence crop.

The whole vision of working the land in Mexico has been romanticized. During the many years that I lived in Mexico, poverty was everywhere. It was not surprising that over the past 50 years, there has been a mass exodus from the countryside to the larger Mexican cities and to the United States. As former Mexican ambassador and prominent agricultural economist Edmundo Flores once told me, "How are you going to keep them down on the farm after they've seen the farm?"

Salinas has bet his presidency and his party on NAFTA, with its $6.5 trillion gross national product and market of 362 million consumers. He is convinced that the real future for Mexico's rural poor, like their urban brethren, is with more efficient and competitive industrial and agricultural enterprises.

Because of NAFTA, the whole world has been watching Mexico and its band of ski-masked rebels. And because of NAFTA, Mexico cares what the whole world thinks.

For Democracy, Mexico's President Needs Power

International Herald Tribune, December 6, 1994

MEXICO HAS A NEW PRESIDENT AND AN OLD PROBLEM: HOW TO MOVE FROM dictatorship to democracy without first plunging the country into anarchy. Unfortunately, the United States isn't helping ease the transition. By pushing Mexico to fully embrace dramatic democratic reforms in the short run, Washington may be helping to ensure the triumph of dictatorship, or worse, in the long run.

Signs of stability were in short supply as Ernesto Zedillo Ponce de León began a six-year term on December 1. The secretary-general of the governing Institutional Revolutionary Party (PRI) was murdered in September. Mr. Zedillo would not be president but for the assassination of the party's first candidate. And the rebellion in the southern state of Chiapas shows signs of reigniting.

Mr. Zedillo is caught between the United States (and many Western-educated intellectuals in Mexico) pushing for a decentralization of power and the dinosaurs in his own party who are not above using violence to maintain their grip. So far he has veered toward those urging quick democratization.

He has pledged to make the PRI independent of the government and to devolve federal powers to the states. But by doing so he will be giving up the very powers necessary to ensure Mexico's democratization.

That is Mr. Zedillo's catch-22. Fundamental change in the PRI and in the role of Congress means surrendering his power to keep Mexico calm through a mixture of patronage and authoritarianism. It is a recipe for resistance, reaction, and violence.

There is another way. It is the way of Mr. Zedillo's predecessor, Carlos Salinas. Mr. Salinas followed the Asian model: good economics before good politics. He used his status of being above the law to dismiss more than half of the country's state governors. But during his reign the budget was balanced, triple-digit inflation came down to a manageable 7 percent, and most

state-owned companies were privatized. As a result, Mexico has a burgeoning middle class and, through the North American Free Trade Agreement,
much closer ties with the United States and Canada.

Today Mr. Zedillo faces problems and opponents even more formidable
than those confronted by his predecessor. He needs to create a safety net for
the tens of millions of Mexicans still living in poverty. He needs to radically
restructure a corrupt judicial and legal system. But first, he must face down
those who have amassed huge personal fortunes based on ties to the PRI.

He must also contend with the Zapatista rebels in the south and the nar-
co-criminals in the north, whose profits from moving drugs into the United
States each year are estimated to be more than twice the total revenues of
Mexico's petroleum industry.

To deal with this unholy triumvirate, he will need to wield more power—
not less.

The United States has much at stake. Mexico is now its second-largest
trading partner, after Canada. Mexico is also its greatest source of illegal
aliens and drugs—problems that will only get worse if conditions become
less stable. And the US relationship with Mexico can set a pattern for relations with the burgeoning democracies elsewhere in Latin America, many of
which are clamoring for inclusion in NAFTA.

What should Mr. Zedillo do? Take a page out of his predecessor's playbook. In his first 100 days, Mr. Salinas attacked the corruption that was at the
heart of Mexico's economic problems. He arrested the gangster head of the
oil workers' union, the top executive of Mexico's largest brokerage house,
and a major drug trafficker. That asserted his authority and gave him the
breathing room for his economic reforms.

President Zedillo, too, should go after his enemies. He must face down
the anti-democratic element within the PRI, pursue and arrest the leading
drug dealers, and tell the Zapatistas that he will treat them fairly but that if
their revolt resumes he will send in the army to restore order. Only then will
he have laid a foundation upon which democracy can be built.

Mexico: Curtain Time for a Political Drama in Three Acts

International Herald Tribune, December 3, 1997

THE CURTAIN RISES ON A THREE-ACT DRAMA IN MEXICO. IN ACT I, Cuauhtémoc Cárdenas takes office this Friday after a landslide victory as Mexico City's first elected mayor. His left-leaning supporters assume that by the end of Act III he will be Mexico's new president and his Party of the Democratic Revolution will be in control.

But first Mr. Cárdenas must get through Act I, demonstrating that he can rescue one of the world's most deeply troubled cities from 70 years of corruption, central planning, and virtual dictatorship by the Institutional Revolutionary Party (PRI).

In undertaking this effort, Mr. Cárdenas must decide whether he is the democratic hero that his party members say he is, or another in a long line of anti-market, nationalistic demagogues.

If he toes his party's populist, statist, Marxist line, he will run straight into the National Action Party (PAN), Mexico's oldest and strongest opposition party, which preaches free enterprise and free elections, holds six governorships in the largest and wealthiest states and mayoralties in nine of the 11 most populous cities.

I know a little something about Mexico—and the theater. Forty years ago I produced Mexico's first musical. It was a smash hit. The only problem was that we lost money with every ticket sold.

The Mexico City authorities had assured us that we could charge whatever we wanted. But just before opening night, the mayor informed us that we could charge only a fixed admission of 4 pesos (32 US cents). Our cost was 10 times that.

He told us that "*el pueblo*" (the people) must be protected. We argued that *el pueblo* didn't have 4 pesos for tortillas and beans, let alone for theater tickets. We offered to hand over the entire balcony gratis and to soak the rich for the rest. No sale.

After some months we ran out of money, the musical closed, and I retired from the theater. It was an expensive lesson in how Mexico worked.

On the surface, not much has changed since the 1950s. Mexico City is still the core of the nation's economic, political, and cultural life, responsible for more than 25 percent of the country's economic output. Congress meets there, and every government ministry is headquartered in the city.

It is home to most of the country's financial elite, international corporations, and leading politicians and intellectuals. Culture is found in the Fine Arts Institute and the National Anthropological Museum, not far from Los Pinos, the presidential palace.

But in reality it is overcrowded, crime-ridden, polluted, and hopelessly in debt.

The bulk of the more than 20 million in the metropolis live in what is termed the "urban stain" encompassing a dozen surrounding cities. These impoverished municipalities form a misery belt from which millions of workers commute daily into downtown Mexico City.

Air pollution, the worst in the Western Hemisphere, is so bad that the city's air ranks as "satisfactory" only 35 days a year. Ozone levels are three times the national standard, and 70 percent of the area's children have unacceptable levels of lead in their blood.

The crime rate has doubled in the last two years. There are 750 robberies and other crimes reported each day, but corruption among law enforcement officials is rampant. A running joke has it that if you get mugged on the street, don't yell or you may attract the police.

It will take a generation—and a miracle—to improve the political, judicial, and environmental conditions in this most ungovernable piece of real estate. Mr. Cárdenas has only two and a half years before the presidential election in 2000. His only hope is to revert to the role of victim that he played so successfully in his run for mayor, blaming the PRI for everything and the PAN for anything.

The least he can do for the venerable old capital is marry his party's principles of social justice with free market reforms, thereby co-opting the basic programs of both his opponents. That means that he must resist the temptation to set prices, including theater prices.

Then maybe, just maybe, the audience will be cheering this namesake of the greatest Aztec hero and son of a beloved former president when the final curtain comes down.

Mexico after NAFTA Becomes a New Home for Democracy

International Herald Tribune, June 28, 2000

I ONCE BRAGGED TO A FRIEND IN MEXICO THAT IN THE UNITED STATES WE know the winner of a presidential election within minutes after the polls close. "That's nothing," he replied. "Here in Mexico we know almost a year before."

On Sunday the joke may be on the Institutional Revolutionary Party (PRI), which has ruled Mexico by hook or by crook for seven decades. Francisco Labastida, its presidential candidate, is running neck and neck with Vicente Fox of the National Action Party (PAN).

Next week the PRI may need its *mapaches*, the so-called devious raccoons who tamper with the votes. Or it can hope that Cuauhtémoc Cárdenas, the third major candidate in the race, will be the spoiler by siphoning off more than 15 percent of the votes, mostly from Mr. Fox.

But no matter who wins the election, democracy wins. Mexico will finally have a vibrant multiparty system with an opposition Congress, an independent judiciary and a free press—developments that would have been unthinkable only six years ago when President Carlos Salinas won approval of the North American Free Trade Agreement, the groundbreaking treaty with the United States and Canada.

Because of NAFTA, the whole world will be watching to see that the elections are conducted fairly. It's a good thing.

When Mr. Fox drew even in the polls, Mr. Labastida exchanged his "softly, softly" approach for the more familiar PRI tactics of vote-buying and coercion. He also called in the old guard, known popularly as the dinosaurs, led by former Interior Minister Manuel Bartlett. Mr. Bartlett was accused of faking a computer crash to steal the 1988 presidential election from Mr. Cárdenas and deliver it to Mr. Salinas and the PRI.

Two years earlier, when polls showed that a PAN candidate for governor of Chihuahua was leading by three to one, the PRI manufactured a victory for its man. Mr. Bartlett explained that a PAN win would open the door to the historic enemies of Mexico—the church, the United States, and the business community. So if there was fraud, he said, it was patriotic fraud.

Because of NAFTA, Mexico can now afford the luxury of democracy. Inflation is relatively low, commercial banks are on their way to recovery, and foreign debt is under control. With an export-led growth strategy, commerce between the United States and Mexico has expanded by more than 150 percent to $220 billion last year.

In 1998, Mexico replaced Japan (which has an economy 11 times its size) as the No. 2 trading partner with America. In less than 10 years it will be *número uno*, replacing Canada. It has free trade arrangements with 28 other countries, including those in the European Union. Given its history as a protectionist economy, this is an extraordinary turnabout.

These economic changes are affecting every aspect of life. Within five years Mexican women will average two children, a sign of a growing middle class. In 1975 women had a fertility rate of six.

New prosperity, zero population growth, and fewer job seekers will reduce the flow of illegal immigrants to the United States.

But Mexico still has a long way to go. Forty percent of its population lives on less than $2 a day. Corruption and violence have gone from bad to worse. The Zapatista uprising in the remote southern border state of Chiapas remains unresolved. And Mexico's multibillion-dollar narco-trade with its addicted neighbor to the north is a powerful destabilizing force.

But because of NAFTA, these problems will be addressed democratically. The next president will not be one of the new breed of authoritarian-style leaders who have taken over in half a dozen Latin American countries. These autocratic so-called populists, who have assumed power through the ballot box, are ultra-nationalistic, militaristic, and impatient with the niceties of constitutional law.

If the United States wants to do more than pay lip service in encouraging democracy in Central and South America, it should negotiate an American Free Trade Agreement that extends all the way from Canada to Argentina.

President Salinas remarked after the NAFTA vote: "For the first time ever, Mexico has a deadline for becoming more efficient. There is no more *mañana.*" Starting on July 2, Mexican democracy will not have to wait for tomorrow, either.

Replacing Mexican Myth with Reality

International Herald Tribune, November 13–14, 2004

"BADGES? I DON'T HAVE TO SHOW YOU NO STINKING BADGES!" the *bandido* posing as a Mexican policeman in the 1948 classic *The Treasure of the Sierra Madre* snarled at a leery American gold digger played by Humphrey Bogart.

As a young man determined to relive Bogart's adventure, I went prospecting in Mexico. Instead of gold, I found manganese (an essential mineral in steel making) and spent more than two decades living and working in Mexico.

A half-century later, the Sierra Madre stereotype of a poor and lawless land endures in the minds of many Americans.

But a visit to this vibrant country reveals a society undergoing dramatic political and economic changes that belie outdated foreign attitudes. Political leaders here wonder whether George W. Bush's second term will mark a new chapter in US-Mexican relations, including US immigration reform and deeper economic integration beyond the North American Free Trade Agreement.

Yet re-energizing this relationship first requires something more basic: dispelling the myths and misconceptions that prevent Americans from fully embracing their southern neighbor.

Myth: Mexican immigration is out of control. In fact, the estimated 4,000 Mexicans who illegally cross the US border every day distort the big picture.

Every day, tens of thousands of Mexicans enter legally on work visas. Every year, some 200,000 Mexican parents, spouses, and children sponsored by US citizens immigrate legally. Mexicans who want to live in America are the exception, not the rule. Nearly 70 percent have no intention of ever heading north, according to a recent survey by the Mexican and Chicago Councils on Foreign Relations.

Myth: The Mexican economy is a basket case. Given Mexico's history of economic protectionism, endemic poverty, and repeated US financial bailouts, Americans can be forgiven for not offering Mexicans an economic bear hug. But the peso remains strong, inflation is under control, and the Mexican economy—the world's 10th-largest—is expected to grow 4 percent this year.

Exports, 90 percent going to the United States, are booming and employ more than a million Mexicans at *maquiladoras*, export assembly plants, mostly along the US border.

Myth: Coming soon, a North American Economic Union. NAFTA can be credited with turning Mexico into America's second-largest trading partner and giving rise to a nascent middle class. But as long as incomes here remain a fraction of those in America, poor Mexicans will seek a better life on *el otro lado* (the other side) and kill any dreams of a European Union–style North American common market with open borders.

As former president Carlos Salinas once said, "Mexicans will either get jobs in Mexico or they will get jobs in the United States. We will send you either goods or people."

Unfortunately, a common North American energy market is also unlikely anytime soon. The United States needs to reduce its Mideast oil dependence, and Mexico needs billions of dollars to develop deep-water oil projects in the Gulf of Mexico. But the Mexican constitution prohibits foreign investment in Pemex, the state-run oil monopoly. And Mexicans overwhelmingly oppose any grand bargain giving the United States greater access to their oil sector, even if it meant increased US investment in Mexican infrastructure or a more liberal US immigration policy.

Myth: "Mexican democracy" is an oxymoron. In fact, the 71-year "perfect dictatorship" of the Institutional Revolutionary Party has given way to an imperfect democracy, with the victory of President Vicente Fox and his National Action Party in the historic election of 2000.

Rigged elections, where the winner was known a year in advance, are a thing of the past. A parade of candidates are off and running for the 2006 presidential election. The biggest problem today is political gridlock between the president and Congress—a problem familiar to some of the world's oldest democracies.

Myth: Mexico doesn't take the drug war seriously. In fact, Mexicans surveyed rank drug trafficking as the most critical threat facing their nation, even more dangerous than economic crises and international terrorism.

American officials have praised Mexico's "extraordinary progress" in crop eradication, interdiction, and extradition.

Myth: Gringo-hating Mexicans will never cooperate with America. Mexicans still obsess over losing half their territory to the United States in 1848 and cherish their independence from "the colossus to the north." Fox irked the Bush administration by siding with France at the United Nations over Iraq.

Still, in the survey, Mexicans expressed more favorable feelings toward Gringolandia than any other country except Japan. Nearly 60 percent of Mexicans support allowing US security agents to help protect Mexican airports, ports, and borders. Indeed, increased cooperation in homeland and border security may offer the best hope for re-energizing US-Mexican ties.

And with greater trust grounded in reality, neither side will have to show their stinking badges.

United States–Mexico: Next-Door Neighbors, Worlds Apart

International Herald Tribune, June 1, 2006

IT REMAINS AN INDELIBLE MEMORY FROM MY 20 YEARS AS AN AMERICAN living and working in Mexico. Visiting a school I helped build in the town of Charcas, in the central state of San Luis Potosí where I operated a manganese mine, I was startled to see a map showing Mexico's borders stretching across the American West.

"Señor Weiss," a young girl asked, "why did you steal half our country?" She was referring to the northern half of Mexico lost to the United States in the war of 1846–1848.

"Just be patient," I half joked. "You'll get it all back."

The divisive debate over illegal immigration to the United States is more than just another chapter in America's long love-hate relationship with immigrants. When virtually 100 percent of the rhetoric focuses on the estimated 50 percent of illegal immigrants who come from Mexico, it's a tragic flare-up between two old neighbors whose historic insecurities make reasoned compromise all the more difficult.

American xenophobes seize on recent immigration rallies as proof that 170 years after Mexico sacked the Alamo, America's "Anglo-Saxon identity" is still under siege. Hearing a few protestors chanting, "We didn't cross the border, the border crossed us," these latter-day American Know-Nothings warn that Mexicans still covet the western United States and are patiently getting it all back through a demographic *reconquista.*

To many Mexicans, America's rush to defend the border—with Minuteman vigilantes, a new 700-mile high-tech fence (*el muro de la vergüenza,* "the wall of shame," the Mexicans call it), and thousands of National Guard troops—validates old strains of anti-Americanism. It's seen as the latest example of America's historic disregard for Mexican sovereignty, dating back to the 1914 landing of US forces at Veracruz and the 1916 invasion to pursue the revolutionary bandit, Francisco "Pancho" Villa.

Election-year politics in both countries exploit these historic insecurities. In the United States, you know things have turned ugly when President George W. Bush has to explain that rounding up and deporting millions of people "is neither wise nor realistic."

In Mexico, Washington's "militarization" of the border has candidates competing in their outrage. Seeking to regain his lead in the polls, Andrés Manuel López Obrador, the leftist former mayor of Mexico City, blasts President Vicente Fox and his conservative party candidate, Felipe Calderón, for not standing up against "a very serious aggression against a sovereign nation."

Rather than mutual recriminations, Americans and Mexicans alike would be wise to recognize their mutual dependency. Under the North American Free Trade Agreement, cross-border trade has soared to $300 billion a year, making Mexico America's second-largest trading partner. The United States needs Mexico for its people and its petroleum, of which Mexico is America's second-largest supplier. Mexico, in turn, needs the United States as the market for 90 percent of its exports and the $20 billion in remittances that Mexican workers in the United States send home every year.

In the "Mexicanization of America," Hispanics have surpassed African Americans as the nation's largest minority group. They are expected to make California the first Hispanic-majority state by 2035 and to comprise a third of the US population by 2050.

The "Americanization of Mexico," in contrast, is fueled by goods, not people. Thanks to NAFTA, Mexican culture is awash in "Made in America." Some 40 percent of Mexicans are employed by US companies—including Wal-Mart, now Mexico's largest employer.

Washington and Mexico City should see illegal immigration as the supply and demand problem it is. Mexico supplies millions of citizens for which it cannot provide well-paying jobs. A growing American economy demands workers and offers low-skill wages 10 times higher than in Mexico.

On the demand side, Americans should remember that a temporary-work program is nothing new. Between 1942 and 1964, the United States allowed some 5 million Mexican *braceros* (men who worked with their arms, or *brazos*) to work legally on American farms and ranches, take their wages home to Mexico during the winter, and return the following season. The program was eventually killed—not because of harm to American workers, but because of physical and financial exploitation of the *braceros*.

On the supply side, Mexico must create the well-paying jobs that give its people a reason to stay. This means shaking off, once and for all, the last remnants of its protectionist past with constitutional, labor, and tax reforms that would attract greater foreign investment, especially to its state-run oil monopoly.

Americans and Mexicans can harp on ancient history, or they can recognize their common responsibility to change the underlying economic forces driving illegal immigration. Until that happens, Mexicans will keep trying to cross to *el otro lado*, the other side. And as recent history teaches, with a tragic wall in Berlin, there is no barrier big enough and no border force strong enough to hold back the desperate.

Hey, Donald Trump: Making Mexico Go Broke Would Actually Be Mucho Dumb

Fortune Magazine, February 6, 2017

IT'S WIDELY KNOWN THAT 19TH-CENTURY MEXICAN DICTATOR PORFIRIO Diaz once said, "Poor Mexico. So far from God, so close to the United States." It's less well-known that his predecessor, Sebastián Lerdo de Tejada, looked at the stretch of land between the two countries and said, "Between the strong and the weak, the desert." There was little doubt who was who.

Starting with Franklin Roosevelt, US presidents have worked to heal those historical grievances and build a closer, more mature partnership. But now, President Donald Trump's talk of sending in troops to deal with "bad hombres," building a wall between our countries, imposing a 20 percent border tax, and re-negotiating the North American Free Trade Agreement in a way that helps the US while hurting Mexico—threatens to return us to the bad old days. This stance won't just hurt America economically. If we humiliate Mexico, a proud and important country, we will undo years of progress; stoke anti-American sentiment; and possibly turn a friend into an enemy—making both countries less secure.

I say this as an American citizen who has seen the relationship from both sides of the border. As an impulsive young college student on the G.I. Bill in the early 1950s, I was inspired by the movie *The Treasure of the Sierra Madre* to move to Mexico in search of gold. Mexicans joked that I was the only American who ever swam the wrong way across the Rio Grande.

I never did find gold—but I did find manganese. It helped me build a global mining business. My customers included the US government, which needed our manganese for its strategic stockpile. For decades, I lived and worked among some of the most famous artists and intellectuals in Mexico, along with old miners, prospectors, and working-class Mexicans of all backgrounds. What I found were people willing to work hard to create a stronger and more prosperous future for their country.

After signing NAFTA in 1993, America formed a partnership with Mexico—our third-largest trading partner—[that] helped build a nation where its citizens don't have to go north to have a future. Contrary to Trump's alternative facts, illegal immigration from Mexico has been falling since 2009, as a *Washington Post* article recently reported. Mexico and the United States have worked to share intelligence and fight drug trafficking and transnational crime. The United States has also relied on Mexico to stop between 200,000 and 300,000 undocumented immigrants from entering Central and South America before they ever reach the US border.

By putting Mexico in the crosshairs, Trump threatens to halt all of that progress. One idea that Trump is considering is a 20 percent border tariff against imports from Mexico to pay for a southern wall. As many wonder how the tariff could get passed along to US consumers in the form of more expensive items in the grocery store and at Wal-Mart, US Senator Lindsey Graham may have captured the sentiment best in a recent tweet: "Simply put, any policy proposal which drives up costs of Corona, tequila, or margaritas is a big-time bad idea. Mucho sad."

But there's far more at stake in our relationship with Mexico. Having a prosperous, peaceful, and friendly neighbor along our 1,900-mile southern border is vital to America's national security. What difference does it make when a neighbor is hostile and unstable? Just ask South Korea.

The stronger Mexico is economically, the less incentive there is for residents to cross the border, and the more resources Mexico has to invest in security, development, and institutions—all of which benefit the United States. The answer to making America great again is not to make Mexico more poor. President Trump's position has already driven the peso to a record low against the US dollar. More isolation could tank Mexico's economy—ironically, creating precisely the conditions that could drive undocumented immigration through the roof.

In just about two weeks as president, Trump has managed to bring old resentments back. His threat to send the US Army to Mexico reminded me of an experience I had in the central Mexican village of Charcas in the mid-1960s. With my business more established, I had helped build a school there and visited a classroom one day, when I saw a map of North America in which the United States looked much smaller. Meanwhile, Mexico stretched over the entire American West. As I gazed in wonder, a little girl looked up and asked, "Señor Weiss, why did you steal half our country?"

She was talking about the half Mexico had lost in the Treaty of Guadalupe Hidalgo that had ended the Mexican-American War in 1848, which the map represented. That legacy is a big part of why Mexico has often had a difficult relationship—to say the least—with its powerful neighbor.

Former Mexican president Vicente Fox says Trump represents the return to that time of "the ugly American" and the "hated gringo." Mexican president Enrique Peña Nieto, who has instituted difficult but crucial reforms supported by the United States, has seen his approval ratings essentially tank after meeting with Trump. Meanwhile, populist and extreme left-winger Andrés Manuel Lopez Obrador, who has been called Mexico's Trump, is gaining ground for the 2018 presidential elections.

What can we do? I agree with *The Economist*'s recent suggestion on how to handle a bully. Mexico should highlight its many positive contributions, try to influence Trump to re-negotiate rather than scrap NAFTA, and strengthen Mexico's domestic economy.

Mexico should also open regular channels with some of the Trump administration's more practical officials—like newly appointed Secretary of State Rex Tillerson and Secretary of Defense James Mattis. In Mexico, US ambassador Roberta Jacobson—a career diplomat—should focus on public outreach to show that our president's disrespect does not represent the American people.

And for the rest of us in the United States, we should all watch a 2004 film directed by Sergio Arau called *A Day without a Mexican*. It imagines what would happen in California if Mexicans suddenly disappeared from every job. The result was chaos. The film's message? We should appreciate what we have before it's gone. To do otherwise wouldn't just be mucho sad, but mucho dumb.

GREAT GAME

Give China Favored Status

Defense News, April 18-24, 1994

"YOU CANNOT BECOME A FAT MAN WITH ONE BIG MEAL." WITH THAT uniquely Chinese aphorism, Chinese President Jiang Zemin summed up to US Secretary of State Warren Christopher the problem of quickly meeting tough US human rights conditions. Even the pro-democracy dissidents agree with the Chinese authorities that the United States should extend China's most favored nation (MFN) trade status.

If US President Bill Clinton does not, he will place the world's fastest-growing economy and one of our largest trading partners in a class reserved for only a few outlaw nations. The imposition of this most dire of economic sanctions against Beijing may or may not improve the plight of persecuted Chinese dissidents and Tibetans. But it will surely undermine our post–Cold War national security interests.

The Clinton government has identified what it considers the major threats to our nation's security: nuclear proliferation, regional conflict, internal threats to building democracy, and a weak US economy. Withdrawing China's MFN status would undermine not only one but all four of these threats.

NUCLEAR PROLIFERATION

North Korea is widely believed to have two crude nuclear devices. Coupled with a now-operational missile delivery system, this would represent a nuclear threat to all of East Asia, including Japan. In exchange for economic aid and expanded diplomatic ties, the United States has only managed to arrange inspection of nuclear facilities hand-picked by Pyongyang. As Defense Secretary William Perry acknowledged, China is crucial to any effort to persuade Kim Il Sung to forgo further development of nuclear weapons.

REGIONAL CONFLICT

Regional conflict is bad enough in Bosnia, where we have few economic interests and no troops. War in South Korea would be catastrophic to one of our largest trading partners and bring the 37,000 US troops stationed there into the conflict. China's help and support are as necessary to settle this potential disaster as they are needed in virtually every major dispute in Asia, including Hong Kong, Cambodia, and territorial and island disputes in the South China Sea.

The Pentagon also is discussing joint US-China military cooperation, beginning with peacekeeping and disaster relief operations in Central Asia, as well as how to transform Chinese and US defense industries from military to civilian use. A least-favored China would not be a cooperative ally.

DEMOCRACY BUILDING

Since opening its economy to trade and investment 15 years ago, China [has enjoyed a] rising standard of living [that] has led to more freedom, not less. While persecuted dissidents and Tibetans attest to how far China's democracy has to go, it is hard to see how limiting Chinese access to the US market and hurting China's burgeoning entrepreneurial and middle class will help.

As development in Asia and Latin America has shown, economic liberalization preceded the legalization of opposition parties in Taiwan, the election of former opposition leaders as presidents in South Korea and Chile, and potentially free elections in Mexico.

DOMESTIC PROSPERITY

Senator Max Baucus, D-Montana, describes rescinding China's MFN status as the "trade equivalent of dropping a nuclear bomb." The fallout would affect China and the United States. China is the key to Clinton's vision of creating jobs through expanded trade in an economically integrated Pacific Rim.

Although China maintains a multibillion-dollar trade surplus with the United States, exports to China are responsible for at least 200,000 jobs nationwide, many in high-wage, high-tech areas such as power plants and aircraft. Trade sanctions would be cutting off America's nose to spite China's face.

In the Cold War effort to blunt Soviet expansionism, the United States maintained good working relationships with a large number of regimes that did not live up to our standards of decency. But we stuck with them anyway. Now, ironically, since good economics makes good politics, not the other way around, most of these countries are on the path to democracy and respect for individual liberty.

Although our national security concerns may be dramatically different today than they were for almost 50 years, the cost of satisfying our sense of self-righteousness about China's human rights policies would be no less great.

Sanctions: Don't Love Them or Hate Them—Make Them Work

UN Chronicle, 1999
(with Zachary Selden)

FEW FOREIGN POLICY ISSUES EXCITE SUCH PASSIONATE AND DISPARATE feelings in the United States as proposals to impose economic sanctions in order to try to influence the behavior of other countries. The business community hates sanctions which cost American firms in terms of lost sales and business relationships. Meanwhile, many politicians love sanctions; how else to take "tough" action against a foreign country without risking American blood or treasure?

The domestic debate, which concerns largely ineffective unilateral sanctions, is mirrored internationally by similar intellectual trench warfare over multilateral sanctions. On one side, critics line up to deride the use of sanctions without admitting those instances in which these measures work. On the other side are those who view sanctions as the default option, with little regard to the type used or the manner in which they are employed. The end result is that sanctions are seen as primarily symbolic gestures. In fact, if done right, they can be a useful, though limited, diplomatic tool.

The problem is that even multilateral economic sanctions, which have a much better chance of achieving diplomatic goals, are rarely done right.

As a result, sanctions are often worse than ineffective. In many cases, they have proven highly counterproductive, creating changes in the target country's economy which make the offensive behavior that brought sanctions to bear even more difficult to reverse. Yet sanctions have met with success in more than a few instances. The key to their more effective use is understanding what they are, and how and why they can produce such divergent results. At the most basic level, there is a distinction between trade sanctions on commodities and financial sanctions aimed at impeding the flow of capital to a target country. Trade sanctions can be further divided into those which prevent the target country from being able to import goods (export sanctions) and those which block exports from a country (import sanctions).

Why are these distinctions important? Because while financial sanctions tend to raise the cost of capital to an offending country, export sanctions tend to induce import substitution. Even if multilateral sanctions are effective in blocking the flow of goods to a particular country, the target state will respond, if possible, by producing substitutes. The 1977 UN-imposed arms embargo on South Africa, for example, prompted the creation of a vast military industrial complex there. The result was that South Africa not only became self-sufficient in weapons, but also became a major exporter of sophisticated arms. Employing nearly 140,000 people at its peak in the 1980s, the South African arms industry was the sixth-largest weapons exporter in the world. Even today, it is a major supplier of weapons to other African countries. Although import substitution is an expensive and economically inefficient practice, it is well worth the cost, especially when sanctions demand significant changes in the target country's policies or behavior.

More important, trade sanctions have political ramifications. Refusing to sell to a country gives it the functional equivalent of a protective tariff. This benefits producers capable of making substitutes and provides a reason for them to support the policies and leaders whose actions keep sanctions in place. In other words, export sanctions tend to create groups within the offending country with a material incentive to see that sanctions remain, and these groups try to influence the target country's government to maintain the policies that prompted the sanctions.

In the 1990s, trade sanctions imposed on Yugoslavia enriched a criminal elite closely tied to paramilitary organizations and arch nationalist political parties. The loosely enforced blockade on gasoline produced an extremely profitable black market controlled by these criminals, including the leader of an infamous Serbian paramilitary group responsible for much of the violence and ethnic cleansing in Bosnia. He is a wealthy man, thanks to sanctions and the illegal profits from the black market.

Financial sanctions have been used successfully to resolve a number of international disputes. In the 1960s, these were effective in securing compensation for expropriated property in Sri Lanka and Peru. In 1980, financial sanctions imposed by the European Community against Turkey helped to moderate the military government's authoritarian policies. Financial sanctions also played a role in pushing Iran, which was eager to regain frozen assets held abroad, to release the American hostages in 1981.

Regardless of the type of sanction contemplated, a few basic rules must be followed. First, sanctions need to be supported by the vast majority of potential suppliers. Near-global unity might be necessary in the case of food, while only the industrialized countries would have to support sanctions involving high-tech goods. In the case of certain war materials, the United States could almost do it alone. Financial sanctions can be particularly effective precisely because capital is the one commodity for which most nations cannot substitute domestically. By blocking the flow of capital from the cheaper lenders, through the World Bank and the International Monetary Fund, the cost of capital goes up. That hurts the elite of the target country, who then have to make some hard choices about where to cut spending—or accede to the wishes of the global majority.

Second, if economic sanctions are to work, it follows that the banned goods must not be easily available internally. Banning oil exports to a leading oil producer is sanctions' version of bringing coals to Newcastle—the loss of access to foreign goods, which are also produced domestically, simply won't cause enough pain to modify behavior. Even countries that do not presently produce the banned product may be able to do so if the stakes are high enough.

Before sanctions were leveled, Iraq was known as a major food importer. In the wake of sanctions, Iraq planted more land with basic cereal crops in the early 1990s and had larger harvests than before the war. In 1991, the grain harvest was 24 percent larger than the previous season.

No matter what sanction is chosen or how it is imposed, it can only work if the cost of the sanction is greater than the cost of the policy change. For example, when the United States threatened to cut off aid to Peru in the 1960s unless the government changed its mind about expropriating American property, the sanctions were effective because United States aid mattered more to the Peruvian government than the value of the property. But sanctions against Yugoslavia designed to depose President Slobodan Milosevic probably won't work if the Yugoslav ruler knows that by giving in, he faces jail or death as a war criminal.

Economic sanctions are a tool that can induce changes at the margins and can be combined with other forms of pressure to exert greater changes. In and of themselves, they succeed only when the goals are modest, the sanctions are chosen properly, and they enjoy the support of key countries. If used properly, sanctions will be neither loved nor hated. That realization alone will go a long way toward making them more effective.

China and India Face Off in Nepal

International Herald Tribune, July 21, 2001

ONLY A PRESENT-DAY WILLIAM SHAKESPEARE COULD IMAGINE THE real-life tragedy in Nepal when the Crown Prince eliminated an entire line of a royal dynasty that had ruled that land for more than 200 years.

In killing his father the king, his mother the queen, his brother and sisters, an uncle—and then himself—the Crown Prince did more than re-create the most dramatic themes of *Hamlet, Romeo and Juliet,* and *Macbeth.* He also plunged Nepal into its most serious crisis ever—one that can affect the rest of this volatile region.

Before last month, Nepal was known in the West primarily for its small size and remoteness. But in geostrategic terms, it is neither small nor remote. The Himalayan kingdom is sandwiched between the world's two most populous countries: China and India. Nepal's 25 million people are divided among more than a dozen ethnic groups that speak 48 languages and dialects. And although the king relinquished most of his powers in 1990 in favor of becoming a constitutional monarch with a parliamentary democracy, the monarchy has been the glue that held the country together. Indeed, in the 11 years of constant political party infighting, there have been 11 governments and six prime ministers.

All of this turmoil has been an open invitation for China and its surrogate, Pakistan, to try and extend their influence both in Nepal and into India's turbulent northeastern states.

The hijacking of an Indian passenger plane taking off from Kathmandu by Islamabad-backed Kashmiri rebels two years ago, the arrest of a Pakistan diplomat allegedly planning to sell explosives to Nepalese insurgents, and the emergence of Nepal as the passage to India for Pakistan's Inter-Services Intelligence furnish more than enough of a security reason for New Delhi not to take its ties with the kingdom for granted.

India is by far Nepal's most important economic, military, and political ally. But Delhi expects complete loyalty in this unequal partnership, especially vis-à-vis China. When Nepal talked of procuring Chinese anti-aircraft guns in 1988, for instance, India responded by closing its markets to Nepal, increasing the landlocked kingdom's economic isolation.

Compounding its recent problems, and virtually unnoticed by the outside world, Nepal has been subjected for the past five years to a Maoist guerrilla insurgency spreading to most rural districts. The insurgency's intellectual godfather boasts that like Mao Zedong's guerrillas, once they control the countryside, the capital, Kathmandu, will fall and "we will hoist the hammer-and-sickle red flag atop Mount Everest." Sadly, with the death of most of the royal family, and the accession of a new king who may use the army to restore law and order, the nation may find itself in a full-scale civil war.

The oxygen feeding Nepal's instability is its abject poverty. Fully half of the population is unemployed and living below the poverty line.

That is Nepal's real tragedy. The country could be rich. It has a crucial natural resource, water. Hundreds of rivers gushing south between the Himalayas have massive hydroelectricity potential to serve all of its domestic needs and the growing demand from India and Bangladesh.

So why hasn't Nepal exploited this limitless, renewable source of energy? A fear of increasing dependence on India, its principal consumer, has been the prime concern.

But with Nepal and nearby Bhutan endowed with enormous water resources, India with its coal, and Bangladesh with its natural gas, these four neighboring countries could develop a mixed energy system for all to benefit. And massive investment capital from the West, the World Bank, and the IMF to build the dams and the hydroelectric plants would surely be forthcoming.

Whether concerned about economics or security, there is too much at stake not to bring peace and prosperity to the kingdom and transform a Shakespearean tragedy into a happy ending.

Get Real: Preserve Artificial Countries

The Straits Times, August 5, 2003

INDIA'S DEPUTY PRIME MINISTER LAL ADVANI TOLD ME THE STORY THIS way. Pakistani president Pervez Musharraf looked at his Indian guests and said, "I was born in India, and after Partition, my family settled in Karachi, the capital of Pakistan's Sindh province. Why not let the people of Kashmir decide whether they want to continue to be a part of India?"

To which Mr. Advani replied, "I was born in Karachi and, after Partition, moved to India. Why not let the people of Sindh decide whether they want to continue to be a part of Pakistan?' At which point President Musharraf changed the subject, knowing full well that the Sindhis would vote for independence.

The terse encounter highlights the central tension underlying much of today's instability from the Indian subcontinent to Afghanistan to Iraq and in many other countries—self-determination versus national preservation.

Frustrated by centuries-old conflicts, some Western observers have advocated redrawing the regional maps and carving up "artificial countries" created by former colonial powers.

At first glance, certain states seem ripe for the picking. Pakistan is an invention—literally an acronym denoting the provinces of the new Muslim state after its 1947 Partition with India: *P* for Punjab, *A* for the Afghan-border region of the northwest frontier, *K* for Kashmir, *S* for Sindh, and *TAN* for Baluchistan.

The dominant Punjabis have never succeeded in forging a Pakistani national identity. Baluchistan, Pakistan's largest province, has chafed under the iron fist of Islamabad. (When I asked a cab driver here in London if he was Pakistani, he replied indignantly, "I am not Pakistani! I am from Baluchistan!") Pashtuns in the Northwest Frontier Province have long dreamed of an independent Pashtunistan with their ethnic cousins across the Afghan border.

Likewise, the dominant Pashtuns of southern Afghanistan have never forged a unifying national psyche. Tajiks, Uzbeks, and Turkmens in the north have more in common with their brethren in neighboring Tajikistan, Uzbekistan, and Turkmenistan. In the west, Herat province is reverting to its historical role as a virtual extension of Iran.

Finally, whether Iraq survives as a multi-ethnic nation may hinge on the Kurds, the world's largest ethnic group without its own state. Today, 30 million Kurds are spread across Turkey, Iran, Iraq, and Syria, and repeated Kurdish rebellions have been brutally crushed.

So why not think the unthinkable and simply dispense with the irrational borders of the past? After all, isn't the birth of new states from the wreckage of Yugoslavia the latest tribute to self-determination?

On the contrary. The orgy of violence that accompanied the breakup of Yugoslavia would be a picnic compared with the carnage if dysfunctional states like Pakistan, Afghanistan, and Iraq fell—or were pushed—apart.

Ethnic minorities should be careful what they wish for: reckless quests for self-determination may only sow the seeds of their self-destruction.

Don't expect Islamabad to give up Sindh and Karachi, Pakistan's financial capital and the source of most of the nation's revenues. Pakistan's eastern wing, now Bangladesh, won its war for independence in 1971, but 3 million Bengalis died in the process. The Punjabis have suppressed past rebellions in Baluchistan and would do so again.

Pro-Taliban Muslims already control the provincial legislatures of Baluchistan and the Northwest Frontier Province. Is the world prepared for two new independent Al Qaeda havens?

In Afghanistan, the Pashtuns may long for unity with their Pakistani cousins, but not at the expense of losing influence over the more fertile and prosperous regions of the north.

The Kurds may have found an answer. The continued presence of Turkish troops in northern Iraq is a blunt reminder that Ankara will forcibly oppose an independent Kurdistan, which could incite Turkey's own restive Kurds. Bowing to reality, Kurdish leaders in Iraq appear to have abandoned their quest for statehood, casting their lot with a federal Iraq that preserves Kurdish autonomy.

Autonomy could also break the Gordian Knot of Kashmir. Lose the *K* in Pakistan to India, and Pakistan loses its *raison d'être* as a homeland for Muslims on the subcontinent.

Similarly, if India gives up its only Muslim-majority state, it risks losing its national identity as a secular state in a predominantly Hindu country. Ceding Kashmir's 4 million Muslims to Pakistan would prompt Hindu extremists to unleash a wholesale ethnic cleansing of India's 150 million Muslims and a flood of refugees that would destroy Pakistan.

So why not compromise? Pakistan controls 35 percent of Kashmir and could accept the present Line of Control, agreed to in 1972, as the permanent border. In return, India could restore to Kashmir the autonomy that it enjoyed for several years after Partition.

In an ideal world, each of these distinct ethnic groups could have its own independent homeland. And some day, they just might. But in today's real world, their security and survival lie not with independence, but with a high degree of autonomy. And there is nothing artificial about that.

Latin America Is No Joke:
US Neighbor Relations

International Herald Tribune, December 27, 2004

WHEN 11 LATIN AMERICAN COUNTRIES TOOK THE FIRST STEPS TOWARD A regional common market in 1960, dismissive US officials predictably joked that the ill-fated Latin American Free Trade Agreement would generate "more tears than LAFTA."

But no one was laughing this month in Peru when all 12 South American nations pledged themselves to an EU-style political and economic community. The South American Community of Nations—which by definition excludes Mexico, the United States, and Canada—envisions a common market, a regional constitution, and a parliament.

Are America's southern neighbors finally on the path to lasting integration?

Recent decades have seen an alphabet soup of acronymic trade agreements designed to bind the region, from LAFTA to NAFTA (North American Free Trade Agreement) to CAFTA (the Central American Free Trade Agreement, awaiting ratification) to AFTA (the Andean Free Trade Agreement, under negotiation) to SAFTA (a South American Free Trade Agreement, still a dream).

The infighting at the recent economic summit in Brazil underscores the rivalries that have plagued the Mercosur customs union between Brazil, Argentina, Uruguay, and Paraguay.

Negotiations to create a hemisphere-wide Free Trade Area of the Americas (FTAA) stretching from Alaska to Argentina are stalled over disagreements between the United States and Brazil.

More likely, the display of unity in Peru was as much about South America as it was about the North—specifically the United States. A more unified group of South American nations is seen as a way to strengthen their collective bargaining power in trade negotiations with the almighty *yanquis*.

Meanwhile, American policy toward the region is "old-fashioned and murky," says Rubens Barbosa, a former Brazilian ambassador to Washington.

"The United States has not recognized the changes in the region after NAFTA. There is a new economic geography in the Americas."

Indeed, always bound more by geography than ideology, America and its Latin neighbors are drifting apart. As Washington moves to the right, the rest of the hemisphere is moving to the left. The presidents of Brazil, Argentina, Chile, Venezuela, and Ecuador were all elected by challenging Washington-driven free market reforms that have done little to reduce the region's endemic poverty.

This spring, Uruguayans will swear in their first leftist president ever. In Nicaragua, mayoral wins by the Sandinistas may herald the return of US nemesis Daniel Ortega. In Mexico, leftist Mayor Andrés Manuel López Obrador of Mexico City remains the man to beat for president in 2006.

In another sign of the changes, Mexico and Chile, with temporary seats on the UN Security Council, resisted intense American pressure to support the invasion of Iraq.

While in Canada recently, President George W. Bush said that "a new term in office is an important opportunity to reach out to friends." How can the United States reverse what Barbosa calls Washington's "policy of benign neglect" toward Latin America?

Washington can reach out to its southern friends by focusing more on Latin American concerns. After the recent Asian-Pacific Economic Cooperation summit in Santiago, Bush's only stop in the region was a four-hour drop-by in Colombia to show support for President Alvaro Uribe's war on narco-terrorism.

In contrast, President Hu Jintao of China spent two weeks traveling the region, signing $30 billion in trade and development deals with Brazil, Argentina, Chile, and Cuba. Last year, China became Brazil's second-largest trading partner behind the United States.

"The US war is against terrorism," Barbosa says, "Latin America's war is against poverty and hunger."

Washington must acknowledge continent-sized Brazil, with South America's largest economy, as the awakening giant it is. In addition to championing the new South American community, President Luiz Inácio Lula da Silva of Brazil has won praise across the developing world for fighting US cotton subsidies, which the World Trade Organization has ruled illegal.

Brazil's refusal to fully open its markets without corresponding US concessions on farm subsidies has so far killed dreams of a hemispheric trade pact.

Regrettably, some in Washington view Brasilia as a strategic competitor. Having once warned that Brazil's only trading partner would be Antarctica if it did not agree to a hemispheric trade zone, US trade representative Robert Zoellick last year labeled Brazil a "can't do, won't do" country.

Washington should instead welcome Brazil as a strategic partner. Brazil is leading the UN peacekeeping mission in Haiti, has been a valued ally in the drug war, and can serve as a diplomatic bridge between the United States and regional bad boy Hugo Chávez of Venezuela. Washington should support Brazil's candidacy for a permanent seat on an enlarged Security Council. And if they really want a hemispheric free trade agreement, Bush and Congress must take on the powerful farm lobby and end unfair agricultural subsidies that make a mockery of free trade.

Washington can no longer afford to neglect Latin American countries like unwanted stepchildren. The United States needs the region—and not just for professional baseball stars. Limited initiatives like free trade agreements with Chile, Central America, and the Andean countries are positive steps, but pale beside the huge benefits of a hemisphere-wide pact.

The smuggling of drugs and illegal aliens, narco-terrorism, and responding to crises in places like Haiti are hemispheric challenges. As Secretary of Defense Donald Rumsfeld observed while meeting with his regional counterparts in Ecuador last month, "No one country can deal with these problems alone."

It's in Washington's interest to treat its southern neighbors as the indispensable partners they are. Otherwise, it will be Latin America that has the last laugh.

Don't Play This Great Game

International Herald Tribune, December 10–11, 2005

TO LISTEN TO WESTERN COMMENTATORS, WASHINGTON, MOSCOW, AND Beijing are in the early rounds of a new Great Game, akin to the 19th-century struggle between Czarist Russia and the British Empire for primacy in Central Asia. Unable to resist the analogy, analysts sound more like sports announcers, calling every play as a gain or loss for the players on the field.

This month's re-election of Kazakhstan's strongman president, Nursultan Nazarbayev, in a vote that was neither free nor fair, will surely be cited as the latest example of Soviet-style authoritarianism resisting the onslaught of Western-style democracy.

The July summit of the Shanghai Cooperation Organization (SCO)—made up of China, Russia, Kazakhstan, Uzbekistan, Tajikistan, and Kyrgyzstan—was billed as a "NATO of the East," a new team to counter American global dominance. The SCO's call for a timetable for withdrawal of US forces from bases in Uzbekistan and Kyrgyzstan was seen as the opening play. Uzbekistan's subsequent decision to evict American forces and to forge a new defense pact with Russia last month was called a strategic loss for Washington and a win for Moscow.

Likewise, China's recent purchase of the second-largest oil company in Kazakhstan and a new oil pipeline and railroad between the two countries have been portrayed as proof of Beijing's unmatched economic prowess in the region.

While colorful, such commentary fails to capture the real situation on the ground. First, the grand prize itself—political, economic, and military influence over these oil-rich republics—may not be the trophy some imagine. Though the Bush administration seeks to turn the region into a "corridor of reform," with Kazakhstan as a "regional leader" (in free markets, if not free elections), Central Asia largely remains a corridor of criminality, oppression, and corruption.

In fact, Uzbekistan's eviction of the Americans and its new bear hug with Russia may turn out to be a blessing for Washington and a curse for Moscow.

After Tashkent's brutal suppression of protests last spring, Washington is now in bed with one less despotic regime that oppresses its Muslim population.

Second, despite old ethnic ties to Russia and new economic links with China, the region increasingly looks west. Kazakhstan, among the world's largest remaining oil and natural gas reserves, plans to tap into the new Caspian pipeline from Azerbaijan to Turkey, thereby reducing its dependence on oil export routes through Russia.

Meanwhile, the United States has become Kazakhstan's largest foreign investor.

Third, Russia, with its declining population, exodus of capital, and demoralized military, is too weak—and China, with its voracious appetite for energy and exploding population, is too feared—to dominate the region.

Rumors about a new Russian-Chinese alliance are also greatly exaggerated. Russian and Chinese troops did indeed this summer conduct their first military exercise ever. But historic mistrust and potentially explosive border disputes between the two powers suggest that closer ties are more a tactical, temporary partnership rather than a long-term strategic alliance. Indeed, the SCO will more likely be a way for Moscow and Beijing to keep a check on each other in Central Asia rather than for keeping the Americans out.

Finally, economic and political jockeying is unlikely to escalate into military conflict. As General Charles Wald, deputy commander of US forces in Europe, tells me, "Although progress is often interrupted by political concerns, our military-to-military relations with the Russians improve every year."

Rather than be lured into a zero-sum Great Game of inevitable confrontation, Washington, Moscow, and Beijing should recognize Central Asia as an opportunity for cooperation against the one danger that threatens all three—Islamic terrorism.

The existential threat to Russia no longer emanates from NATO to the west, but from Islamic militants to the south, from Chechnya, and across its southern republics. China is facing increasingly vocal demands from the Uighur, Kazakh and Tajik Muslims in its western province of Xinjiang, which separatists call "East Turkestan."

The United States, Russia, and China could also counter the appeal of Islamic extremism by working to reduce the region's economic misery. Recent progress in negotiations to expand the Caspian Pipeline Consortium from Kazakhstan to the Black Sea via Russia proves that cooperation is possible in the name of economic development.

Washington's goal of promoting regional cooperation would benefit from the involvement of two other powers: Rather than its self-defeating policy of trying to isolate Iran, the United States should recognize it as a potential partner in stabilizing and developing the region, as Tehran has done in Afghanistan. And rather than a futile attempt to diminish the SCO, Washington should encourage Indian membership so that New Delhi can offer a democratic voice for reform and stability.

Dropping the alarmist rhetoric about Great Games and recognizing the reality of the world's common interests in this vital region would be a strategy worth trying. It also might be the one game where everyone wins.

The Power of Water:
The Untapped Might of the Himalayas

International Herald Tribune, May 11, 2005

WHAT DO THE FOLLOWING HAVE IN COMMON? NEPAL'S BRUTAL MAOIST rebellion. India's violence-racked northeastern states. China's global energy race with India. Warming ties between Pakistan and India. Bangladesh's increasing Islamic extremism.

Answer: water.

Specifically, the thousands of glacier-fed rivers of Nepal and Bhutan, the tiny Himalayan kingdoms sandwiched between India and China. The vast hydro-electric potential of these raging rivers could serve as the centerpiece of a long-term regional energy strategy promoting stability and prosperity across South Asia.

Poverty-stricken Nepal and Bhutan as a regional energy hub? Admittedly, these countries at the top of the world rank near the bottom of virtually every measure of development. Most Nepalese and Bhutanese literally live in the dark without electricity or potable water.

In Nepal, the nine-year-old Maoist insurgency has occasionally shut down power plants and spooked foreign investors. Having harnessed less than 1 percent of its hydropower potential, Nepal last year imported electricity from India. "Water, water, everywhere," locals could lament, "but not a drop to drink—or export."

Such dire conditions make development more urgent, not less. Just as extreme poverty fuels the Maoist insurgency, better economics can make for better politics. As Farooq Sobhan, president of the Bangladesh Enterprise Institute, told me, "Energy is an area where all the countries of South Asia have much to gain through cooperation."

For Bhutan and Nepal, exporting hydroelectricity to energy-hungry India could generate wealth beyond their dreams. "Water is to us what oil is to the Arabs," King Wangchuck of Bhutan has said.

For Nepal, using hydro dollars to bring roads, electricity, drinking water, health clinics, and schools to the countryside would also be the best way to fight poverty—and the Maoists. "The insurgency can be neutralized if the benefits of hydropower development are shared by all in an equitable manner," says Janak Lai Karmacharya, head of the Nepal Electricity Authority.

For India, which is aggressively pursuing an annual economic growth rate of 8 percent, hydroelectricity could end the power shortages that shrink its gross domestic product by an entire percentage point every year. Job-creating hydro projects could also temper secessionist movements in the country's volatile northeastern states.

How can these countries turn their water into white gold?

First, natural resources must not be seen as a zero-sum game. "The real problem is the lack of political trust between nations and the reluctance to deal with energy as a shared opportunity," explained Uday Bhaskar of India's Institute for Defense Studies and Analyses.

Indeed, the 1960 Indus Waters Treaty, which has survived several wars between India and Pakistan, proves that even adversaries can bridge troubled waters.

To tap the natural bounty of the Himalayas, Nepal must get over its inferiority complex that prevents closer economic ties with its big Indian neighbor. Bangladesh must get over the irrational nationalism that prevents it from exporting natural gas to India and using the revenues for development projects that could avoid its Talibanization.

India must be more sensitive to the legitimate water worries of its smaller neighbors. What's good for New Delhi must also be good for the region, economically and ecologically. For example, as part of their new "strategic partnership" and plans for joint energy ventures, China and India should stop treating Nepal and Bhutan as buffer zones and instead see them as future hydro-based economic zones.

Second, current strife in Nepal should hasten, not halt, development. King Gyanendra's decision last week to lift the state of emergency he imposed in February should be welcomed in New Delhi as a first step toward resuming military and development assistance to Nepal. Likewise, the World Bank, the International Monetary Fund, and the Asian Development Bank should continue, not cut off, aid projects that help Nepal realize its hydropower ambitions.

Third, India should champion a regional energy strategy. As the region's biggest energy consumer, New Delhi has little to lose and much to gain from linking the power grids of the seven-nation South Asian Association for Regional Cooperation.

To the east, Bangladesh has conditionally agreed to open its territory to a pipeline carrying natural gas from Myanmar to India. In return, New Delhi should open its power grid to carrying Himalayan hydropower to Bangladesh. And to the west, connecting the electrical grids of India and Pakistan could complement plans for a "peace pipeline" carrying natural gas from Iran to India across Pakistan.

"The technology is there to start connecting these countries tomorrow," says Hugh McDermott, who manages the South Asia Regional Initiative for Energy, sponsored by the US Agency for International Development. "All that's missing is the political will and the financial commitment."

Finally, hydro dollars should end the paradox of countries being resource-rich but people-poor. Bhutan could be a model. Under King Wangchuck, famous for favoring Gross National Happiness over Gross Domestic Product, exports of hydroelectricity to India now generate nearly half of all government revenues and fund critical improvements in health and education.

The icy rivers of the Himalayas are not holy water that will miraculously cure the region's ills. But for those seeking practical answers to some of the urgent challenges facing South Asia, it would certainly be a blessing.

Azerbaijan: The Key to the Caucasus

International Herald Tribune, December 9, 2008

"WELCOME TO HOUSTON ON THE CASPIAN," SAID ANNE DERSE, THE US ambassador to this booming, oil-rich nation, as our delegation of American business executives arrived on the final leg of a visit to Georgia, Armenia, and Azerbaijan.

After days of discussion with political, military, and business leaders across the region—including a talk with President Ilham Aliyev of Azerbaijan, whose office overlooks the Caspian Sea, home to perhaps a quarter of the world's new oil production—it all seemed obvious. As one US diplomat put it, Azerbaijan "is central to all we're trying to do in this part of the world."

Azerbaijan is the indispensable link to reducing European energy dependence on Moscow, with the only pipelines exporting Caspian oil and gas that bypass Russia altogether, with routes through Georgia and Turkey.

Without Azerbaijan, there will never be what the US energy secretary Samuel Bodman calls "a new generation of export routes" bypassing Russia. Known as the "southern corridor," it includes plans by Kazakhstan and Turkmenistan to ship oil and gas by barge across the Caspian to Baku, as well as the EU's long-planned Nabucco gas pipeline from Turkey to Europe.

Aliyev stresses that (unlike President Mikheil Saakashvili of Georgia) he will not taunt the Russian bear, continuing instead to walk a fine line between East and West. This policy includes allowing his military to train with NATO, but not rushing to become a NATO member.

Aliyev insists that "time is up" for the return of the Azerbaijani territory of Nagorno-Karabakh—the Armenian-majority region occupied by Armenia, with Russian support, since the war over the area in the early 1990s. Still, he seems determined not to give Moscow a pretext to intervene, as it did with its invasion of Georgia this summer.

Azerbaijan—like Turkey, with which it shares deep ethnic and linguistic ties—is one the world's most secularized Muslim countries, with a strict separation between mosque and state. Moreover, the nearly 20 million ethnic Azeris living in neighboring Iran—about a quarter of Iran's population—are culturally closer to their brethren in Baku than their Persian rulers in

Tehran. Azerbaijan also draws the ayatollahs' ire as one of the few Muslim nations with diplomatic ties with Israel.

Yet for all its strategic significance—and its support for the US war on terrorism, including sending troops to Afghanistan and Iraq—Azerbaijan remains the neglected stepchild of US Caucasus policy.

Despite Saakashvili's miscalculations with Russia, Georgia remains the darling of the West, garnering another $1 billion in post-war aid from the United States atop the nearly $2 billion Washington has bestowed over the years. The powerful Armenian-American lobby has not only secured some $2 billion for Armenia to date, it has succeeded in limiting US aid to Azerbaijan because of the dispute over Nagorno-Karabakh.

To be sure, this country is no democracy; the 46-year-old Aliyev learned well from his authoritarian father, who ruled Azerbaijan both as a Soviet Republic and after independence. Indeed, not long before our delegation arrived, Aliyev claimed re-election with 89 percent of the vote.

But if Azerbaijan is "central" to everything Washington is trying to accomplish in the Caucasus, then Azerbaijan should be at the forefront of US Caucasus policy.

To help Azerbaijan—and the region—realize its full economic potential, the incoming Obama administration should make a major push to resolve Nagorno-Karabakh, which—as one development official here tells me—"is the main issue that prevents regional integration."

A breakthrough is possible. Every member of the so-called Minsk Group charged with resolving the conflict—Azerbaijan, Armenia, Russia, several European countries, and the United States—has powerful incentives for compromise.

Aliyev wants Nagorno-Karabakh back, but understands that Moscow won't allow him to take it by force. Landlocked, impoverished Armenia desperately wants Azerbaijan and Turkey to end a 16-year economic blockade of its borders. Turkey wants to improve relations with Armenia. Europe wants to avert another crisis that would complicate plans for its Nabucco pipeline. And with new competing diplomatic initiatives, Turkey and Russia clearly want to play a leadership role in the region.

This "frozen conflict" will not thaw easily. But through a gradual process backed by the major powers, the Caucasus countries could finally focus on economic cooperation rather than military confrontation. And the trade routes of the old Silk Road could become a new energy corridor of the 21st century.

Rivals and Partners

The New York Times, January 9, 2010

LAST FALL, A RARE OPINION POLL WAS CONDUCTED ACROSS CHINA. IT ASKED a simple question: *What do you perceive as the greatest threat facing China?* The range of answers was interesting—but even more interesting was the way the survey was reported in India.

Among Indian newspapers, the thrust of the stories said that 40 percent of the Chinese polled think India presents the greatest security threat after the United States. Yet Indian business journals emphasized that 60 percent of Chinese saw no threat from India. The *Indian Business Standard* explained that while India was seen in China as the second-biggest threat, six in 10 Chinese citizens didn't mention India at all—a reflection of the broader concerns of a wealthier populace.

The contradictions come as no surprise—India is a kaleidoscope of competing realities. But as China and India begin preparations to mark 60 years of diplomatic ties, that same schizophrenia has come to characterize their bilateral relations.

Where does the heart of the relationship between the dragon and the elephant lie?

Is it in their increasingly public bickering over disputed land on the Himalayan border, where Indian officials have accused China of 270 line-of-control violations and 2,285 instances of aggressive border patrol last year?

Or is it in a burgeoning economic relationship that has seen China become India's largest trading partner, with bilateral trade leaping from $15 billion to $40 billion in the past five years—and is expected to grow to as much as $60 billion in 2010?

Does it rest in China's aggressive support of India's arch-rival, Pakistan; Beijing's strategy of building roads and ports in countries around the Indian Ocean as a "string of pearls" designed to choke India; and its efforts to block a $2.9 billion Asian Development Bank loan to India?

Or is it anchored in the remarkably united front India and China presented in Copenhagen, where they stood together to ensure that developed countries did not extract unilateral concessions on climate change from developing ones?

Right now, the answer seems to be both. "Indians generally agree that we must have excellent economic and diplomatic relations with China, but we must also keep our powder dry," Vice Admiral A. K. Singh, the former chief of India's Eastern Naval Command, told me. "We feel our foreign policy must be backed by sufficient power—a steel fist in a velvet glove."

Whether the future of this relationship is fashioned in velvet or forged in steel, three truths are emerging.

First, China seems committed to a vision of a multipolar world, but a unipolar Asia. It is no accident that China's posture toward India hardened in 2006. Just days after the United States and India unveiled a defense framework and then a nuclear agreement, China's ambassador to New Delhi began referring to the Indian state of Arunachal Pradesh as "Southern Tibet," a provocation not heard since the two nations fought a 32-day war over the territory in 1962.

"China has always believed that India lacks the will to resist a sharp-pointed thrust," says Brahma Chellaney, one of India's leading strategic thinkers. "But a US-India military alliance has always been a nightmare for China because it fears India becoming a new Japan to America." China's regional brinksmanship seems designed to distract India and box it in, allowing China to emerge as the voice of Asia.

Second, India seems determined not to be pushed around by China. Since 2006, India has beefed up its border security, reiterated its border claims, and deported thousands of unskilled Chinese workers. It also has deepened support for the Dalai Lama, welcoming him to a historic Buddhist monastery in Tawang last fall, despite Beijing's protests. Rather than weakening India's resolve, Chinese intransigence may be strengthening it.

Third, it is in America's interests to maintain good relations with both nations. After President Obama's travels to China and the Indian prime minister's state visit to Washington, the joke in New Delhi was that "China gets an agreement, Pakistan gets funding, and India gets a nice dinner." With China acting as America's banker, it would seem, as a prominent Indian diplomat said to me, that "for the foreseeable future, the United States is unlikely to act as a countervailing power to China, and India will have to look after its interests the best it can. But there is also a sense that the United States will recover, and its passivity toward China will be temporary."

"The truth is," a high-ranking US State Department official told me, "both India and China have important roles to play in the emerging global architecture."

"We are concerned about the border," he added, "but in the next decade, the United States will likely be involved in a different issue on the Himalayan border—which is the dire shortage of water in both nations, and the role Tibetan waters can play in addressing it."

Which brings us back to that opinion poll: When asked what most threatened them, the majority of Chinese cited nontraditional threats, like climate change, water, and food shortages.

China and India might yet end up in the same boat.

The Mao Doctrine

The Huffington Post, August 15, 2011

HE STUDIED LAW UNDER THOMAS JEFFERSON, SERVED AS SECRETARY OF state and secretary of war under John Adams, was elected president of the United States in 1816, and was so fondly hailed that his eight years as chief executive were dubbed the "era of good feelings."

The question is not why James Monroe is remembered by history—but rather, why he is being thrust once more into the spotlight, during this era of decidedly less-than-good feelings. The answer: China.

Last week, China sent its first-ever aircraft carrier to sea—yet another move in a year that has seen Beijing establish a much more combative stance in the South China Sea, alarming the United States and its regional allies.

Meanwhile, locals are wondering: is this the beginning of China's version of the Monroe Doctrine?

The famous policy articulated by Monroe in 1823 declared that any effort to subjugate any republic in the Western Hemisphere by any outsiders would be interpreted as a hostile act toward the United States, and responded to in kind. The Monroe Doctrine sought to keep foreign powers out of the waters surrounding America; the "Mao Doctrine" seems designed to deny US naval access to Asian waters. The danger, of course, is that if Chinese aggression sparks any conflict with US allies, the United States will be forced to respond.

"The Chinese want to play the game that they aren't threatening and there's no need for the United States to remain," Bambang Harimurti, the editor-in-chief of *Tempo* magazine, tells me. "But once they are strong enough, they will be aggressive. In China's constitution, it says these waters are theirs." Adds Adam Schwarz, an Indonesian historian and a McKinsey & Company strategist, "It's hard to see a scenario where it's in China's benefit to escalate this further, because the United States would be asked to come help the Philippines and Vietnam. But look at China's actions recently: this is their version of the Monroe Doctrine."

China has done much to undo a decade's worth of good neighbor diplomacy in Asia. In Pakistan this year, China began building two nuclear reactors, which will allow Pakistan—the world's number one nuclear proliferator—to build 24 nuclear weapons each year; in Myanmar, China's hand is evident in the renewed civil war in the northern Kachin State; in North Korea, it refused to condemn Pyongyang's murder of South Korean civilians and soldiers; in the territory around India, China's "String of Pearls" policy supports new ports in Myanmar, Bangladesh, and Pakistan; after Japan agreed to Beijing's demands to release a Chinese fishing captain arrested for ramming a Japanese ship, China suspended diplomatic relations.

"All of Southeast Asia has a fear of the giant to the north," the former chief of Indonesia's special forces, Lieutenant General (retired) Prabowo Subianto, says to me. "I asked a senior Malaysian official, what will Malaysia do if China occupies the South China Sea? He said, 'What can we do?'"

Last year, Beijing laid claim—for the first time in two centuries—to the entire South China Sea, including islands in the territorial waters of five other nations, as a "core national interest." Washington saw this as a naked power grab at the region's shipping lanes, one of the most heavily traveled waterways in the world. In March, two Chinese patrol boats were accused of intimidating a Filipino exploration ship searching for oil within the Philippines Exclusive Economic Zone. In May, a Vietnam vessel searching for oil was damaged by three Chinese surveillance vessels.

Some believe the presence of oil under these waters is the real prize: one Chinese estimate puts the possible oil reserves as high as 213 billion barrels—10 times the proven reserves of the United States. Others believe the South China Sea is integral to its nuclear submarine strategy. Having quadrupled its military expenditures in recent years—the new aircraft carrier is the first of four—the South China Sea is integral to China's intentions to develop a blue-water navy. "But," as Anies Baswedan, the president of Paramadina University, tells me, "this is, above all, a challenge to the unity of ASEAN."

If this is China's Mao Doctrine, then the Association of Southeast Asian Nations, or ASEAN, needs its NATO, or "SEATO." The question is, will this bring the 10-member association closer together, or drive them apart? At its meeting last month in Bali, Ted Osius, the US chief of mission in Jakarta, told me that "ASEAN officials spent 70 percent of their time focused on the South China Sea"—and reached agreement on a Code of Conduct with China, with a follow-up meeting planned for October. For a Chinese government that prefers bilateral agreements to split ASEAN members, the joint stand in Bali communicated a strong message: ASEAN will stand as one.

What can the United States do? Continue to support the work of ASEAN. Make the South China Seas a focus of the recently initiated talks between the US and Chinese militaries. And maybe even help ASEAN members build up their own navies.

For a nation that suffered endless invasions and offenses from 1840 to the founding of the People's Republic of China in 1949, the new swagger is also about something else, as former Indonesian Minister of Defense Juwono Sudarsono tells me: "pride." In truth, the Mao Doctrine is making real an influence in the region that Mao's China itself never achieved—something James Monroe himself would have understood.

Asia's Quiet War

The Huffington Post, May 1, 2012

IT IS ONE OF HISTORY'S GREAT IRONIES THAT THE BUDDHA GREW UP, attained enlightenment, and taught in India, while Buddhism has gained its greatest number of adherents—nearly 40 percent of the population—in China. This discrepancy was on full display last December, with New Delhi and Beijing each jockeying to be the site of the new International Buddhist Confederation. Swayed by India's status as Buddhism's birthplace, and displeased by China's treatment of the Dalai Lama, 900 Buddhist delegates to a conference in India voted to establish Buddhism's de facto world capital here in India's capital.

Angered that the Dalai Lama had been allowed to speak at the Indian gathering, China broke off diplomatic talks with India—talks to negotiate a boundary dispute that has festered for 50 years, ever since China invaded the northeastern Indian state of Arunachal Pradesh in the month-long Sino-Indian War.

This mildly farcical battle over Buddhism is merely one manifestation of a broader struggle, an ongoing "Quiet War" between Asia's rising superpowers. Overshadowed by high-profile incidents—such as India's recent test launch of its Agni 5 ballistic missile with a 3,100-mile range that includes Beijing and Shanghai—it is in little-noticed trans-border activity and diplomatic skirmishes that Asia's elephant and dragon are posturing and probing one another, seeking advantage in the new "Great Game" unfolding on the Asian continent and its surrounding seas.

Last year, for example, the capture and confession of a top Indian separatist leader roiled New Delhi with revelations that Chinese arms dealers were arming and financing insurgents in India's restive northeast. Add to this explosive disclosure of "China's secret war with India" that China's five largest arms buyers—Pakistan, Myanmar, Bangladesh, Iran, and Sri Lanka—are India's immediate neighbors.

Coupled with Chinese railroads encroaching through Bangladesh and Nepal, as well as a $2.5 billion pipeline through Myanmar, these moves have made clear Beijing's intention to encircle India while securing key resources for itself. When India recently asked the Asian Development Bank for loans to develop coveted hydropower resources in Arunachal Pradesh, China blocked them (much as Beijing has prevented India from becoming a permanent member of the UN Security Council).

In the meantime, China has staked a claim to the Indian Ocean region—through which 40 percent of the world's energy and 50 percent of its merchant shipping travel—as its "Ocean of Destiny." Dubbed its "String of Pearls" strategy to surround India, China is constructing commercial ports in Myanmar, Sri Lanka, Bangladesh, and Pakistan, which Indian analysts fear ultimately will be turned into military bases. The latter partner is especially worrisome to India, which has seen China consistently support Pakistan—in international disputes, and even with nuclear technology—as a major check on India's influence in Southeast Asia.

Consequently, though it has largely kept quiet, India has not been quiescent. Just as the 16th-century Mughal Emperor Akbar once moved courtiers around a life-sized chessboard, India has maneuvered with great care to protect its assets and counter the encirclement China envisions.

This has primarily been accomplished by hewing to a more assertive version of India's decade-old "Look East" policy, engaging more closely with its smaller eastern neighbors to strengthen its hand in the region.

During an October 2011 state visit, India and Vietnam signed energy and security cooperation agreements to counter Chinese intimidation in the South China Sea. India has likewise begun strengthening economic ties with Vietnam's neighbors, Laos and Cambodia, while using newly liberalizing Myanmar as a bridge between South and Southeast Asia. Reacting to China's growing naval footprint in the Indian Ocean, Indian troops have stepped up exercises in the strategically critical waterway. In short, India is presenting China with a significant countervailing sphere of influence.

It would be naïve to think that very real geopolitical concerns—particularly ones as acute as access to vital energy and water resources—can be glibly dispensed with. There is little love lost between China and India. As the world's two largest countries and fastest-growing economies emerge from the shadows of their colonial pasts onto the world stage, both have some shaking out that needs to be done.

But we can take heart that the sabers are at least rattling relatively softly, and both New Delhi and Beijing seem willing to sheath their swords when there are greater economic gains to be made.

When Chinese premier Wen Jiabao visited India in 2010, for instance, he brought with him a delegation of 400 businessmen, larger than equivalent delegations from the United States, the UK, or France. Despite present barriers to doing business, both countries anticipate that bilateral trade—which grew 20 percent last year to hit a record $74 billion—will roughly double by 2015. In a gesture of good faith, and in recognition of its increasing utility, India has even begun offering Mandarin classes in secondary school. As the columnist James Lamont notes, "'Indo-Pak' was a hyphenation born out of 62 years of bruising hostility. 'Chindia' is shorthand for rising prosperity."

For all the seemingly inevitable flashpoints born of geopolitical growing pains, a war that is carried out quietly may yet be concluded as quietly. When I recently met with India's foreign secretary, Ranjan Mathai, he characterized his country's relationship with China as "stable," especially in light of China's upcoming elections. And, experience shows, the promise of prosperity often speaks loud enough to drown out decades of belligerence and mutual unease.

Just a week after India tested the Agni 5, China and India concluded a long-delayed deal to import Indian basmati rice, ignoring Pakistan's strenuous objections.

Who knows? When China and India have settled into their own a few decades from now, Buddhism and basmati may trump ballistics and brinkmanship. After all, in Buddhist teachings, Siddhartha Gautama's acceptance of a bowl of rice is the turning point that led him down the path to enlightenment. Perhaps this latest exchange of rice, too, hints at a Middle Path for India and China in the years to come.

Imagining Eastphalia

Strategic Review, January/March 2012

INTRODUCTION—INNOCENT ABROAD

IT BEGAN IN THE NETHERLANDS, AS OUTRAGED CALVINISTS SMASHED statues to protest the wealth and excesses of Spain and the Catholic Church. In Germany, starving soldiers laid waste to entire regions. The ensuing war engulfed all of 17th-century Europe in 80 years of bloody religious conflict.

After the assassination of generals and the death of kings, after nearly one-third of Germany's population lay dead from the plague or the sword, Europe's rulers finally came together. They intended only to end the wars; they did not expect to create a new global order. But when they finally signed the Peace of Westphalia in 1648, Europe—and the world—was on its way to being transformed.

Westphalia proclaimed the rule of *cujus regio ejus religio* ("Whose realm, his religion"), meaning that citizens of a respective country were subject primarily to the laws and actions of their respective governments. Westphalia established fixed territorial boundaries for countries for the first time, with neither church nor chancellor able to interfere in another nation's affairs. These tenets ushered in our modern system of nation-states.

Pope Innocent X memorably denounced Westphalia as "null, void, invalid, iniquitous, unjust, damnable, reprobate, inane, empty of meaning and effect for all time." Despite this papal condemnation, the modern system of sovereign nation-states inaugurated by the Westphalian treaties endures over three and a half centuries.

The 20th century, however, gradually chipped away at the Westphalian idea. The principle of *cujus regio* gave rise to the corollary that government is sovereign to rule its people as it sees fit. It led to order among states, but also enabled three centuries of atrocious human rights abuses. Out of the ashes of World War II and the Holocaust, countries came together to create the United Nations. In 1948, exactly 300 years after the Peace of Westphalia, the UN ratified its Universal Declaration of Human Rights. It was the first global expression of rights fundamental to all human beings and a challenge to the Westphalian concept of sovereignty.

For half a century, it was applied delicately, often through sanctions, in places like South Africa. It wasn't until the 1990s when the international community intervened directly on behalf of humanitarian principle in Haiti and Kosovo—a thread that runs through NATO's recent intervention in Libya. Meanwhile, the same decade witnessed the creation of a unified European Union (EU) in 1993, accelerating the trend toward international organizations and regional associations.

It was at this moment that historians began speaking of a post-Westphalian world.

The question now facing us is not whether Westphalia is "empty of meaning and effect for all time," but rather what meaning and effect it will have for our time, the globalized world of the 21st century. For insight, we need look no further than the Association of Southeast Asian Nations (ASEAN), which David Carden, the first resident US ambassador to ASEAN, believes "is making the case for a new definition of 'regionalism.'"

The movement to integrate the 10 nations of ASEAN—Indonesia, Singapore, Thailand, Vietnam, Brunei, Malaysia, Cambodia, Laos, Myanmar, and the Philippines—into a single entity represents a different model of regional cooperation from the EU. Unlike the EU, ASEAN is less rooted in democracy, more tolerant of human rights violations, and more committed to individual sovereignty. If successful, it may redefine how other regions—from Latin America to the Indian subcontinent to the Middle East—evolve in the 21st century.

It may also give rise to a new framework for a new century: Eastphalia.

THE LAGGING FLAG

On August 8, 2011, 44 years to the day after ASEAN was founded, the colorful ASEAN flag was hoisted for the first time alongside the banners of all member states at hundreds of embassies and diplomatic missions around the world. It kicked off what ASEAN secretary-general Surin Pitsuwan describes as "our drive to raise our own bargaining power from a larger base." At a time when the EU's struggle to rescue free-spending members Portugal, Ireland, Italy, Spain, and Greece has threatened to bring the whole continent tumbling down, ASEAN is rushing headlong to create a single economic community by 2015.

It may seem strange that flying the flag should lag so far behind the organization's founding, but for many years, ASEAN was a flagging confederation.

The forum has been derided as little more than a "talk shop" whose deference toward sovereignty allowed successive waves of atrocity, from bad actors like the Khmer Rouge and Myanmar generals. Collective action on economic or security policy was virtually unheard of. ASEAN, a former Indonesian foreign minister dismissively noted, is a mere diplomatic "cocktail party."

The people of ASEAN frequently reflect this sentiment. A young Filipino professional confided that ASEAN is only discussed in school textbooks, never in everyday conversation. It is telling that when Indonesia, ASEAN's largest member, held its 2009 presidential election, not one of the candidates mentioned the regional alliance headquartered in Jakarta.

Yet in the past few years, ASEAN has made itself progressively more relevant across the region. The "talk shop" still focuses on dialogue, but it has begun letting its actions do the talking. As the global financial system struggles and China asserts itself in the South China Sea, ASEAN's increasingly vulnerable member states are seeking a future in cooperation.

At the same time, ASEAN has so far maintained "the ASEAN Way"— the region's traditional respect for national sovereignty—while using the prospect of economic prosperity to incentivize concerted action on a range of policy goals. Though ASEAN's halting steps toward regional unity remain difficult to predict with certainty, its growing readiness to act on critical regional challenges heralds a new vitality. The lagging flag appears to be the leading indicator of a new model of economic-centric regionalism.

ASEAN ASCENDANT

As the saying goes, trade follows the flag. Since implementing its ambitious integration plan, ASEAN member states have eliminated 95 percent of tariff and non-tariff barriers, in an effort to increase intra-ASEAN trade from 25 percent to 35 percent in the next four years. It has been working. After [the organization] reportedly implemented 75 percent of its blueprint to become an economic bloc, trade among ASEAN nations rose 33 percent in 2010, while trade with China grew 25 percent in the first half of 2011.

While its vision doesn't yet include a unified currency, ASEAN has floated the idea of a common visa and the free flow of skilled workers. The latter is not an easy sell to ASEAN's wealthier members. As the EU has learned the hard way, wealthier nations tend to become beacons for job seekers from poorer nations in a way that isn't always manageable. A new

$500 million infrastructure bank funds the building of roads, railways, and ports to knit together the islands and archipelagos of the Pacific Rim. These efforts have begun to make real the prospect of rapid growth and access to the global marketplace.

By many measures, ASEAN is ascendant. Whereas European nations formed the EU to arrest a continental slide into stagnation—stemming from a loss of economic power in an increasingly global economy—ASEAN hums with the sounds of a region on the rise. Its 600 million people produce a combined gross domestic product of $1.7 trillion, exceeding that of India. ASEAN nations weathered the global economic slowdown well, growing at 7.4 percent in 2010 with healthy future growth projected. From 2009 to 2010, total trade ballooned by a third, to $2.09 trillion. Savvy investors have caught on, leading to a 38 percent increase in foreign direct investment in 2010.

Economic integration has also served as an instrument for improving governance and social policy. Though ASEAN's Secretariat still boasts only 70 professional employees overseeing a region of 600 million, its regional architecture—in Professor Paul Evans's characterization, a "noodle bowl" compared with the EU's more complex and interwoven "spaghetti bowls"—is becoming richer and more robust. In 2009, ASEAN established an Intergovernmental Commission on Human Rights—which the *Wall Street Journal* rightly criticized as "toothless," but which is nonetheless indicative of new attitudes and institutions coming to the fore. Plans are also underway for a new ASEAN Supreme Audit Institution that would reduce graft and promote good governance. It is an important development in a region where six of 10 members scored in the bottom third of the 2010 Transparency International Corruption Perception Index—a potential disincentive to global investors seeking to put their money in emerging markets.

With these institutions has come a willingness to address taboo subjects. At regional meetings last fall, for instance, several delegates spoke out in their hope that Myanmar's November 2010 general election would be free and fair. Last spring, the UN delegated to ASEAN a role in resolving the ongoing border dispute between Thailand and Cambodia, a regional first. And rather than cowing to China's preferred method of dealing with each nation bilaterally, delegates have presented a unified voice in opposition to

China's aggressive move into the South China Sea. This more unified posture has been noticed across the region by former critics like Anies Baswedan, the president of Indonesia's Paramadina University, who says that "more difficult issues [are] being tackled through official meetings."

Important partners, such as the United States, have taken note. President Obama, who grew up in Indonesia just three houses down from former Indonesian president Abdurrahman Wahid, has made the region a priority. And his secretary of state, Hillary Clinton, in the words of the Center for Strategic and International Studies' Ernest Bower, considers ASEAN "the focal point where the most important geostrategic chess games of the 21st century will be played."

Along with these developments, Baswedan notes that "there's more involvement of people, not just governments." Within higher education, the ASEAN University Network promotes cross-country collaboration, with a credit transfer system for students. Indonesia holds a competition for young Indonesian students to become young ASEAN ambassadors. As the *Jakarta Post* noted last July, ASEAN has hosted so many conferences in Bali that its flag has become familiar to residents.

Recognizing that ASEAN integration must stem from the people, the Secretariat has organized regional events ranging from small business conferences to batik festivals. In October 2010, 80 talented musicians from around the region joined together at the Hanoi Opera House to play in the first ASEAN Symphony Orchestra. The beautiful strains of Brahms and Dvorak symbolized a broader harmony emerging among the people of the Pacific.

But as much as playing Antonin Dvorak's *New World* Symphony epitomizes ASEAN's new regionalism, it is new social media that offers a real opportunity for ASEAN citizens to meet and communicate across vast expanses of ocean and distance. Recently, Indonesian president Susilo Bambang Yudhoyono urged the people of ASEAN to do just that, noting that Indonesia boasts the world's second-most Facebook users (24 million) and third-most people on Twitter. ASEAN's own Facebook page—"liked" by 2,877 (as of this writing), a fraction of ASEAN's total population—provides updates on ongoing initiatives and dialogues. These online spaces are among the best ways for Pitsuwan's hope for fulfilling his vision "to make ASEAN a household word," and for people to "identify their futures with ASEAN, or with the potentiality of ASEAN."

AN ASIAN SPIN ON REGIONALISM

All of which raises the question: Is the ASEAN Way going away? ASE-
AN's charter emphasizes "noninterference in the internal affairs of ASEAN
Member States" and "respect for the independence, sovereignty, equality,
territorial integrity, and national identity of all ASEAN Member States."
Which sounds wonderful—and quintessentially Westphalian—on paper,
but has proven less pretty in practice.

ASEAN's Asian spin on regionalism has presented unique opportunities,
but also vexing challenges. As Pitsuwan often notes, "The European model
is not our model; it is only our inspiration." For all its recent steps toward
greater institutionalization, few have contemplated anything approaching
the EU's multitude of multilateral and supranational governing bodies.
As the EU pulls out its collective hair trying to restructure its intransigent
members, looser association has kept ASEAN free from Europe's current
troubles. However, ASEAN faces other difficulties challenging its traditionally hands-off approach.

Chief among these [is] addressing [both] the authoritarianism of Myanmar and the aggressiveness of China.

ASEAN's leadership, to an extent, recognizes this. They have leveraged
Myanmar's scheduled turn to chair ASEAN in 2014—the chair is selected
alphabetically—as an opportunity to encourage Myanmar's government
to institute reforms and release political prisoners. Yet recently, Myanmar
announced that it would be releasing 6,300 prisoners, in addition to increasing communication with pro-democracy leader Daw Aung San Suu Kyi, and
halting construction on a dam condemned by environmentalists. Though
Myanmar's sincerity remains an open question, these steps do indicate that
newly energized ASEAN may have some potential to promote progress on
human rights: rather than applying the "stick" preferred by Western nations,
who have sanctioned Myanmar with little effect—ASEAN is in a much
stronger position to promote the "carrot" that membership can bring.

As a rising regional player, ASEAN holds the keys to tremendous economic growth. In addition to signing free trade agreements with China,
Australia, and New Zealand, the United States has expressed interest in a
possible trade deal. But as Secretary Clinton made clear at a regional security
forum in Bali, Myanmar challenges the "cohesion and future" of ASEAN—
and to US-ASEAN partnership.

Nor is Clinton alone. "The foreign business community is anxious to be part of the rebuilding of (Myanmar)," an editorial in the *Nation* magazine declared. "But we need to see peace and the rule of law applied." Time will tell if Myanmar is willing to revise past habits if it means future economic success.

As a local business owner says, "The biggest proponents toward change in Myanmar are the young, who know what is happening with the Arab Spring in the Middle East, and want to join the world."

Where Myanmar poses a test to ASEAN's internal affairs, China challenges its outward unity. Last year Beijing claimed the entire South China Sea, including islands in territorial waters of five other nations, as a "core national interest." It has been interpreted as everything from a naked power grab at the region's shipping lanes (through which a third of all transit ships pass) to an attempt to seize possible oil reserves estimated at 213 billion barrels to a cornerstone of China's nuclear submarine strategy. But "above all," as Baswedan contends, "it represents a challenge to the unity of ASEAN."

It is still undetermined whether a belligerent Beijing will bring the association closer together or drive them apart. But what is certain is that ASEAN is acting, and acting together. At its meeting in Bali last July, ASEAN officials spent 70 percent of their time on the South China Sea, and reached agreement on a Code of Conduct with China. The joint stand in Bali communicated a strong message to its giant neighbor: for now, ASEAN will stand as one.

As it has evolved organically over the last 44 years, ASEAN, Singapore's ambassador K. Kesavapany asserts, has been "nothing if not pragmatic." It appears that the association now understands that there are cases where an iron-clad regard for sovereignty threatens regional goals, especially economic ones. When such instances arise, ASEAN is inclined to continue its familiar dialogues and back-channel discussions, using the carrot of economic growth to encourage compliance and collective action. As an Australian embassy official put it, "The ASEAN approach is right—strength in numbers, and all have shared interests."

CONCLUSION—IMAGINING EASTPHALIA

In the inaugural volume of the *Strategic Review*, President Yudhoyono envisioned Indonesia on its centennial in the year 2045. Given the above developments, it is worth considering what ASEAN—and other regions influenced by its model of regionalism—might look like in 2048, four centuries after Westphalia, and a century after the UN Declaration of Rights hinted at a post-Westphalian departure. To use a provocative term coined by University of Chicago law professor Tom Ginsburg and others, it is worth imagining "Eastphalia."

Eastphalia is where sovereignty and association meet, holding the promise of integration as well as independence. ASEAN's biggest weakness and biggest strength have always been its inclusivity. It is, commentator Leon Hadar writes, "a mosaic of . . . old and new civilizations in various stages of economic development." Singapore, one of the world's richest nations per capita, coexists alongside repressive and impoverished Myanmar. Indonesia, a nascent democracy with the world's largest Muslim population, and Thailand, with its Buddhist constitutional monarchy, abut the tiny sultanate of Brunei.

It is also a mosaic of various political systems. Indonesia and Thailand are nascent democracies—yet in Thailand, one can be jailed for speaking out against the Crown. Vietnam, Cambodia, and Laos are all dictatorships. Singapore is semi-autocratic. All 10 members are different. Yet these disparate nations are steadily forging an integrated community—which should give hope to other regions around the world, many of which more closely resemble the patchwork of ASEAN than the relative homogeneity of the EU.

There is also an emerging market reality that is hard to ignore: unlike the EU, which is trying to maintain its place in the global order and stop its descent as a global power, emerging market nations like the 10 members of ASEAN are ascendant. For a world shifting from West to East, the challenges, aspirations, and growing clout of ASEAN seem eminently more familiar to other emerging regions than old-world capitals like Paris and London, which enhances ASEAN's ability to serve as a role model.

It's also a time when the once-thriving models of the West aren't held in the same regard. While Western observers condemn ASEAN over Myanmar and argue that a wobblier version of the EU will never work because it lacks central authority to enforce common rules, ASEAN supporters darkly point to democracy's present struggles. "Authoritarian leaders and their populations here are appalled by America's lack of discipline and massive debt," wrote Yohanes Sulaiman, a lecturer at Indonesia's National Defense University, in a recent essay. "If democracy provides nothing but economic crisis, political squabbling, and gridlock, why would anyone want it? Better to stick with the authoritarian system of China or the semi-authoritarianism of Singapore."

It's not hard to imagine, for instance, a South Asian confederation of India, Pakistan, Bangladesh, Nepal, Bhutan, Sri Lanka, and the Maldives— or a future bloc in the Middle East—modeled on ASEAN. Present conflicts may suggest they are improbable, given the bloodlust between Pakistan and India alone. But 60 years ago, few would have imagined France one day being joined at the hip with Germany.

The makeup of the modern Middle East—monarchies, military regimes, multi-ethnic states—reflects that of ASEAN. If ASEAN's trajectory over the last few years is any indication, an Eastphalian world, by accommodating difference and deferring to national sovereignty, could facilitate the formation of regional associations. They could begin as free trade areas and common markets—Israelis and Iraqis trading with Indians and Indonesians—and gradually evolve into something more cohesive and more vibrant.

As Ginsburg put it well, "Eastphalia may be Westphalia without the universalism. A kinder, gentler Westphalia."

Because as troubling as the implications of non-interference can often be in our post–UN Declaration world, it may be the only way to begin. Theorists from Seymour Martin Lipset onward have hypothesized that a baseline of economic security may be a necessary precursor to democratic and human rights reforms. Though others have challenged this theory, the trajectory of the region's "Asian Tigers"—Singapore, Taiwan, Korea—support this line of thinking. All have democratized as they become wealthier. By 2048, perhaps ASEAN's human rights commission will be as vigorous as South Korea's.

Projecting so far into the future, as Pope Innocent's 17th-century prognostication reminds us, naturally has its risks. As the region that gave us both Westphalian and post-Westphalian paradigms convulses, the future of regionalism remains very much in doubt. The EU could emerge stronger; Myanmar could retrench; Beijing could play a cynical game of bilateralism and belligerence that rends the fabric of ASEAN unity. Or the ASEAN model, if present encouraging trends continue, may yet prove itself viable and desirable. In 2048, students from Myanmar could travel and study freely in the United States; trade between ASEAN and other regional blocs could exceed our wildest imaginations; and what began in 1967 as a loose association of nations could model a new regionalism for a changing world.

As it creates its own passage between the Westphalian model on one side and the EU on the other, ASEAN might one day replace the principle of *cujus regio ejus religio* with an expression popular in Indonesia—*mendayung antara dua karang,* or "rowing between two reefs."

China's Indian Ocean Strategy
Not a Danger—Yet

The World Post, July 8, 2013

WHEN THE CHINESE ADMIRAL ZHENG HE SET OUT ON THE FIRST OF SEVEN historic voyages of exploration 608 years ago, the sails of his 317 ships blotted out the horizon. Included in the fleet were several colossal, football field–sized vessels—large enough to fit 65 of Columbus's ships end-to-end—whose holds would eventually bring home mountains of gold, ivory, and porcelain for the glory of the Ming emperor. Sailing to a dizzying array of coastal countries over the next three decades, Zheng's flotilla made its way across the modern-day Middle East, ultimately reaching the Cape of Good Hope some 4,000 miles away.

Such expeditions had never been seen before—and would not be seen again. Internal instability, Mongol threats, and high financial costs conspired to cripple China's Age of Exploration. Zheng died and was buried at sea. His magnificent ships were burned. Records of his voyages were destroyed. For nearly six centuries China turned inward, away from the ocean.

That is, until now. With its release last month of a 350-page "blue book" detailing China's strategy in the Indian Ocean, Beijing has served notice that—while insisting its interests are strictly economic—it is not content to ignore the waters to its west any longer. And India, which relies on the Indian Ocean for most of its trade and has long suspected China of pursuing a so-called "String of Pearls" strategy in the region—encircling the subcontinent with a network of commercial and military facilities—is understandably wary.

Despite the blue book's conciliatory tone, it has become clear, as the journalist and geopolitical analyst Robert Kaplan observes in his book *Monsoon*, that as "China expands vertically [and] India horizontally . . . the Indian Ocean is where the rivalry between the United States and China in the Pacific interlocks with the regional rivalry between China and India." To explore Kaplan's view that "together with the contiguous Near East and Central Asia," the Indian Ocean "constitutes the new Great Game in geopolitics," I reached out to a man who has trained three generations of Indian diplomats.

Maharaja Krishna Rasgotra, a former foreign secretary under Indira Gandhi in the early 1980s and ambassador to six countries—a courtly Indian version of Henry Kissinger—is a keen student of this "new Great Game." Rasgotra joined India's Foreign Service in 1949, just two years after India's independence, the same year the People's Republic of China was established. He has witnessed the entirety of the two Asian giants' modern relationship, from the heady years of *Hindi-Chini bhai-bhai*—a popular Hindi slogan meaning "Indians and Chinese are brothers"—to the brief but bitter Sino-Indian War of 1962 to the simmering border disputes that carry into the present day, including a baffling Chinese incursion into Indian territory in May that reportedly left New Delhi on the verge of crisis with Beijing.

"I look at the Indian Ocean as a projection of India's landmass—all of it vital for India's security, stability, and progress," Rasgotra says. Likewise: "The Chinese have an interest in the Indian Ocean. New Delhi is watching the developments. If the Chinese get militarily interested in dominating the Indian Ocean, then India is strong enough to resist that."

Certainly, there have been developments worth watching. No sooner had the ink dried on the blue book, for instance, than China offered Iran $78 million to upgrade its Chabahar Port, which is near the Iranian border with Pakistan and a stone's throw from the Straits of Hormuz—a strategically vital chokepoint through which 20 percent of the world's oil passes. This comes amid China's $200 million investment in the Pakistani port of Gwadar, a $209 million airport in Sri Lanka, and plans to build another port on the coast of Tanzania.

While China's Ministry of National Defense has dismissed the "String of Pearls" theory as "totally groundless," India has observed 22 recorded instances of Chinese nuclear submarines encroaching into the Indian Ocean—as recently as February 2013, and as close as 50 miles off Indian soil.

Still, for all China's newfound assertiveness in India's backyard, Rasgotra remains skeptical of Beijing's belligerence. The "String of Pearls," he tells me, "is part history, part poetry, and part mythology."

"China's strategy is motivated by two major factors," he says. "First, to project power in the Indian Ocean in rivalry not only with India but primarily with the United States; and second, to safeguard supplies of much-needed energy and other material sources from the Middle East and Africa." Neither is cause for hysteria, though Rasgotra feels India should do more to modernize its military. Indeed, plans are underway to spend nearly $45 billion to build 103 new warships over the next two decades while strengthening naval cooperation with friendly countries. Echoing Rasgotra, a Western diplomat in Sri Lanka says confidently of the island off India's coast, "This isn't going to become India's Cuba."

Rasgotra adds that the Chinese "are beginning to realize that containing India is not a practical proposition," and sees "signs of China becoming less aggressive, even less assertive, in its dealings with India." China has seemed eager to downplay border disputes, preferring to focus on economic engagement. Trade between the two countries topped $66 billion last year, a figure China and India hope will reach $100 billion by 2015. To promote tourism, India is also considering a proposal to ease visa restrictions for Chinese citizens.

Chinese premier Li Keqiang visited New Delhi in May, on his first trip abroad since assuming office. After several days of meetings and signing agreements on issues ranging from urban development to religious pilgrimages, Prime Minister Li declared that "our two countries fully possess the will, wisdom, and ability to together nurture a new bright spot in Asian cooperation."

Until China begins establishing military bases in Sri Lanka, Myanmar, or the Maldives, Rasgotra will sleep easy. "There is a desire with China to get along, and I know there is such a desire in India," he says. "Commerce will help soften political attitudes."

As these two rising giants navigate the rocky geopolitical shoals, both countries would do well to remember the stone stele Zheng erected in Sri Lanka in 1410, not far from where a Chinese-financed shipping center now stands. Written in Chinese, Persian, and Tamil, the inscription "invoked the blessings of the Hindu deities for a peaceful world built on trade." Here's hoping that out of the irritants of today's maritime maneuvering, true pearls may yet grow.

INDONESIA

What the United States Should and Should Not Do in Indonesia

International Herald Tribune, August 15, 1998

THE KEY TO UNDERSTANDING INDONESIAN POLITICS IS THE JAVANESE shadow play called *wayang*—stories about mythical battles between gods and kings, good and evil, with the common people standing aside in powerless awe.

A shadow play is more than mere entertainment; it is a deeply ingrained way for Indonesians to view events in their world. The driving force behind each performance is the *dalang*, the puppet master. He has control over the destinies of all the characters.

For 32 years, President Suharto was the *dalang*, a king who possessed *wahyu*, the divine light signifying a Javanese leader's power. He ruled his nation as a benevolent despot, consulting frequently with his spiritual advisor and tapping the deep cultural roots of the *wayang*.

Last year, he lost his *wahyu*: There were fires, droughts, locusts, and plane crashes. This year, the economy crashed. Now he is gone.

He has been replaced by B. J. Habibie, who appears to be trying to open the way to democratic reform. This new puppet master does not hold all of the strings and seems to be making up his stories as he goes along. Neither Javanese nor mystic, he is more comfortable communing with his computer, exchanging e-mail with friends. Mr. Habibie rules at the pleasure of the military commanded by General Wiranto, a former aide to President Suharto. As Mr. Habibie says, "I take General Wiranto with me everywhere; as long as he is smiling, I know I'm OK."

The general was an architect of the constitutional coup that forced the 76-year-old Suharto from office. He became a hero for his role in ending the numerous riots and for purging Lieutenant General Prabowo Subianto, Mr. Suharto's son-in-law and the former commander of the special forces who was accused of numerous human rights abuses.

But this is Indonesia, where intrigue is as much a part of daily life as *wayang* myths. So it is not entirely clear how the dance between General Wiranto and President Habibie will turn out. At the request of the new president, General Wiranto and his brain trust abandoned their preferred candidate for chairman of the government party, Golkar, in favor of Akbar Tanjung.

Now there will be no parliamentary elections until next May and no selection of a president until December 1999. Mr. Habibie has more time to consolidate his power with the appointment of loyalists, such as General Faisal Tanjung, coordinating minister of defense and security.

America should resist any temptation to become a major actor in this continuing drama. "The Indonesians did an impressive job of getting rid of President Suharto without any help from us, and they are engaged in a profound and lively negotiation about their political future," said Paul Wolfowitz, former US ambassador. "For now, I believe, we should leave the negotiating to them and focus our efforts on preventing starvation."

And starvation is a real possibility in a country facing a shortfall of more than 5 million metric tons of rice. The response of the international community has been to pledge less than one-fifth that amount.

Mr. Wolfowitz urges immediate action and points out that the United States is far more likely to be listened to later if it takes the lead now in providing desperately needed food and medical assistance.

"A massive emergency assistance program can also serve political as well as humanitarian purposes," he said. "If creative use is made of nongovernmental organizations in Indonesia for food distribution, it can strengthen some of the organizations critical to the success of political and economic reform."

Feeding Indonesia's hungry is the equivalent of stopping the bleeding in a critically wounded patient: It must be done first. Only then can the issue of political reform be addressed.

One of the sad legacies of Mr. Suharto's regime is that rather than foster the growth of political parties, he ensured that the opposition was weak and disorganized.

There are more than 50 registered parties in Indonesia, each with a single focus. This is a recipe for anarchy. But there are positive signs that Parliament is working to create a process for building broad-based parties capable of winning working majorities in next year's parliamentary elections.

The United States should develop a number of programs to train and educate Indonesia's military—the greatest stabilizing force in the country.

Indonesian officers should be encouraged to participate in the International Military Education and Training program. The program exposes officers to international norms of human rights, the concept of civilian control of the military, and respect for the rule of law.

In addition, America should create scholarship programs for midlevel officers at colleges and universities around the United States to give these future leaders a broader view of democratic values.

There is nothing mystical about the importance of a stable, prosperous Indonesia to the United States and its Asian partners. And there is nothing magical about helping Indonesia write a happy ending to a real-life *wayang*.

How to Help Indonesia Prosper in the Free World

International Herald Tribune, September 21, 1999

WHICH SET OF COUNTRIES IS MORE DEMOCRATIC: GREECE AND SOUTH Korea, or Cuba and Iran? Understanding why it is the first set may go a long way toward determining whether or not Indonesia moves firmly toward democracy and human rights.

A truism of 20th-century statecraft is that good economics makes good politics. Country after country in Europe, Asia, and Latin America has turned toward democracy, civilian control over the military, and greater respect for human rights only after developing some form of market economy. Precious few democratic success stories have grown out of centrally planned economies.

Which brings us to Indonesia. So enraged were American human rights activists and their friends in Congress by the militia and military violence in East Timor that, along with suspending US links with Indonesia's armed forces, a bill was introduced in the US Senate to cut off all aid to Indonesia.

Jakarta's acceptance of international peacekeepers may short-circuit that proposal. But the apparent willingness on the part of the United States to end such contacts, just as Indonesia was beginning to show signs of recovery from the last two years' financial meltdown, is troubling.

An American focus on human rights, independent of sound economic policies, will not lead to a lasting solution.

The aftermath of the events in East Timor may yet spark a nationalist backlash, anti-Western sentiment, more human rights abuses, and a longer and more difficult transition to democracy. This would be an enormous opportunity lost, not only for Indonesia but for the United States as well.

Indonesia's geopolitical importance cannot be overemphasized. The world's fourth-most populous country has been a moderate force in the Islamic world. And it is a counterweight to China, as the keystone of the Association of Southeast Asian Nations.

About 40 percent of the world's shipping goes through one of the four straits in the Indonesian archipelago, as does the bulk of the oil that Japan and South Korea import. These are the same straits through which China will need to import oil from the Middle East to fuel its economic growth.

To punish Indonesia's military for its role in East Timor by isolating it further will do little to make it a more democratic institution or to increase security in this vital region. The United States should invite the Indonesian armed forces commander, General Wiranto, to the meeting of the Asia Pacific defense chiefs in Hawaii next month. Ties with the Indonesian military should be renewed and expanded, including exchange and training programs that expose key military officers and emerging leaders to the nature of civilian-military relations in a democracy.

On a recent visit to Jakarta, I met with Yunus Yosfiah, a retired lieutenant general [who is] now the minister of information. He is responsible for Indonesia having one of the most outspoken media in Southeast Asia. An open-minded thinker, he told me that a free press was more important than a government. Perhaps this was one of the lessons he learned as a young officer at Fort Leavenworth and Fort Bragg, as a participant in America's International Military Education and Training program.

The United States should now ensure that Indonesia turns toward a sound market economy and democracy.

First, it should engage in quiet diplomacy, not public ultimatums. "Go to hell with your aid," was the reaction of President Sukarno to threats that the United States might cut off economic assistance in the 1960s. The same response would probably come from present and future Indonesian leaders.

Second, America should pressure both the IMF and the World Bank not to postpone financial aid to Indonesia. International institutions that exist to create economic opportunity and prosperity should not use financial sanctions to pursue political goals.

Third, the United States and the IMF should help Jakarta develop internal banking reforms and other mechanisms to cut down on rampant corruption and restructure Indonesia's large foreign debt in order to restore faith in doing business there, for both domestic and foreign investors.

Fourth, Indonesia should return to the free market course that President Suharto's first generation of economic technocrats (known as the "Berkeley

Mafia" for their links to that American university) charted 30 years ago. The economy boomed until Mr. Suharto's clan and cronies established monopolies in practically every business sector.

Jakarta should continue to break up these monopolies, get the military out of both its many business enterprises (estimated at $9 billion) and politics, and induce the ethnic Chinese to return—with their money. Above all, Indonesia needs to establish the rule of law and the transparency that comes with a free press.

In essence, Indonesia must think reconciliation, the future, democracy—not revenge, the past, authoritarianism. And America must work with its post-Suharto leaders.

Since the end of World War II, the United States has put aside short-term misgivings about military and civilian leadership in Greece, South Korea, and elsewhere and concentrated on helping those countries develop economically, thereby planting seeds for democracy later. In contrast, it has tried to isolate Cuba and Iran, with far less laudable results. Cuba remains a secular dictatorship, Iran a theocratic one.

How Washington responds to the ongoing crisis in Indonesia may well determine to which set of countries—democracies or dictatorships—the largest nation in Southeast Asia will belong 10 years from now.

Be Quiet While Indonesia's Chess Master Makes His Moves

International Herald Tribune, March 6, 2000

INDONESIA'S PRESIDENT IS A CHESS MASTER IN THE GAME OF POLITICS— a man with a thousand maneuvers.

Abdurrahman Wahid, an ailing, nearly blind Muslim scholar, is Indonesia's most admired and beloved individual. He is known to all as Gus Dur, or honored brother. Many venerate him as a living saint. To some he is the just king, the most mysterious of Javanese shadow play heroes, whose appearance signals the end of times of chaos and the beginning of periods of peace.

To others he is the Javanese puppet Semar, a buffoon-like character who killed his enemies with razor-sharp intelligence. Like a knight on a chessboard, Semar knew—and Gus Dur knows—that the best way to move from A to B is not in a straight line.

The queen is the most powerful piece. Megawati Sukarnoputri was the princess, waiting all too regally for her coronation. The daughter of Indonesia's first president, she was brought up in the palace and then witnessed her father's overthrow, humiliation, and death.

A housewife, she entered politics in 1987 and became the only longtime opposition leader to her father's oppressor, President Suharto. When he fell, Mrs. Megawati saw the chance to transform her mass support into a return to the palace. Her party won a large plurality in parliamentary elections, with three times the votes for Gus Dur.

The saint and the housewife formed a partnership. But she spent the presidential campaign in sphinx-like silence, never reaching out to the Muslim leaders and underestimating the chess master. Gus Dur won the presidency and, in a move to stop pro-Megawati riots, named her as his vice president, saying they made a perfect team: "I can't see and she can't talk."

The rook is the second most important piece. General Wiranto, former head of the military, tried to be kingmaker. Playing that game with

President Wahid, he ended up being plucked from the political chessboard like a lowly pawn.

General Wiranto had adroitly moved from presidential adjutant to commander of the armed forces, effectively running the government of transitional president B. J. Habibie after the East Timor massacres began.

At first he supported Mrs. Megawati's run for president, but when Mr. Wahid was elected, he turned on her so that he could become vice president and control the new government. His fatal miscalculation was dropping out of the race and giving up the state's coercive apparatus on Mr. Wahid's promise of a key cabinet position.

Curiously, this vain, dapper general, a past master at walking political tightropes, underestimated the chess master. The two clashed over how to deal with violence in the remote provinces and General Wiranto's refusal to resign his commission. When the match ended, the general was no longer the coordinating minister for defense and security, and his military and political careers were finished.

The bishop never moves straight. Amien Rais was a Muslim firebrand. Charismatic and self-promoting, he often shoots from the lip with anti-Christian, anti-Chinese, or anti-Semitic statements. With Mr. Wahid and others, he was a leader of the pro-democracy Muslims, the single largest constituency involved in the effort to overthrow Mr. Suharto.

Mr. Rais created the Islamic coalition that Gus Dur skillfully manipulated to win the presidency, and is now chairman of Indonesia's highest legislative body. He has alternately befriended and undermined Mr. Wahid, but he has never underestimated the chess master. He represents the mainly urban white-collar professionals and intellectuals espousing a less tolerant, more doctrinaire Islam.

Gus Dur's followers practice an inclusive, accommodating, Sufi-like Islam. He may be the only leader capable of bringing these two major competing strains of belief together.

He has thus far successfully neutralized his political opponents. He is taking important steps to bring the military under civilian control. But there is much more to be done to secure the future of Indonesia's 212 million people.

It is less a nation than a random string of islands, and there are separatist movements in provinces throughout the archipelago. The economy is shaky at best. Ethnic violence after the fall of President Suharto caused Chinese Indonesian bankers and businessmen to flee the country.

Most important, there are those who reject Gus Dur's "sweet face of Islam" with its tolerance for all religions. Islamic fringe groups are trying to destabilize the government.

The United States should be like the audience at a chess match—quiet. But Washington should expand aid, support World Bank and IMF projects, and reinstate programs for advanced education of Indonesian officers in America. It should encourage public and private foundations to join with Indonesian organizations to create community programs, scholarships, and other services.

The endgame should bring a prosperous, tolerant, democratic Indonesia. So far, President Wahid has shown that he knows the right moves.

Indonesia: The Military Can Shape Up if Washington Helps

International Herald Tribune, August 20, 2001

THREE YEARS AND THREE PRESIDENTS SINCE THE FALL OF PRESIDENT Suharto, the latest palace turnover is an important reminder that Indonesia's quest for democracy remains a work in progress.

Indonesia has replaced two autocratic chief executives with a gang of five party bosses, who control a largely unaccountable super-parliament, the People's Consultative Assembly. Indonesians do not vote for individuals but for parties, which dance to the tune of their bosses.

The bosses recently traded in President Abdurrahman Wahid, who talked too much and never listened, for Megawati Sukarnoputri, daughter of the country's first president, who never talks and who, the gang of five expects, will listen. The makeup of her cabinet is encouraging, but it is not at all clear how stable the nation will become.

One institution that does provide stability is the military, the TNI. It is the most powerful organization in the nation, with a territorial structure reaching all the way to the remotest village. With the army as its backbone, it has been the glue that keeps this sprawling archipelago of 215 million people with diverse cultures from falling apart.

Under President Suharto, the military suppressed dissent and often acted as an instrument of repression, but it also has done some things well: resettling refugees, supplying disaster relief after floods and landslides, and putting down extremist actions. The armed forces could do even more if given training and responsibility for jobs that take advantage of their logistics and organizational skills, such as fighting forest fires and replanting trees. Army strategic reserves and special forces, well trained and disciplined, could be used as UN peacekeepers or peace enforcers.

What limits the TNI from becoming more accountable to its civilian bosses and more effective as a servant of the nation is that only 25 percent of its funds come from the defense budget. The rest is made up from the military's own business enterprises, both legal and crooked.

A former defense minister, Juwono Sudarsono, tells me that an estimated 65 percent of the revenues from these businesses is siphoned off. That leaves the average soldier with little choice but to go into "business" for himself: illegal logging or mining, smuggling, gambling, drugs, prostitution, extortion. Unfortunately, the US Congress has banned military aid and training to Indonesia until its armed forces introduce reforms and punish the officers responsible for the killings and mayhem that devastated East Timor after its vote for independence from Indonesia in 1999.

The result of Washington's shortsighted and one-dimensional thinking is that it now has little leverage to promote positive changes in the military. Yet providing assistance to redefine the role of the TNI is key to America's goal of helping to build democracy here.

Even José Ramos-Horta, East Timor's foreign minister and [a] Nobel Peace Prize holder, supports Jakarta's request for resumption of US supplies to the Indonesian military.

The Bush administration would like to renew ties and is asking Congress to approve limited contacts. That would allow Washington to help the TNI professionalize its legal businesses with regular audits, broad oversight, and transparent reporting. Then it should help Jakarta convert the military companies to state-owned enterprises. And finally, the central government should privatize these businesses and use the tax revenues to finance the military entirely through the defense budget.

America should work with Indonesia to create an elite coast guard. A maritime nation with 13,000-plus islands, Indonesia loses some $6 billion a year to illegal fishing, not to mention losses from piracy. A well-trained and -equipped coast guard with high-speed patrol boats, air support, and over-the-horizon radar could pay for itself with what it saves, and then some.

America could provide assistance in building a professional civil service within the Ministry of Defense. Few officials have training in planning, budgeting, and administration. These are all steps leading to civilian control of the military.

Indonesia has greater geostrategic value than any other country in Southeast Asia. The world's biggest Muslim nation has been the moderate face of Islam. It can be a valuable counterweight to China, especially in the South China Sea. Nearly half of the world's commercial shipping goes through one of its key straits, as does the bulk of oil that Japan and South Korea import.

Egypt and Turkey are also large, strategically located, secular Muslim countries with miserable records of human rights abuses. Egypt, a police state backed by the army, gets $2 billion a year from America in military and economic assistance. Turkey, whose generals make or break the duly elected governments, gets America's military support as a valued partner in NATO. Indonesia gets American lectures.

The United States must balance its policy on human rights with its interest in having stable allies in strategic areas of the world. Here America can have it both ways. By helping Indonesia's military, it can help this nation to become the world's third-largest democracy.

Indonesia's Progress Will Continue Despite the Bombing

International Herald Tribune, August 8, 2003

"THIS COUNTRY," MY INDONESIAN HOST SAID TO ME, "IS A GOLD MINE IN A mine field. Avoid the mines and you will reap the reward." Just days later, one of those mines exploded down the street—at the Marriott Hotel in the terrorist attack Tuesday that killed at least 10 people and wounded more than 150.

Can the government of President Megawati Sukarnoputri navigate the dangerous terrain ahead and prevail against the Islamic extremists within Indonesian society? Will Indonesia—and the world—reap the rewards that would follow if the country with the largest Muslim population succeeds in its bold experiment in democracy?

My discussions with political, business, and military leaders shortly before the attack suggest that while many land mines litter the landscape, the gold mine of a peaceful, prosperous Indonesia is closer than many Western observers believe.

To be sure, the capital has been on high alert since Islamic terrorists killed more than 200 people in Bali last October. In recent months, explosions ripped through the Jakarta airport and Parliament. Luxury Western hotels have installed metal detectors. Encircled by barbed wire and concrete barriers, the US embassy resembles Fort Apache. Foreign tourists and investors are taking their money elsewhere.

Yet for all the uncertainty, Indonesia continues its slow march to becoming the world's third-largest democracy. Economically, the country appears poised to recover from the 1997 Asian meltdown. Rampant corruption, nepotism, and poverty persist. But money from the ethnic Chinese community, which fled the murderous riots of 1998, is returning. The rupiah has firmed up against the dollar. Gross domestic product is up. Inflation and interest rates are down. Privatization of state-controlled companies continues. The Jakarta stock market is bullish.

Politically, this former dictatorship inches closer to genuine democracy. A free press and independent political parties flourish. Ideologues who would impose Islamic law remain, as always, divided and disorganized. Asked who will win the presidential election next year, Jusuf Kalla, the coordinating minister for people's welfare, tells me, "Whoever wins the most votes." For the first time, the Indonesian people will choose their president in a direct election.

In terms of security, the Bali bombings finally roused Jakarta to the terrorist threat within its porous borders. Authorities have aggressively pursued Jemaah Islamiyah, the extremist group linked to Al Qaeda that is suspected in the Marriott and Bali attacks, and have put on trial the Bali bombers and their spiritual leader, Abu Bakar Bashir. The guilty verdict delivered Thursday for Amrozi, accused of helping to plan and carry out the Bali bombings, is a sign that the Indonesian judiciary will not be intimidated.

Indeed, the massacre at the Marriott, apparently intended to thwart the government's crackdown, will probably achieve the opposite, generating a renewed determination in Jakarta to combat terrorism and to deepen US-Indonesian cooperation, discreet though it may be.

Paradoxically, the biggest land mine on the way to a stable Indonesia may be the one institution capable of preserving its territorial integrity: the military.

Determined to avoid the disintegration of her ethnically diverse country, Megawati has given the army a free hand in the rebellious provinces of Aceh and Papua and has installed former generals as governors across Indonesia. Its appetite whetted, the military proposed controversial legislation granting itself authority to take action in times of national emergency without prior presidential approval.

So what is Washington doing to increase its influence with this powerful institution? Nothing. Congress and now, apparently, the White House continue to raise barriers to resuming the International Military Education and Training program, or IMET, suspended in 1992, under which more than 3,000 Indonesian officers expanded their views on democracy and human rights while learning how to handle insurgencies and terrorism.

The murder of two Americans in Papua last year, apparently by renegade soldiers, must be fully investigated, as Congress insists. And by all accounts, Jakarta is cooperating with the FBI. Yet discussions with two members of the last IMET class illustrate how resuming the program would enhance American influence.

Lieutenant General Agus Widjojo fondly recalls training with the US Army Rangers, whom he describes as "warriors with a respect for human rights." Susilo Bambang Yudhoyono, a retired general who is now coordinating minister of security and political affairs, speaks of America in glowing terms: "I love the United States, with all its faults. I consider it my second country."

As it wages a global campaign to win Muslim hearts and minds, Washington needs as many Widjojos and Yudhoyonos as it can get. And as Jakarta wades through the dangerous terrain ahead, it needs as much help combating terrorism as it can get.

From the charred wreckage of the Marriott comes a lesson for Indonesia and America: If these two natural partners can work together to deftly sidestep the political and economic mines that remain, a treasure awaits . . . in the form of a peaceful, prosperous, and democratic Indonesia.

Washington Is Neglecting a New Friend

International Herald Tribune, August 16, 2005

"INDONESIA IS NOT A COUNTRY," DEFENSE MINISTER JUWONO SUDARSONO tells me. "It's a happening." As a regular visitor here for two decades, I've always admired the dynamism and diversity of 225 million people comprising 300 ethnic groups, speaking 500 languages and dialects, spread across 17,000 islands.

Still, on my first visit since last year's devastating tsunami, I've been startled by the new mood of optimism among political, business, and military leaders here. After decades of dictatorship and years of political and economic drift, Indonesia finally seems poised to start realizing its potential as the world's third-largest democracy.

There's genuine hope that this week's peace agreement in Helsinki between Jakarta and Acehnese rebels may finally end the fighting that has killed 15,000 in the rebellious province since 1976.

Susilo Bambang Yudhoyono, the country's first directly elected president, remains popular for his "pro-growth, pro-poor, pro-employment" and anti-corruption agenda. Erry Riyana, deputy chairman of the Corruption Eradication Commission, tells me that the number of investigations and prosecutions of business and political elites is "unprecedented."

Although still rebounding from the 1997–1998 Asian economic meltdown, the Indonesian economy is defying expectations with 6 percent growth so far this year. Foreign investment is on track to nearly double this year to $7 billion, according to Muhammad Lutfi, chairman of the Investment Coordinating Board.

Microsoft recently announced it will build its fourth international research lab in Indonesia, putting Jakarta in the ranks of Cambridge, Beijing, and Bangalore.

In one recent poll, 81 percent of Indonesians described their quality of life as "good" or "very good." This, in a country where December's tsunami killed 130,000, where 40 million are chronically unemployed, and where 110 million subsist on under $2 per day.

Yet it is precisely this schizophrenic nature of life here that makes Indonesia so vital. If it succeeds as a prosperous democracy, this strategically located archipelago with the world's largest Muslim population promises enormous political, economic, and security dividends for the entire world.

Alternatively, Indonesia can simply stumble along, proving—as Charles de Gaulle famously said of Brazil—that it has "great potential, and it always will."

Indonesia's neighbors are not taking that chance. Six years after Australian-led UN troops battled Indonesian-backed militias in East Timor, Australia's ambassador, David Ritchie, says that relations between Canberra and Jakarta have "never been better."

China is getting over its own dark history with Indonesia, which has often treated its small Chinese minority business class as a scapegoat. After a failed communist coup in 1965, tens of thousands of ethnic Chinese were slaughtered and Jakarta severed ties with Beijing for a quarter century. An estimated 100,000 Chinese Indonesians fled the country during deadly anti-government riots in 1998.

Nevertheless, Beijing and Jakarta this spring unveiled a new "strategic partnership" bringing together the world's second-largest consumer of oil (China) with one of the world's largest producers of oil and liquefied natural gas (Indonesia). Last month in Beijing, Yudhoyono secured a Chinese pledge to invest $7.5 billion in new oil, gas, coal, and railway projects.

But while neighbors like China and Australia are paying attention to Indonesia, refusing to let old disagreements obscure common strategic interests, America risks squandering the good will it engendered here for its tsunami relief efforts.

Congressional neglect toward Indonesia has gone from benign to malign. Indonesians are still enraged by a vote of the House International Relations committee in June questioning the circumstances of Papua's 1969 integration with Indonesia. One Indonesian suggested to me that his Parliament revisit the Cherokee Indian nation's "integration" with the United States.

In the Senate, a few members continue to oppose the Bush administration's attempt to restore full military ties with Indonesia even though Secretary of State Condoleezza Rice certified earlier this year that Jakarta is cooperating with the investigation into the murder of two Americans in Papua in 2002. Despite personal appeals to senators by Yudhoyono and Sudarsono, the $800,000 requested by the Bush administration to train

Indonesian officers next year under the International Military Education and Training program may never see the light of day.

Indonesians tell me they don't understand the selective self-righteousness of US politicians who deny their struggling democracy access to a small program to help professionalize their military, while throwing billions of dollars in military support to serial human rights abusers like Saudi Arabia, Egypt, and Pakistan.

In addition, many here see the US war on terrorism as a war on Islam. It's easy to see why more Indonesians have a positive view of China (73 percent) than the United States (38 percent), according to the Pew Research Center.

At the White House this spring, President Yudhoyono told the story of an American student who sent a letter to a child in tsunami-ravaged Aceh, along with a bracelet used to raise donations for victims. To which the young girl from Aceh replied, "I am so glad you are paying attention to us here." She would wear the bracelet, she wrote, "to remind me that I have new friend."

Perhaps she should send her bracelet to politicians in Washington who don't seem to realize what others in Asia already know. You have a new friend in Indonesia, and it's time to pay attention.

Indonesia: Why Pluralism Will Prevail

International Herald Tribune, September 14, 2006

YOU COULD BE FORGIVEN FOR THINKING THAT INDONESIA, LONG ADMIRED as a beacon of Muslim moderation, is descending into an Islamic theocracy.

Christian churches are torched. Western resorts, hotels, and embassies are bombed. Abu Bakar Bashir, the radical cleric imprisoned for inspiring the Bali bombings of 2002, receives a hero's welcome home from fellow jihadists.

Across the country, more than two dozen cities and districts have imposed variations of Shariah, Islamic law, requiring women to wear headscarves and banning alcohol, gambling, and adultery.

But a visit with Dr. Zulkieflimansyah (who, like many Indonesians, uses one name and is more commonly known as Zul) reveals the more complex face of political Islam here. As vice chairman of the Justice and Prosperity Party, a rapidly growing Islamic party with two cabinet ministers, he speaks of the need for an "Islamic moral code" in a country that is more than 80 percent Muslim.

But the 34-year-old British-trained economist equivocates when I ask if his party will push for Shariah: "This is difficult. If we say no, we will be rejected by the Muslims. If we say yes, there are too many definitions of Shariah."

So Zul, now a gubernatorial candidate whose running mate is a well-known actress-turned-politician, speaks of fighting corruption and poverty and creating jobs and investment. "All this can be considered Shariah," he says. "We are not trying to create a new society like the Arabs. Pluralism is a fact of life, and radical Islam is our enemy."

Zul's deft balancing act mirrors that of Indonesia—the country with the world's largest Muslim population but which, as a state, is officially neither secular nor Islamic. Indeed, history suggests that Indonesia's unique brand of pluralism ultimately will prevail over today's "creeping Islamicization."

After Indonesia proclaimed independence in 1945, attempts to forge an Islamic state were thwarted when nationalists removed from the new constitution the famous "seven words"—"with obligation for Muslims to practice Shariah."

Instead, the official ideology of Pancasila—"five pillars": belief in one God, humanitarianism, national unity, democracy, and social justice—was a quintessential Indonesian compromise, acknowledging the role of religion in public life while guaranteeing the freedom of six state-recognized faiths: Islam, Protestantism, Catholicism, Hinduism, Buddhism, and Confucianism.

Ever since, attempts to create an Islamic state or impose Shariah nationally, whether by bullet or by ballot, have been soundly defeated. As recently as 2002, Parliament overwhelmingly rejected amending the constitution to allow for Shariah.

Defeated nationally, Islamists have gone local, empowered by a decentralization movement allowing greater regional autonomy—most notably in conservative Aceh, where canings of Shariah offenders have drawn international condemnation. But "Aceh does not represent Indonesia," as an Australian diplomat told me. In a nation of 240 million people, Shariah in a few cities and districts is an aberration.

In fact, there already are signs of a backlash against Shariah among Indonesian Muslims, who largely espouse a less rigid form of Islam that blends Hinduism, Buddhism, and Javanese mysticism. "Democracy can be noisy," Vice President Jusuf Kalla tells me, but in Indonesia "there are far more moderates than radicals."

Indeed, a major poll last month showed that the vast majority of Indonesians reject Shariah and still embrace Pancasila. But in treating the symptoms of extremism, Jakarta must not ignore underlying causes.

With 40 million chronically unemployed and perhaps 100 million living in poverty, "we are running out of time," says Defense Minister Juwono Sudarsono, who oversees a military that considers itself a guardian of constitutional pluralism.

President Susilo Bambang Yudhoyono, accused of being indecisive on the economic front, now appears to understand the urgency. Jakarta is alive with rumors that he plans a dramatic October surprise, reshuffling his cabinet with an eye toward a bold New Deal–style program to create jobs and combat poverty.

The murderous acts and militant agenda of a radical few here are making headlines. But historically, culturally, religiously, and politically, Indonesians give hope that the center will hold—that they will succeed in what Sudarsono calls "the big challenge of daring young Muslims not to die for Islam, but to live for Islam."

Indonesia's Security Burden

International Herald Tribune, September 4, 2009

LOCALS HERE QUIP THAT WHILE INDONESIA IS THE WORLD'S LARGEST archipelago nation—by definition, a nation of islands—it is not a maritime nation. Imagine, they say, a stretch of land covering the distance from Seattle to New York, or Lisbon to Moscow. And then imagine having fewer than 100 police cars responsible for patrolling that entire area, to respond to emergencies and protect national borders.

It seems inconceivable. And yet that is the equivalent mission that weighs on the Indonesian navy today. Its fleet of ships reportedly numbers around 120. If you discount the vessels in dry dock due to funding shortfalls, far fewer than 100 patrol at any given time. And with those vessels, the navy is expected to protect a nation with more than 17,000 islands, covering 5 million square kilometers.

When the navy appeals to the air force for help, the situation is equally dire. The air force has about 220 aircraft and helicopters, a number of which are unserviceable. Among its fleet of C-130 Hercules aircraft are some that first flew in the 1960s. Planes have been known to simply fall out of the sky.

This would be a regional issue if it weren't for the increasingly central role that Indonesia is playing to American security interests, the fight against global terrorism, and its potential as a check on China's growing footprint.

"Indonesia is as strategically important to the United States as Israel and Egypt," Endy Bayuni, the editor of the *Jakarta Post*, tells me.

The case can be made on several grounds. There is the maritime argument: More than half of the world's merchant fleet tonnage passes through the straits around Indonesia, including the vital 805-kilometer stretch of water between Peninsular Malaysia and the Indonesian island of Sumatra, known as the Strait of Malacca. More than 80 percent of the critical "maritime pipeline" of fuel from Gulf suppliers to US allies in Japan, South Korea, and Taiwan comes through the strait.

There is the democracy argument: With more people than the Arab Middle East, Indonesia is the world's largest Muslim-majority nation, its third-largest democracy, and the only Muslim democracy besides Turkey.

"If democracy can work in this vast, plural society, it can work elsewhere," says Ted Osius, deputy chief of mission at the US embassy.

Then there is the reform argument: This nation has made strides against former President Suharto's 32-year dictatorship. The national police have arrested hundreds of suspected terrorists, the nation just observed another peaceful presidential election, and the military "has come a long way from the days when it was the political tool of President Suharto," says Mr. Bayuni.

And yet Washington seems stuck in 1991, when Indonesian troops were accused of killing unarmed East Timorese civilians. Since then, cases of human rights abuses have focused almost entirely on the "Indonesian green berets," the controversial special forces group Kopassus, even though most abuses occurred when today's soldiers were in knee pants. Nevertheless, nongovernmental organizations in Washington have largely painted the entire Indonesian military with a Kopassus brush.

As a result, US military aid to Indonesia is more than 200 times less than military aid to Israel and Egypt. While President Susilo Bambang Yudhoyono recently proposed an increase in the 2010 defense budget, and funding from Washington is expected to climb $10 million by 2011, it's still a pittance. What to do?

First, the United States should increase military financing to Indonesia to levels equivalent to [US aid going to] Israel and Egypt. To get beyond the Kopassus conundrum, aid should be specifically directed to the Indonesian navy and air force, to improve security in the Strait of Malacca and other sea lanes on which US interests depend.

Second, the primary goal of US aid should be to build the "coast guard" capabilities of the Indonesian navy and air force, not its weapons systems.

Third, the United States should increase by tenfold the number of Indonesian military personnel participating in the State Department's International Military Education and Training Program. Prior to 1991, dozens participated. Only six do so now.

Finally, the United States should enter into a formal strategic partnership with Indonesia when President Obama visits in November. Mr. Yudhoyono opened the door to such a partnership in a Washington speech last November, as did Secretary of State Hillary Clinton in her visit here in February.

When Mr. Obama lived in Jakarta as a boy, the United States didn't appreciate Indonesia's problems. As Mr. Obama prepares to return as president, the United States doesn't understand its progress. The United States should begin to see Indonesia for what it really is: America's Israel and Egypt on the Strait of Malacca.

Indonesia, America, and China's Nine-Dash Line

The World Post, September 8, 2014

WHEN THE HISTORY OF THE EARLY PART OF THE 21ST CENTURY IS WRITTEN, one of the great heroes of the People's Republic of China might turn out to be an anonymous mapmaker from the late 1940s whose work is helping to drive increasingly dangerous confrontations today between China and its neighbors across the South China Sea.

The question at issue is: Who owns what across this 1.3 million-square-mile stretch of water, through which passes more than half of the world's nautical trade? Numerous studies reveal that maps of the region, including some carved in stone that date back to the 10th century, show China consistently laying claim to just one island in the sea: Hainan Island, just off the mainland, which defined China's southern border for centuries. But as journalist Andrew Browne recently illuminated, in 1947, somewhere deep in the cartography division of the Kuomintang regime, a mapmaker added 11 heavy dashes to the familiar atlas encircling 90 percent of the South China Sea and connecting it back to China. No explanation accompanied this change. No Chinese territorial conquest drove it. No treaty enabled it. No other nation acknowledged it. No global body even knew about it.

And yet, as Brown argues, after forcing Generalissimo Chiang Kai-shek's Kuomintang to flee to Taiwan in 1949, Chinese communists turned the 11-dash map into a nine-dash line in 1953 and claimed ownership. It sat passively until 2010, when Beijing revived the map, assigned historical weight to the concocted line, and used it to declare "indisputable sovereignty" over the same 90 percent area of the sea. It did so in spite of the fact that huge swaths of the territory are claimed by—and recognized by the United Nations as owned by—five other nations.

While headlines often tiptoe around the map's murky origins, there is little question that the nine-dash line is, in the words of one Filipino judge, a "gigantic historical fraud."

Even so, China has used the nine-dash line as justification to make mayhem across the South China Sea. In 2014 alone, it tried to build a new oil platform in waters claimed by Vietnam. It blocked ships supplying the Philippine navy. It announced plans to build lighthouses on land claimed by the Philippines, began construction on islands claimed by Vietnam and the Philippines, and issued new rules for access to fishing off its shore that the United States has described as "provocative and potentially dangerous." In fact, China claims almost the entire South China Sea, rejecting rival claims not only from Vietnam and the Philippines, but also from Taiwan, Malaysia, and Brunei.

And this is not to mention China's continuing claim in the East China Sea to five islands known as Senkaku in Japanese and Diaoyu in Chinese. While the dispute over the uninhabited islands goes back more than a century, tensions flared in 2010 after Japan arrested the captain of a Chinese fishing boat for ramming Japanese patrols boats in the waters off the islands. They flared again after Japan purchased three of the islands from a private Japanese owner, and got ratcheted up again last month when Japan quietly gave names to the five islands and published them on a maritime website. With Chinese and Japanese ships and planes regularly playing a dangerous game of cat and mouse, credible foreign policy analysts have asked if these five tiny islands could spark war.

But sitting here in the Defense Ministry of Indonesia, the region's biggest potential counterweight to China's aggressive actions, it's difficult to see any easy solutions. Like Russia's aggressive actions in Ukraine, this is about power politics, pure and simple. China—thirsting for oil and unquestionably driven by the vast store of oil and natural gas that reportedly lie beneath these ocean waters—waited until it was strong enough economically and militarily to reassert the nine-dash line. It is all but daring the rest of the world to stop it. And Indonesia hasn't been excluded—this past spring, China lay claim to parts of the Indonesia-held Natuna Islands, including a segment of Indonesia's Riau Islands. Far from a full-throated response, Indonesian officials went out of their way to publicly deny that Indonesia had any maritime dispute with China (while quietly and quickly working to strengthen its forces on Natuna).

For a nation like Indonesia—which counts China as one of its largest trading partners, its largest purchaser of Indonesian products, and a strong partner of its military—it is a difficult balancing act.

"I've been the chief of bilateral defense relations with China since 2007," the deputy minister of defense, Sjafrie Samsudin, tells me in his office. "I visit China every year and they visit us to enhance the bilateral relationship . . . We want the Chinese to implement a stable dialogue and increased efforts (in the South China Sea). The Chinese tell us that they agree with us, but feel they are surrounded by countries such as the United States."

This point comes as something of a surprise. What I hear repeatedly in conversations across this island nation is that China might be the only Asian country that believes the United States will use its influence to deter the ambitions of Beijing here. Despite high-profile joint exercises between the US and local militaries and a marked increase in US military hardware postmarked for Southeast Asia, many leaders here believe that there is more sizzle than steak when it comes to the US's highly touted "pivot" to Asia.

"Privately, at the highest levels of the government here, they are concerned about China and see the train coming at Indonesia in four years," says a high-ranking Western diplomat. "China is trying to pick off each country one by one, and they know the US threshold. Indonesia realizes this and thinks that the United States is not going to stand up against the Chinese, and doubts the United States has resolve in Asia."

With China's leadership taking a with-us-or-against-us mentality across the region, the burden placed on China's neighbors is excruciating—particularly when it comes to the United States. "No one wants to be told by the Americans what to do," a longtime diplomat from the Asian subcontinent tells me, explaining that to be seen as compliant with Washington invites scorn. "There's a negative perception of America over the past few years. We are looking forward to increased interaction with the United States after Obama."

For many years, America was able to circumvent such concerns because its relationship with the Indonesian military was so strong—essentially training two generations of Indonesian leaders. But in the wake of reported human rights abuses here 15 years ago, the United States—under the leadership of Vermont Senator Patrick Leahy—cut off relations with the military. While some training and support have since been restored, US training for Indonesia's elite special forces has yet to resume.

In fact, Sjafrie, the deputy minister himself and a decorated special forces officer, cannot get a visa to visit America. While he leads Indonesia's military delegations to Russia, China, and other nations, he's not allowed to meet with his US counterparts—and when US elected officials visit Jakarta, they rarely meet with the military. It prompts Sjafrie to ask, "How can you have a fair understanding (of each other) if you don't meet and talk to us?"

"Our office is now very close to China as a result of America's bad behavior," says a high-placed aide to the ministry, adding, "Many good opportunities have gone to China instead." That's not a good formula for convincing local governments to side with America against their 800-pound neighbor to the north.

"The next Indonesian president needs to strengthen relations with both the United States and China," says Sjafrie, pointing out that US ambassador Robert Blake is working hard to establish full military-to-military support and relations, a priority he deems "vital."

"The macro relations are being enhanced and have been developing for a long time," continues Sjafrie. "But on the micro side, we need more work and development. We have suffered for 15 years under sanctions, and we want to move on."

In October, Sjafrie will move on as deputy defense minister. But unlike some previous occupants of his office, he won't be going to America to train with military leaders at Fort Bragg or the Army War College. Instead, he says, "I'll be going to Beijing to enhance my knowledge in defense studies. I'll study (revered Chinese military general) Sun Tzu again because it can be used in all aspects of life."

It was Sun Tzu who said, "Supreme excellence consists of breaking the enemy's resistance without fighting." Time will tell if the same may be said about the South China Sea.

Resisting the Arabization of Islam in Indonesia

The World Post, December 7, 2015

IT IS A SIGN OF THE VIOLENT AGE WE LIVE IN THAT THERE IS A WEBSITE IN the United States devoted to updating daily deaths by gunfire. Last week, the Mass Shooting Tracker reported that in the first 334 days of this year, America had experienced 351 shootings in which four or more people were killed or injured—an average of more than one a day. And yet, aside from wondering what it will take for America to end its insane addiction to guns, few of these tragedies have garnered as much attention in the South Asian nation of Indonesia than last week's horrific shooting in San Bernardino, California, where 14 were killed and 21 wounded at the hands of a young Muslim couple who were reportedly radicalized in Saudi Arabia.

For Indonesia, the world's largest Muslim-majority nation—with more adherents of Islam than Saudi Arabia, Iran, Iraq, Syria, Afghanistan, Jordan, Libya, Lebanon, and Palestine combined—the story of citizens returning home from the Middle East more extreme than when they left is an old one. But it is also a story generating fresh concern as a number of Indonesian Muslims are choosing to travel to Iraq and Syria to fight for the jihadists of the Islamic State (also known as ISIS).

As in other countries witnessing a similar migration, the fear isn't what they will do when they get there—but rather, like the alleged shooters from California, what they might do when they get home. But the tolerant, secular, and democratic Indonesia is the nation best positioned today to challenge the clash within Islamic civilization, and there are lessons from how Indonesians are fighting this battle that we can all learn from today.

Some of those lessons go back nearly a century. For 600 years, since it first arrived in Indonesia with traders from India in the 13th century, Islam grew quietly and locally across many of the islands that make up this archipelago nation. But trouble began in the late 1800s, when Jakarta's colonial Dutch overlords began building steamships and investing in ports, enabling many Indonesian Muslims to make the pilgrimage to Mecca for the first time. By 1885, Indonesians quickly became the largest contingent of pilgrims from any nation to visit the holy place revered as the birthplace of the prophet Mohammad, where he first received instruction from God.

While at Mecca, the pilgrims were exposed for the first time to the teachings of 18th-century Saudi cleric Muhammad ibn Abd al-Wahhab, who advocated a medieval interpretation of Islam that promotes the subjugation of women and encourages the violent deaths of all "infidels" who believe differently by such barbaric practices as stoning and beheading.

Many of these travelers returned to Indonesia much less tolerant of the Hindu-infused brand of Islam practiced at home and horrified by local rituals and superstitions that had been layered on the practice of Islam over the centuries. Many sought to purify it, often violently, by advocating a turn to Wahhabism while calling for the state to adopt a strict form of Muslim, or Shariah, law.

By January 1926—90 years ago next month—moderate Indonesian Muslims had had enough. They came together to found an organization, called Nahdlatul Ulama, which is known as NU and translates to "The Renaissance of Islamic Scholars." NU was dedicated to a more humane, more tolerant interpretation of Islam while calling out Wahhabism as a gross distortion of God's commands. For the next nine decades—as Indonesia eventually won its independence from the Dutch in the 1940s, lived under military dictatorship starting in the 1960s, and started on the road to becoming the world's largest Muslim democracy in the 1990s—NU waged a constant battle against fundamentalists.

For two of those decades, NU was led by Abdurrahman Wahid, fondly know as Gus Dur. Blind and irreverent, Gus Dur was the grandson of an NU founder and the son of a former NU leader. He and I became friends in the early 1990s, nearly a decade before he was elected president of Indonesia in the country's first presidential election after three decades of authoritarian rule.

"Too many Muslims willfully ignore the true teachings of Islam," he said to me many times before his death in 2010. "Right Islam" as he liked to call it, isn't fanatical, but instead is open and tolerant, recognizing that all religions in the modern world must exist alongside, and often within, secular society. "Democracy is not only not *haram* (forbidden) in Islam," he once wrote, "but is a compulsory element of Islam. Upholding democracy is one of the principals of Islam."

This very openness has made Indonesia a target in the age of Al Qaeda and ISIS, both of which espouse a nihilistic version of Wahhabism. Over the past 15 years, a homegrown strain of Al Qaeda, called Jemaah Islamiyah, has brought Middle Eastern violence to Indonesia, often targeting Western symbols. In 2000, bombings in 11 churches across Indonesia took 19 lives. In 2002, two explosions occurred at a popular Balinese nightclub my wife and I often frequented, killing 202 people. In 2005, 20 more were killed in another bombing at a Bali resort. In 2003 and again in 2009, explosions at hotels in Jakarta took more lives.

In recent years, extremists have targeted symbols of the state itself, attacking Muslim police and military personnel. As the ISIS threat has grown in Syria and Iraq, NU—which is now the largest Muslim organization in the world, with 50 million members—has worked with local officials to combat what journalist Elizabeth Pisani has called the "Arabization of Islam in Indonesia." While government officials estimate that about 700 Indonesians have gone to fight for ISIS in the Middle East—including, in a few cases, entire families—widespread ISIS videos advocating violence haven't yet found a broad audience.

In fact, a recent global study by the Pew Foundation found that 79 percent of Indonesians condemn the actions of ISIS and only 4 percent support it—numbers much different from other Muslim majority nations like Pakistan, where just 28 percent of respondents voiced any disapproval of the Islamic State at all.

NU understands that opposition to radicalism needs to be constantly reinforced. Last week, just as their predecessors had done 90 years ago, the leadership of NU announced that it was time for the world to fight back against ISIS. It released a feature film that directly challenges the idea of ISIS, stressing that the Koran instructs true believers of Islam to love, not hate. Called *The Divine Grace of East Indies Islam,* the film, as NU head Mustofa Bisri said last week, will counter "the spread of a shallow understanding of Islam," [whose adherents] "justify their harsh and often savage behavior by claiming to act in accord with God's commands" but "are grievously mistaken."

For Indonesia, the lessons for fighting a false and barbaric form of Islam are simple.

First, it's not enough to speak out against radicals only when tragedies happen. As a well-known general says, when prompted, "An insurgency can't be ended by eliminating the last supporter. It's not about killing them all and using the military. You need a political solution, and use smart power. You need to speak out against them every single day."

Second, cooperation counts. Indonesia's most effective counterterrorism squad, known as Densus 88, was established by the Indonesian National Police, funded by the American government, and trained by the Central Intelligence Agency, and coordinates constantly with the Australian Federal Police. In recent years, such coordination has stopped a 2012 plot to bomb the Indonesian Parliament building and a planned 2013 attack on the embassy of Myanmar.

Third, lies need to be exposed publicly and immediately. In a country where the majority lives in poverty and the economy is struggling, ISIS is promising to pay thousands of dollars each month. One motorcycle taxi driver made news recently when an ISIS representative told him he'd earn the equivalent of $3,800 per month if he joined. It was countered with highly publicized stories from other Indonesians who returned early from Syria—because they were never paid the high wages they were promised.

As American officials struggle to understand what radicalized alleged San Bernardino shooters Syed Farook and Tashfeen Malik in Saudi Arabia, Indonesia will continue to work every day to make clear [that], as a former US secretary of state once said, "if you want to know whether Islam, democracy, modernity, and women's rights can co-exist, go to Indonesia." Hillary Clinton was right when she spoke those words in 2009—and with the NU's leadership, it will continue to be true for many decades to come.

It's Time for the United States to Pivot to Indonesia

The Huffington Post, September 23, 2016

AS AMERICA ENTERTAINED ITSELF WITH THE VITAL QUESTIONS OF whether Hillary Clinton's temporary absence from the campaign trail due to pneumonia constituted a character issue (it didn't), or whether Donald Trump finally admitting that Barack Obama was born in America meant that the "birther" conspiracies he spun against the president for the past five years were just one long racist lie (it did), Russia and China came together to conduct the single largest joint maritime military exercise between the two nations—ever.

The fact that they did so in the hotly disputed waters of the South China Sea was just the latest evidence that whoever occupies the Oval Office next January is going to face a rapidly growing danger in Asia. That fear was compounded when Philippine President Rodrigo Duterte announced during the Sino-Russian wargames that his country would no longer take part in joint naval patrols with the United States. While not as inflammatory as his appalling statement two days earlier that Obama was "the son of a whore"— an unconscionable thing for any world leader to say about another, let alone the leader of an ally responsible for 75 percent of all Philippines arms imports since 1950—his reasoning for the severance was more damning: "China is now in power, and they have military superiority across the region."

When Trump or Clinton becomes president next year and considers how to reassert American power in the region, the most important face looking back will be that of an unassuming man who started working in his family's furniture shop at 12, was evicted from his home on three occasions, and was best known just four years ago as the mayor of a city the size of Cleveland. In truth, Joko Widodo, known here as Jokowi, was as unlikely a candidate to be elected president of Indonesia—which he was, in 2014—as there's ever been.

Yet there is no nation in Southeast Asia better positioned to provide the counterweight to China and Russia that America needs in the South China

Sea than the world's fourth-most populous country, one that's not only strategically located in the region but growing economically in ways that will increase its ability to assert its interests. And there is no nation in the world that provides a more powerful example in this era of global extremism and instability than the world's largest Muslim-majority democracy which, at 250 million strong, proves every day that democracy and Islam can not only co-exist, but thrive.

If the story of the Obama years was about America's supposed pivot to Asia—which critics say is sinking—the story of the next eight years needs to be America's pivot to Indonesia. And after two years of false starts and concerns about his leadership, Jokowi is ready for his close-up. And not a moment too soon.

As we were starkly reminded last week by China and Russia's seventh joint naval exercises since 2005, tensions are rising in the South China Sea, and Indonesia is right in the thick of it. The trouble started in 2010, when Beijing, trumpeting a widely debunked 1953 map that laid claim to 90 percent of the South China Sea as Chinese territory, declared "indisputable sovereignty" over the same territory.

That came as news to the five other nations, including Indonesia, which the international community has long recognized as the owners of the land and water being claimed by China today. But that hasn't stopped China from throwing its considerable weight around the past six years, constructing oil platforms, boarding ships, and, most ominously, seizing islands claimed by Vietnam and the Philippines—on which it has put up buildings, constructed airstrips and huge aircraft hangars, and deployed military planes and other armaments.

In July, an international tribunal in The Hague rejected China's claim to 90 percent of the South China Sea—through which half of the world's nautical trade passes—ruling in favor of the Philippines in a maritime dispute. China has responded with more bluster, vowing that it will "never stop" construction while all but daring the international community to force it to leave. And "it's not hard to understand why," a journalist here tells me. "More than half of China's reserves go through the South China Sea. It's a weak spot and it's vital that they have control."

China also continues to build up its coast guard and fishing fleets, which is where Indonesia directly enters the fray. Over the past five years, there have been a number of clashes between Chinese fishing vessels and the Indonesian navy over the Indonesia-owned Natuna Islands, which China now also claims. As one journalist recently observed, "Beijing uses these fishing ships as a kind of militia to harass and block other nation's vessels from accessing the vital trade routes and fishing grounds."

Indonesians have had enough. Beginning in late 2014, led by Jokowi and fisheries minister Susi Pudjiastuti, this island nation has taken the extraordinary step of blowing up more than 220 seized fishing vessels in public events that have sent an unmistakable message to Beijing. In June, to reinforce that show of strength, Jokowi made a high-profile visit to the Natunas.

"Taking sides on the South China Sea issue is not something we traditionally do," a respected editor says to me. "We won't take the US side on this. But we may lean." However, a well-connected consultant confides that "Jokowi recently told (me) in a private meeting that he is now ready to face South China Sea issues. He is interested in China now and being assertive."

It fits with other moves the president has made that reflect a growing strength. Dismissed in 2014 as an inexperienced puppet for the leader of his party, the former president Megawati Sukarnoputri—memorialized in the *Wall Street Journal* headline "Mega's Message to Jokowi: I'm the Boss"—Jokowi was criticized for rubber-stamping controversial allies of Megawati's for his cabinet. That, too, is changing. He recently brought back Sri Mulyani, a bold reformer whom Jokowi had exiled to the World Bank for ruffling feathers, as finance minister. He also appointed a widely respected police chief and shuffled a powerful gatekeeper to a different post.

"Jokowi is frustrated and needs good people to assert authority," says a well-placed confidante to the president, who adds that Jokowi's profile began to change when he built a stronger relationship with the military a year ago. "He is tired of this political drama that has been going on since he became president. He is consolidating power."

It's a moment tailor-made for the United States to strengthen relations with Jakarta. How? Three ways.

First, our next president should visit Indonesia as soon as possible, and make clear: while Obama's focus was on expanding alliances with Japan and Korea, facilitating change in Myanmar, and improving relations with Vietnam and India, the top priority for the next four years is Indonesia. That's especially important for Clinton, whose time as Obama's secretary of state left people here "skeptical of her," one insider confides. A substantive presidential visit would bolster her standing and signal that the United States is serious about pivoting to Indonesia.

Second, the United States should support Indonesia's emerging assertiveness on South China Sea issues. That includes offering Indonesia more maritime capabilities so that it can stand up for itself at sea—including modernized coast guard vessels and training. Former minister of defense Juwono Sudarsono believes this is something Trump would do, expressing confidence that "Trump will win and he will change."

Finally, the next administration must articulate a creative strategy for our economic relationship that contrasts with China's strategy of "exploit and extract." There is a fear here that Indonesia's growing dependence on China—it recently ranked 10th in a *Forbes* list of the "Top 10 China-Dependent Countries"—could compromise its assertiveness on the South China Sea. US economic and business-to-business engagement should offer a vision that empowers, instead of extracts from, Indonesia. That means investing in education and development, supporting innovation and entrepreneurship, and giving Jakarta an alternative to China in its race to improve its gridlocked economy. It also means finding a way to make the proposed trade pact between the United States and 11 Pacific Rim nations, known as the Trans-Pacific Partnership—which is projected to bring $26 billion in trade to Indonesia—work.

Lastly, no matter who wins in November, there is one thing the next president should do: invite Jokowi to visit and work to secure an invitation for him to address Congress. The last, and only, time an Indonesian leader spoke to Congress was in 1956—when Trump was nine, Clinton was eight, and Jokowi was five years from being born. Sixty years is too long. It's time to bring the relationship between the world's oldest democracy and the world's largest Muslim-majority democracy into the 21st century—no matter who sits in the Oval Office.

IRAN

Toward Normal Links Between Iran and America

International Herald Tribune, March 31, 1998

WHAT DO THE PRESIDENT AND FOREIGN MINISTER OF IRAN HAVE IN common with the president and secretary of state of the United States? They all want a dialogue.

Mohammed Khatami wants to establish a "thoughtful" dialogue; Kamai Kharrazi, one that is "constructive." Bill Clinton wants it to be "honest"; Madeleine Albright, to be "direct." And the European Union has now agreed to a dialogue that is "open" rather than "critical."

But A. N. S. Khamooshi, head of Iran's state-supported Chamber of Commerce, told me when I began my visit, "Forget dialogue. Let's do business." To an American businessman, that sounded very promising.

The problem has been that when I try to discuss specifics, I hear the same mantra from almost every Iranian I meet—top government officials, opposition leaders, professionals, economists, journalists, conservatives, and moderates, including those who spent time in the shah's and the ayatollahs' prisons.

It goes like this: Just as President Khatami expressed regret over the seizure of American hostages in 1979, President Clinton must apologize for the part the United States played in overthrowing the Mossadegh regime in 1953 and bringing back the shah.

Surprising as it may seem in a country where half the male population is too young to shave, the coup that took place almost half a century ago is a fresh memory, and a national obsession.

Iranians feel like a woman deceived. The United States had been a hero since the beginning of the century for its anti-colonialist stance, and a savior immediately after World War II for helping get the Russians out of Iran. But in 1951 Mohammed Mossadegh, an anti-communist nationalist, became prime minister and nationalized the Anglo-Iranian Oil Company.

At the urging of political mullahs and British intelligence, the CIA served as paymaster to help overthrow Mossadegh and reinstall the shah. The line from that event in 1953 to the taking of the US hostages in 1979 runs straight and true in the minds of practically every Iranian I speak to.

Americans seem equally stuck in time. The fact is that the Islamic "revolution for export" died on June 3, 1989, and is buried along with Ayatollah Ruhollah Khomeini. Today Iran has a president who speaks openly for the rule of law, a civil society based on the constitution, and individual rights for all Iranians.

He was elected by 70 percent of the electorate, 90 percent of whom voted last May. He is resisted by Ayatollah Sayed Ali Khamenei, Iran's supreme leader. But their "good mullah, bad mullah" partnership seems to be working. It is time that the United States began to readjust its policies based on this new reality.

Unfortunately, the Iranian economy is "sick," as President Khatami said recently. The state controls 85 percent of an economic system that is mismanaged, bloated, over-regulated, and corrupt. The budget policies of the Parliament are subject to the final say-so of a mullah-dominated Council of Guardians.

It is as if the US Supreme Court, made up members of the Moral Majority, had to approve congressional decisions. One doesn't have to be an ayatollah to know that this doesn't have a prayer of working.

Worse, 80 percent of the government's hard currency earnings and 70 percent of its revenues come from oil exports, and world oil prices have dropped to the lowest levels in a decade. The rial has gone from 70 to the dollar at the time of the 1978 revolution to a market rate today of more than 5,000.

Half the population lives below the poverty line. At least half of young Iranians are unemployed or underemployed. Annual inflation is 50 percent, more than twice the official rate.

And then there are the semi-governmental "foundations." These financial organizations, purportedly charitable and run mostly by merchant-traders, operate at least 750 companies and command assets second only to those of the state. Much of their profits go to high-ranking government officials and clerics.

Yet of the 120,000 mullahs, 95 percent confine themselves to religious, not political, pursuits. You can tell who they are; they ride on buses, not in chauffeur-driven limousines.

In 10 days in Tehran, Isfahan, and Shiraz, I have not seen a mugger or a beggar, or anyone looking remotely like the homeless people I see when I walk down Connecticut Avenue in Washington. The wide streets are clean and free of potholes. Iranian family values would make the most devout Christian or Jewish fundamentalist proud.

The literacy rate among Iranians under 30 is an astounding 93 percent. Unlike Islamic countries like Saudi Arabia, where women cannot drive or vote, Iran does not write off half of its population. Iranian women are doctors, lawyers, teachers, psychologists—and vice president. Daughters of Ayatollah Khamenei and former president Hashemi Rafsanjani are feminists.

Iran is of enormous strategic importance to the United States. Sixty-four percent of the world's known oil reserves lie below and around the Gulf. This most populous nation in the Middle East has the second-largest natural gas reserves in the world.

And there is the Caspian Sea, with potential oil and gas reserves worth as much as $4 trillion. The shortest and cheapest pipeline route to the Gulf and to Western markets runs through Iran.

Containment is no longer US policy toward China, whose record on human rights and the proliferation of weapons of mass destruction has been criminal. So why does the United States continue to try to "contain" Iran?

Whatever the rationale for a hard-line policy during the 1980s, today it only isolates the United States and Israel. America should lift its trade embargo and repeal its secondary sanctions on non-US companies that invest in Iran. This would be a blow to the reactionary forces which at present control almost all of Iran's domestic income.

They would like nothing better than for the United States to continue its current policies, because if President Khatami does not succeed in attracting foreign investment and delivering a better standard of living for most Iranians in the next two years, the moderates will be out.

Normalizing US-Iranian relations would bring cheers from Iranians as loud as those that recently greeted the US wresting team—and a mad scramble from the German, Italian, Norwegian, and Japanese business executives operating here. The ones I meet love the US sanctions. They are working frantically to get their contracts finalized, because the day Washington gives the green light for US business to invest and trade, they say, "we might as well pack up and go home."

It is time for Bill Clinton and congressional leaders to have a serious dialogue about renewing the close and historic links between two great nations.

Widen the Focus and See the Big Picture in Iran

International Herald Tribune, February 11, 2000

IN ADVANCE OF IRAN'S PARLIAMENTARY ELECTIONS NEXT FRIDAY, MOST Western analysts are under the illusion that who controls the legislature will determine whether Iran moves from clerical dictatorship to representative democracy. By focusing exclusively on an electoral sideshow, outsiders miss the main event.

The prevailing vision reduces Iran's domestic scene to a convenient plot of good versus evil, with the good guys called reformers and the bad guys called conservatives. Oversimplification in Washington has narrowed the dialogue with Iran to focus on the "reformers" alone, which helps explain why US relations with Iran never seem to go anywhere. America has lost sight of the big picture in Iran.

Conservatives may be as open as reformers to improving ties with the West. But neither group is likely to have much effect, either on foreign relations or on its own society, as long as the ultimate political authority rests not with any popularly elected Parliament or president but with a "supreme leader" chosen by fellow clerics.

In other words, the Iranian political dynamic is not democratic in the sense that the term is understood in the West.

Nor is Iran's current constitutional structure merely the product of the whimsical fantasies of a few theocrats. Washington should not treat the notion of a head of state being a member of the clergy as an aberration. Separation of church and state does not have strong roots in most Islamic societies.

Washington should try altering its approach to promoting change in Iran. That means engaging Iranians across the political spectrum. Not all conservatives are opposed to relations with America, just as not every reformer wants to see a rapprochement. The reality is less cut and dried.

For example, Ayatollah Hussein Ali Montazeri recently called for the position of supreme leader to be popularly elected. This senior cleric was the designated successor of the late Ayatollah Ruhollah Khomeini, who fathered the revolution that overthrew the shah in 1979, until Ayatollah Khomeini shoved him aside.

And the current president, Mohammed Khatami, for all his populist style, has within his camp such figures as Ayatollah Sadegh Khalkali, a man notorious in Iran for sentencing thousands of people to death for violating Islamic doctrine.

The diversity of Iranian politics makes labels almost meaningless. Hard-line conservatives, traditional conservatives, independents, old leftists, new leftists, liberals, and reformists abound. But what unites most of them is pragmatism, and the master of this political art is Ali Akbar Hashemi Rafsanjani, the former president, current chairman of the powerful Expediency Council, and probable next speaker of Parliament. He is now running as an independent.

A popular story in Tehran points up his ability to be all things to all people. In 1988 he was riding with the president and the prime minister when they came to a T junction in the road. The driver asked which way to turn. The president said, "Right." The prime minister said, "Left." Mr. Rafsanjani said, "Signal left but go right."

He recently suggested that Tehran and Washington would one day bridge their differences.

But in Iran, it is two steps forward, one step back. Until his conviction for heresy, Abdullah Nouri was a leading candidate to become speaker of Parliament. Mr. Nouri, a popular cleric who published a widely read newspaper, had openly challenged the idea of Islam as a monolithic ideology subject to interpretation by a select few. His assertion that the supreme leader is "just another Iranian and not above the law" is reminiscent of the 17th-century movement in Britain that challenged the power of the king to override the laws of Parliament.

Increasing numbers of Iranians who supported the revolution are challenging the supreme leader's claim to be God's representative on earth and refusing to accept the notion that arbitrary arrests and executions are the will of their God. The frustrations of ordinary Iranians, especially women and young people, can only further democratic reforms if these are fostered constructively.

Rather than take sides in a largely meaningless election and tailor sanctions to the result, America should take a more practical approach. This means continuing to expand the sale of agricultural and other products as a step toward lifting all sanctions and normalizing relations.

The best way to advance reform in Iran is by offering the Islamic Republic a remarkably simple commodity that has been sorely lacking—respect.

How to Promote People Power in Iran

International Herald Tribune, March 20, 2002

I REALIZED THAT AMERICA WAS MISSING THE MAIN EVENT IN IRAN WHEN I saw the mullah hailing a taxi. When I had met him days earlier, he wore the unmistakable uniform of the clerics who rule the Islamic Republic. But there on a busy Tehran street, he blended with the masses. No turban, no flowing robe. I asked him why. "Because," he answered, "no cab driver would pick me up."

The pivotal battle in Iran is not between "good" and "bad" mullahs. It is between the mullahs and the people. A proverb says: "Do not step on Persian carpets or mullahs, for they will increase in value." Iran's rulers must satisfy both its Persian and its Islamic cultures. But the shah stepped all over the mullahs, which led to the Islamic Revolution of 1979. Since then the mullahs have been stepping all over the carpets.

Today's Iranians want a modern, moderate Islamic society which preserves the country's Persian identity.

How best can the outside world encourage those Iranians who want to moderate their society and modernize their economy? A few suggestions:

Don't waste time favoring the reformers. The Battle of the Mullahs is a sideshow. A grassroots reform movement created President Mohammed Khatami, not the other way around. He has a mandate but no power.

It seems that the indecisive struggles of the past five years will continue so long as power—the courts, the Revolutionary Guards, the state radio and television, the Islamic business conglomerates—rests with the "supreme leader," Ayatollah Sayed Ali Khamenei. Only Iranian people power, not Washington, can change that.

Don't play into the hands of the extremists. Confrontation with the Great Satan is all the tired revolutionaries have left. Every time the reformers and the White House start talking about talking, the old guard stirs things up (arresting reformist parliamentarians) to provoke Washington ("axis of evil") and whip Iranians into another anti-American frenzy (the recent state-sponsored demonstrations were the biggest since the revolution).

These are desperate old men taking desperate measures—the last gasps of their dying regime.

Engage the real force in Iranian politics. The technocrat-pragmatists and clerics from the upper social classes have been keen to direct the government away from an all-consuming commitment to Islam and toward Iran's national interests, including deeper ties with the West.

They are allied to Iran's class of bazaari merchants, with their strong entrepreneurial spirit.

Chief in this camp is Hashemi Rafsanjani, heir to a pistachio family fortune, a former president (1989–1997) and now head of the powerful Expediency Council, which resolves disputes between competing branches of government. The West could do business with the likes of Rafsanjani, who keeps his finger to the wind and has shown an ability to be all things to all people.

Tehran legend holds that he was riding with the president and the prime minister when they came to a junction in the road and the driver asked which way to turn. The president said, "Right," and the prime minister said, "Left." Said Rafsanjani, "Signal left but go right."

He has suggested that Tehran and Washington will one day bridge their differences. Nixon opened the door to Red China. Reagan negotiated with the Evil Empire. Bush should reach out to the Islamic Republic.

Unleash Ronald Reagan's "forward strategy for freedom." Reagan recognized that trading with the enemy could help tear down walls and unravel totalitarian regimes from within. Bush recognizes that trade "reinforces the habits of liberty that sustain democracy."

If contact and commerce are the thin end of the democratic wedge in China, then why not in Iran? Why veto Iran's application to join the WTO, which the United States did again last month? Secretary of State Colin Powell says it is because "we can talk to China—we have ways of dealing with China in a sensible way; with Iran, no."

Of course, you can't really talk to a nation when you are busy damning it as evil. Instead of tirades, try trade.

The ayatollahs love Washington's trade embargo, which aids and abets their increasingly vulnerable grip on economic power. They have repeatedly shot down reform bills that would have encouraged foreign investment.

A million youngsters join the labor force each year looking for jobs that don't exist. Greater US investment and trade would transform one of the mullahs' main constituencies, the bazaari merchants, into a powerful influence for greater openness and freedom. Winston Churchill once remarked that Americans always do the right thing, after they've tried everything else. Loosening the embargo three years ago to allow import of Iranian caviar, pistachios, and carpets was a small step forward. Iran has since become a major customer for American corn.

In contrast, continuing the embargo and secondary sanctions against foreign companies doing business in Iran was a leap backward.

When Vice President Dick Cheney was chief executive of the world's largest oil field service company, he called for an end to the ban on investment by US companies in Iran, calling the policy a "mistake."

Not enforcing the secondary sanctions only makes matters worse. European and Asian oil companies invest in Iran with impunity, leaving US companies out in the cold.

Even Israel—whose destruction Rafsanjani recently said could be achieved with "one nuclear bomb"—trades with Iran, under European cover. An old lesson is learned anew: unilateral trade sanctions hurt only America.

It is not too late to do the right thing. While working to keep weapons of mass destruction from falling into Iranian hands, the United States should lift all non-military trade sanctions. A wave of blue jeans and videos could do more to loosen the grip of the extremists than two decades of weak sanctions and strong rhetoric.

Finally, embrace what Bush has called "the Iranian people's hope for freedom"—especially that of the young. Sixty-five percent of Iranians are under 25, with no memory of the late Ayatollah Ruhollah Khomeini. Iranian youth are more interested in "Made in the USA" than in "Death to America."

They wear Michael Jordan T-shirts and Nike sneakers.

A young man I met during my visit said he wanted to go dancing, hold hands with his girlfriend, and watch movies. In a nation where the voting age is 16, these young men and women surfing the Internet with one hand and holding their cell phones with the other will decide Iran's fate.

It is time for America to help the Iranians get the mullahs off their back. Time to help free Iran with free trade.

Nuclear Iran: The Principle Is Set—Now, What's the Price?

International Herald Tribune, April 6, 2005

"I'VE GOT PRINCIPLES," GROUCHO MARX ONCE QUIPPED. "IF YOU DON'T LIKE them, I've got other principles."

Since Iran's 1979 Islamic Revolution, Washington has made much of its self-righteous principles. No negotiations. No lifting of the US economic embargo. No diplomatic relations. At least not until Tehran stops supporting terrorism and pursuing weapons of mass destruction.

But these high principles yielded low returns. Washington's do-nothing, say-nothing stance toward Shiite Iran failed to change Tehran's behavior yet succeeded in depriving the United States of a valuable partner, from combating the Sunni terrorism of Al Qaeda to stabilizing Iraq.

So now that Tehran is perhaps three years away from having a nuclear weapon, Washington has wisely decided it has other principles. With the recent decision to join the European Union in offering Iran economic incentives to give up its nuclear program, the Bush administration is now negotiating with the Islamic Republic, with Europe as the middleman.

Negotiations will reveal the answers to key questions.

Does Tehran see a nuclear weapon as an end in itself or as a bargaining chip for economic and security concessions from the West?

Is the EU prepared to embrace the one stick that Tehran fears most—not American air strikes against its nuclear sites (which would only rally all Iranians around the clerical regime), but Security Council sanctions backed by Europe and Japan, Iran's main trading partners?

Is the Bush administration willing to offer perhaps the only carrot for which the Islamic Republic might give up the bomb—meaningful US economic and security guarantees?

A grand bargain with Tehran? As George Bernard Shaw said in another context, the principle has been established, and all that remains is the haggling over price.

Exemptions to the US embargo have already made Iran a major customer for American wheat and corn. Americans already buy more than $150 million worth of Iranian dried fruits, pistachios, carpets, and caviar every year.

The Bush administration now says it is prepared to stop blocking Iran's application to the World Trade Organization and to allow the sale of spare parts for Iran's aging civilian aircraft.

Iranian negotiators predictably dismissed this opening offer as "ludicrous" and "insignificant."

President George W. Bush concedes that the principle of all sticks, no carrots has failed. Explaining why he has let Europe take the lead in nuclear negotiations, he recently said, "We're relying upon others because we've sanctioned ourselves out of influence with Iran."

Washington learns an old lesson anew. Multilateral sanctions can succeed in changing behavior (as with the end of South Africa's apartheid regime and Libya's decision to give up weapons of mass destruction). But unilateral sanctions almost always fail (as with the 45-year US embargo against Fidel Castro's Cuba and sanctions to prevent Pakistan from going nuclear).

The US embargo has failed in its primary purpose of isolating Iran economically. While American companies watch, European companies have invested heavily in Iran's energy sector. Iran has agreed to a $40 billion natural gas deal with India and a $70 billion gas deal with China. So much for American threats to penalize foreign companies that invest in Iran's oil and gas sector.

Worst of all, the American embargo perversely reinforces the very regime it was meant to undermine. Why do Tehran's theocrats sabotage every step toward rapprochement with the United States, thwart privatization of state enterprises, and oppose foreign ownership of Iranian companies? Because the embargo props up the mullahs' own business monopolies.

Iran's supreme leader, Ayatollah Sayed Ali Khamenei, and his fellow kleptoclerics pocket billions from *bonyads*, corrupt Islamic "charities" that control an estimated 70 percent of Iran's non-oil economy. The Revolutionary Guards, the iron fist of the regime, profit from black market smuggling. The dilapidated banking system has meant a windfall for bazaari merchants and money lenders, another pillar of the regime.

Want to really undermine this mullahtocracy? Lift the embargo and begin a business invasion. But with the mullahs unlikely to sign their own death warrant and Iran's reformist movement all but dead, who's left to strike a grand bargain with Washington?

Re-enter Hashemi Rafsanjani, the powerful former president who is expected to run in June's presidential election. A leading pistachio exporter, the ever-pragmatic Rafsanjani knows that reducing the country's double-digit unemployment requires ties and trade with America. Iranians know that he is perhaps the only leader with the political clout and revolutionary credentials to strike a bargain with the Great Satan without being tagged a traitor—precisely why hard-core clerics have tried to keep him from running.

A Rafsanjani victory would be Iran's way of saying to the world, "Let's make a deal." But regardless, Washington should act in its own national interest and put all options on the table—major diplomatic and economic carrots included.

If Tehran is willing to submit to intrusive international inspections to assure the world that its nuclear program produces energy, not bombs, restoring diplomatic relations and lifting the trade embargo would be a price worth paying. Let the haggling begin.

Iran's President Is Playing a Weak Hand

International Herald Tribune, March 15, 2006

TO LISTEN TO MANY WESTERN OBSERVERS, IRAN'S HARD-LINE PRESIDENT Mahmoud Ahmadinejad has reignited the Islamic Revolution and is catapulting the world toward nuclear confrontation. Elected last year in a "landslide," his triumph supposedly returns all power to a unified clique of clerical reactionaries, dealing a death blow to Iran's reform movement.

Emboldened by record oil revenues and divisions within the UN Security Council, which will address Iran's nuclear activities this week, Tehran brazenly resumes enriching uranium for a nuclear weapon. Ahmadinejad, deemed the new Hitler for calling the Holocaust a "myth," then has the means to fulfill his pledge to "wipe Israel off the map."

Perhaps no headline captured this hysteria more than a recent cover of *Newsweek*, from which Ahmadinejad peered menacingly at the world and which asked, alarmingly, "How Dangerous Is Iran?"

The answer? Not as dangerous as many in the West believe.

An Iranian bomb is neither imminent nor would it be apocalyptic. According to the latest US intelligence estimates, Tehran is a decade away from possessing a nuclear weapon. Moreover, the Cold War logic of containment and deterrence still applies to Iran's ayatollahs, who are survivors, not suicidal.

Washington, having denied itself diplomatic and business eyes and ears in Iran since the 1979 revolution, is driving blind—unable to see, but hypersensitive to the sound of saber-rattling in Tehran.

"Misunderstanding the other side's ultimate intentions isn't a unilateral problem," says Siamak Namazi, a Tehran-based political analyst. "Both sides tend to misread the other's hand." Indeed, recognizing the weak hand now being played by Ahmadinejad is a prerequisite for a more rational US policy toward the Islamic Republic.

Myth: Ahmadinejad's "landslide" win reflects the aspirations of Iranians. In the first round of voting last spring, Ali Akbar Hashemi Rafsanjani, the centrist former president, received more votes than Ahmadinejad.

Faced with the lesser of two evils, most Iranians boycotted the runoff, allowing Ahmadinejad, who campaigned as an anti-corruption populist, to claim victory thanks to a mere third of eligible voters. Some mandate.

Myth: All power now rests with a united clerical regime. The regime is rife with institutional divisions and personal rivalries. Under the Iranian constitution, absolute power still rests with the supreme leader, Ayatollah Sayed Ali Khamenei, who may fear a challenge to his authority from the radical Ayatollah Mohammed Taqi Mesbah-Yazdi, Ahmadinejad's spiritual mentor.

Khamenei and the clerical elite already seem to be tightening the screws on the new president. Parliament rejected Ahmadinejad's first three nominees for oil minister, and Khamenei has given the Expediency Council, which is headed by Rafsanjani, new authority to supervise Ahmadinejad's administration.

Myth: Ahmadinejad's incendiary rhetoric is the rambling of a madman. The president's nuclear saber-rattling and Holocaust denials are, in fact, deliberate provocations. He's playing the only card he has—nuclear nationalism. Lacking a popular mandate, he uses his nuclear posturing to align him with the vast majority of Iranians who insist they will never relinquish their "right" to a nuclear program.

In fact, Ahmadinejad might welcome punitive action by the West. Economic sanctions would afford him a scapegoat for failing to make good on his wide-eyed campaign promises to redistribute wealth to the poor.

US or Israeli air strikes against nuclear targets would unite Iran as never before and give Tehran another excuse to suppress domestic dissidents.

Myth: Oil-rich Iran can go it alone. Despite Ahmadinejad's chest-thumping boasts of Iran's self-reliance, the world's fourth-largest oil exporter desperately needs foreign investment to modernize its dilapidated refineries and reduce crushing unemployment and inflation. Regionally, it needs Washington's help to counter the greatest threat to Shiite Iran—not a nuclear Israel, but a nuclear, Talibanized, Sunni Pakistan.

Faced with these realities, it's time for Washington to call Ahmadinejad's bluff by playing the card the hard-liners fear most: a dramatic US offer of reconciliation, including a security guarantee like that offered North Korea. Such a move would expose the rifts in the regime, deny the hard-liners the confrontation they court, and deprive the bankrupt revolutionaries of their Great Satan.

Bold moves have never been a part of Washington's game plan toward Tehran. But a power play like rapprochement may be the best chance to deal a new deck that includes mutual respect rather than the same old cards of mutual confrontation.

Dealing with Iran: Finally, a Stick

International Herald Tribune, July 27, 2007

IN THE CARROT-AND-STICK WORLD OF INTERNATIONAL DIPLOMACY, IRAN and its controversial nuclear program seem impervious to both.

The theocrats of Tehran have dismissed every economic and trade carrot that Europe has dangled before them. And knowing that the stick of a US or Israeli military strike against its nuclear facilities would rally Iranians behind their discredited regime, hard-liners like President Mahmoud Ahmadinejad practically invite an attack.

So even as American and Iranian officials meet again in Baghdad to address their deepening proxy war in Iraq, Tehran refuses to halt its controversial nuclear activities and Washington refuses any direct nuclear talks until it does.

"There's really nothing the Iranians want from us," explained Secretary of Defense Robert Gates earlier this year. "We need some leverage, it seems to me, before we engage the Iranians."

Recent months, however, reveal that the West does have an economic stick that could yet change Tehran's calculations. Despite widespread portrayals of Iran Rising—its historic rivals the Taliban and Saddam Hussein ousted, Tehran bolstered by record oil prices, and Iranian allies ascendant from Iraq to Lebanon to Gaza—today's Islamic Republic is actually Iran Slipping.

Unemployment and inflation are soaring, and oil production, which generates more than 80 percent of export revenues, is steadily dropping due to decades of neglected infrastructure. Recent riots that followed gasoline rationing may be a sign of bigger troubles to come.

But while average Iranians suffer, nearly three decades of unilateral US trade sanctions have ironically perpetuated the mullahs' grip on power by helping prop up the business monopolies of key pillars of the regime—the conservative bazaari merchant class and the brutal Revolutionary Guards. Through *bonyads*, corrupt Islamic "charities," Tehran's kleptoclerics control the vast majority of the Iranian economy.

Now, the United States may have found a way to exploit Iran's economic Achilles' heel by hitting the regime where it hurts—the wallet. Alongside recent UN resolutions freezing the assets of Iranian organizations and individuals involved in the country's nuclear and missile programs, Washington has launched a full-scale financial assault on the mullahs. Since last year, the Bush administration has blacklisted two major state-owned Iranian banks and warned foreign governments and financial institutions against doing business with Tehran.

"As a result, the Iranians are beginning to feel that pinch," according to Under Secretary of State Nicholas Burns. Fearing a third round of UN sanctions, the regime is reportedly withdrawing millions of dollars from European banks. France, Germany, Italy, and Japan have reduced export credits and lending to Tehran.

Dozens of financial institutions, many in Europe and Asia, have either halted or curbed their business with Iran. Companies like British Gas, Japan's Inpex Holdings, and South Africa's Sasol have abandoned billions of dollars in energy projects.

A growing movement in the United States aims to tighten the financial screws on Tehran even further. Modeled after the 1980s anti-apartheid divestment campaign against South Africa, the effort aims to force the $1 trillion pension-fund industry to divest from multinational corporations with business in Iran. In particular, divestment advocates hope to deprive Tehran of the nearly $100 billion it needs to modernize its oil and gas infrastructure and keep its petrodollars flowing.

Some public employee pension funds—in Missouri, Florida, and Ohio—are already divesting from hundreds of foreign firms, including energy giants with Iranian operations such as Royal Dutch-Shell, France's Total, Russia's Gazprom, and Malaysia's Petronas. More than a dozen other states—including California and Texas—may follow suit.

It's not certain that divestment will persuade these firms to end lucrative deals with oil-rich Iran. Moreover, divestment is opposed by the Bush administration, which argues that targeting foreign firms risks undermining the fragile international coalition against Iran.

Still, after years of fruitless diplomatic engagement with the Islamic Republic over its nuclear ambitions, targeted financial sanctions and divestment offer a road not yet traveled.

Until now, Tehran's theocrats have thumbed their nose at the world, knowing their petrodollars have been beyond reach. Depriving the mullahs of their money could change that old assumption and maybe, just maybe, force them to rethink their nuclear calculations.

America and Iran's Taba Moment

The World Post, December 17, 2014

AS PRESIDENT BILL CLINTON TELLS IT, YASSER ARAFAT WANTED TO WEAR something controversial to the White House ceremony in which Israelis and Palestinians signed the Oslo Accords in 1993: his handgun. While Clinton convinced Arafat, then chairman of the Palestinian Liberation Organization, to leave his firearm behind—and then convinced Israeli prime minister Yitzhak Rabin to shake hands with Arafat—in truth, a gun abandoned only for a few hours is a good symbol of the tortured road that Israelis and Palestinians have traveled ever since. The closest the two sides have come to realizing the promise of a peaceful two-state solution imagined by Oslo was during a two-month period in the closing days of Clinton's presidency that began 14 years ago this week.

In negotiations that started at Camp David and continued in the Egyptian town of Taba, Palestinians were offered a solution that met 97 percent of their demands. Both sides declared that they had "never been closer to peace." But then, negotiations were halted for a looming Israeli election, with the two sides expressing "a shared belief that the remaining gaps could be bridged." But it was not to be: Israelis elected a prime minister who had no interest in restarting talks, and the hope of Taba died. In the 14 years since, more than 1,180 Israelis and 9,100 Palestinians have been killed, Jewish settlers in the West Bank have doubled, and one in four Palestinians remains mired in poverty.

All of this reinforces a fundamental truth: when two sides take political risks and strain to reach agreement, only to see negotiations fall apart, they don't go back to where they were before—they go back to a much angrier version of where they were before. It is a vital lesson to keep in mind this week as representatives from Iran and America reconvene with officials from five other nations in Geneva to restart talks on what has been called "the sanctions-lifting-and-nuclear-weapon-halting accord."

While it's difficult to use the word "urgent" about decade-long negotiations that had their latest deadline pushed back for the second time this year, the Iran nuclear talks are entering "now or never" territory. With hard-liners on both sides emboldened by the seven-month delay announced on November 24, it is no exaggeration to say that America and Iran have reached their Taba moment.

It was reported last month that Iran has five times the number of advanced centrifuges capable of spinning uranium into bomb-grade nuclear material than it has previously acknowledged. While Iran claims it only wants to use nuclear power to generate electricity, uranium only needs to be enriched to 6 percent—and not the near bomb-ready 20 percent that Iran had achieved before diluting it last July to comply with the ongoing nuclear talks. It is also constructing a heavy-water nuclear facility at Arak, which could be used to produce plutonium to make a nuclear bomb.

On these facts, Western negotiators both for and against an agreement largely agree. But from there, the arguments take a sharply different turn.

Those who oppose an agreement with Teheran say:

Iran has been our enemy for 30 years. It is a state sponsor of terror. It is a country responsible for the deaths of thousands of American soldiers. Developing a nuclear bomb has been a priority of its mullahs for decades. The only reason we found out back in 2002 that Iran had secret nuclear facilities was because a dissident exposed it. The United Nations immediately called for a total dismantling of Iran's uranium-enrichment capabilities. When negotiations began 10 years ago, Iran didn't have the ability to build a bomb. But our negotiators abandoned the UN's call and told Iran it could enrich uranium. And today, Iran has the knowledge and the components it needs to produce a bomb. It also has ballistic missiles capable of delivering nuclear weapons to Tel Aviv or even Europe.

We also know that Iran lies. It agreed to freeze its nuclear program, but then built more advanced centrifuges. It claims to have no interest in building a bomb, and yet we recently learned that it is five times more capable of creating bomb-ready fissile material than it has admitted to. It agreed not to develop its nuclear weapons capacity, but it keeps building the heavy-water reactor at Arak, and it is reportedly developing nuclear weapons at a military facility in Parchin. The worst part is, since Iran won't let inspectors from the International Atomic Energy Agency into the country to catalog its nuclear program, we have to take its word for it. Yet Obama is trying to ram these negotiations through—writing a secret letter to Iran's supreme leader Ayatollah Sayed Ali Khamenei—while bypassing America's elected representatives in Congress.

This is a country that now has control over capitals in Iraq, Lebanon, Syria, and Yemen. The only reason they are going through with the farce of negotiations is to buy time to build weapons. And if Iran has nuclear weapons, then nobody is safe. We should call off these negotiations, bomb Iran's existing nuclear facilities, and intensify our economic sanctions until the country is on its knees, abandons its nuclear program, and lets inspectors in. This is a country that only understands strength, not weakness.

On the other hand, those who favor negotiations argue:

With no agreement, there will be no restrictions on Iran's nuclear program, no leverage to force inspections, and no ability to monitor developments. There will be nothing stopping them from building a bomb. With all the tools at our disposal, why would we leave bombing Iran as our only option? Every president has understood the chain reaction it will set off—not only inviting Iran to retaliate, but inviting Iranian allies like Russia and China to retaliate, too.

What the hard-liners don't understand is that this issue has revealed two different Irans. There are the hard-liners—mostly old men, 35 years removed from the revolution. But they are a minority: nearly 70 percent of Iran is under the age of 35. You might have noticed that in October, a leading mullah died—and despite a state-declared, two-day mourning period, nobody turned out. But in November, when a young pop star died, so many young people turned out in the streets that Iranian authorities were caught off-guard.

These young people want to join the world. Studies show that 70 percent of young Iranians use illegal software to access the Internet and satellite TV. These are the young Iranians who turned out in 2009 to protest Iran's reactionary government, and they provided the winning margin for Iran's moderate president, Hassan Rouhani. Meanwhile, Iranian businesses, the bazaaris, are tired of bribing the Revolutionary Guards and dream of foreign investment coming to Iran. They are looking for reasons to believe in America. By siding with negotiators, we are siding with them and with a different kind of future. If we turn our backs, we send Iran directly back into the hands of Russia and China.

In other words, one choice is to increase sanctions, threaten to bomb facilities, and hope a wider war doesn't break out. The other choice is to accept that the Islamic Republic of Iran may one day have the "breakout capacity" to produce nuclear weapons—knowing that it could start a nuclear arms race in the Middle East. So far, there is no third choice.

So which path is better? I lean toward pursuing an agreement.

Turning our backs on Iran now will only hand power back to the hard-liners who fear the changes underway in Iran and want to remain on a permanent war footing with the West. On the other hand, a comprehensive agreement would give the West some say over Iran's nuclear program while opening the door to Iran's cooperation in ending the war in Syria and overcoming Islamic State terror in Iraq. It could lead to normalized relations and see Iran pass Russia as Europe's supplier of oil and gas. It could lead Iran to better control Hezbollah, which would be good for Israel. It may also mean that Saudi Arabia becomes more dependent on the United States, as we would likely assure Riyadh that we would provide cover for them, as we have for Japan, South Korea, and Taiwan.

The Israelis and Palestinians had a chance at Taba for a historic breakthrough—and instead, they made the perfect the enemy of the good. They had a moment, and it closed. And that moment has never returned again: just more violence, more suffering, and more unrest against the backdrop of a global economy that is passing them by.

This is the best chance the United States and Iran have had in three decades to create a new and better future for in the Middle East. We should take advantage of it.

INDIA

India Should Be at the Top of Washington's Contact List

International Herald Tribune, November 16, 1998

THIS HAS NOT BEEN A VERY GOOD YEAR FOR THOSE IN WASHINGTON who want to focus on foreign policy issues. Congress, the White House, and the media have been preoccupied with Monica Lewinsky and talk of impeachment. Now official attention has turned to the Republican leadership struggle.

There seem to be only two ways in which foreign affairs get attention these days. First, if there is an explosion—the nuclear variety in South Asia, terrorist attacks and US retaliation in Central Asia and Africa, suicide bombings amid hopes for peace in the Middle East, or the on-again, off-again threats of military force against Saddam Hussein for flagrant violations of agreements.

The second way is if the subject is China, a country whose economic potential holds out the promise of enormous trade ties. Relations with China have become the sine qua non for an American president seeking to show that he is "presidential."

But if explosions and economic opportunities are what it takes to get American attention, India should be at the top of the list. This new member of the nuclear club is also a potentially huge market for American goods and investments. Already the United States is India's largest trading partner, with about $11 billion in two-way trade and, most important, investment. Both partners benefit.

America accounts for roughly 30 percent of all the foreign investment in India. Meanwhile, India, which has educated the world's second-largest pool of scientists and engineers (after America's), invents more sophisticated software for American computer makers than any other country.

Yet when Madeleine Albright went to India last November, she was the first US secretary of state to visit in 14 years. For one long period, the United States was not even represented by an ambassador. And the envoys it did name came and went quickly. Thomas Pickering, a popular ambassador in New Delhi, was pulled out in 1993 after less than a year. No American president has been to India since Jimmy Carter in 1978. President Bill Clinton flew over India last June to make his unprecedented nine-day tour of China.

Now he has scrubbed a long-planned, long-overdue trip to the subcontinent. One US official, trying to explain this decision, said it was not cancellation as punishment for India's nuclear detonation but "postponement because of progress."

The comparison with China, a popular travel destination for US presidents since Richard Nixon in 1972, is striking.

India was the first country to call for global nuclear disarmament. And the Indian government has never sold missile or nuclear technology to anyone. From 1974, when it first exploded an atomic device, to last May, when it came out of the closet with five underground explosions, it watched China conduct more than 40 nuclear tests.

India has not broken any international treaties, because it never signed either the 1970 Non-Proliferation Treaty or the 1996 test ban treaty.

China, however, has been the world's biggest proliferator of weapons of mass destruction. From 1987 until Mr. Clinton's recent summit meeting in Beijing, China repeatedly pledged not to sell nuclear and missile technology and equipment, went back on its word, and then agreed never again to do what it had already agreed never again to do.

Despite this record of repeatedly violating its international commitment under the Non-Proliferation Treaty, China receives virtually unrestricted American high-technology exports and equipment that can be used for military purposes. So why not India?

India makes up almost a quarter of the world's population. What national security advisor Samuel Berger stated about China is also true about India: "You can't turn your back on a quarter of the world's population."

After testifying about proliferation, Karl Inderfurth, US assistant secretary of state for South Asia, recently told Congress: "The economic and commercial investment part of our relationship should be the centerpiece of our relationship with India." The administration should follow up on those words by starting to treat India as one of the great powers that it is. President Clinton should visit—the sooner, the better.

Meanwhile, Congress should remove the sanctions that prevent US firms from providing India with much-needed help in replacing, or even managing, its aging, potentially dangerous nuclear power plants. The new Congress must then put aside some of its squabbles and develop a policy toward India commensurate with the country's growing importance.

Should it really take explosions to get noticed?

Develop Separate Policies for India and Pakistan

International Herald Tribune, January 28, 2000

PRESIDENT BILL CLINTON SHOULD MAKE ONE MORE NEW YEAR'S RESOLUTION: Stop thinking of India and Pakistan as Siamese twins. These two nations were separated at birth on August 15, 1947. Today, India has one foot firmly planted in the 21st century; Pakistan has both feet planted in the past.

During the Cold War, Pakistan was the darling of the United States. But a decade after the collapse of the Soviet Union, and with the emergence of pro-Western Indian governments, it is time Washington ends its policy of treating these two countries as if they were of equal geopolitical importance.

India is set to become a major regional power with the ability to influence events throughout Asia. Should China become expansionist, India will be the only country that America can count on to act as a counterweight.

On the other hand, Pakistan has alienated everyone in the neighborhood by training and supporting the Taliban militia, whose tactics have alarmed India, Iran, Russia, and the former Soviet Central Asian republics. Even China, Pakistan's "most reliable and trusted friend," does not relish becoming a victim of Islamic fundamentalism in its Muslim-majority Xingxiang province.

The British bequeathed democracy to India and Pakistan. A highly educated middle class in India preserved that legacy by taming the might of the feudal landowners. The result has been a flawed but vibrant democratic society ever since. And when New Delhi began to loosen its control of the economy in 1991, India started to take off.

The World Bank and the International Monetary Fund estimate that India will be the world's fourth-largest economy early in this century. It has the second-biggest pool of English-speaking, scientific manpower after the United States. Its software exports should increase from $4 billion today to $50 billion by 2008, revolutionizing India's balance of payments position and allowing an even more liberal attitude toward trade.

Pakistan has become a basket case. Its feudal families transformed themselves after independence into powerful political families, while keeping a grip on almost all land and wealth. Less than 1 percent of the 140 million Pakistanis and almost none of the country's landowners pay any tax.

Benazir Bhutto and Nawaz Sharif have taken turns as the elected head of state for the past decade and made a sham of democracy by showing themselves to be autocratic, kleptocratic, corrupt, and irresponsible. They left the nation in the midst of an identity crisis, economic meltdown, political fragmentation, and ethnic warfare. Pakistan is becoming increasingly "Talibanized" and is disintegrating as it pursues its suicidal obsession with India and Kashmir.

Ironically, the best hope for Pakistan's survival as a country, let alone a democracy, rests with its only effective modern institution, the military. Last October, General Pervez Musharraf, a liberal Muslim, seized power in a bloodless coup, suspending the constitution and arresting the prime minister, Nawaz Sharif. Since then, General Musharraf has made some surprising moves, such as naming civilians with experience in banking, finance, and law enforcement to key posts in his cabinet and the powerful National Security Council.

He has made even more surprising statements: "Let those who have the resources contribute to the betterment of the poor. After all, who has let Pakistan down? It is the elite, me included—the bureaucratic elite, industrial elite, military elite, religious elite."

General Musharraf has clamped down on bank loans to the nation's powerful families, introduced measures to make them pay their fair share of taxes, and vowed to fight corruption.

America should stop lecturing Pakistan about signing the Comprehensive Test Ban Treaty and insisting on a time frame for a return to a democracy that never existed. Instead, the United States should encourage and help finance specific economic reforms. A place to start would be by breaking up the immense land holdings of the feudal families and turning over political power to its middle class—the bulwark of the nation's stability. Pakistan must also ban terrorist groups operating from its soil, take steps to halt the supply of arms into Afghanistan and the $4 billion-a-year heroin trade flowing out, and provide education.

Mr. Clinton is eager to visit India, and he should go. He should also make a separate, later trip to Pakistan. Only then can the United States develop policies which recognize that India and Pakistan share a past but face very different futures.

America and India Are Getting Together, and It's About Time

International Herald Tribune, February 9, 2001

AFTERSHOCKS FROM INDIA'S DEVASTATING EARTHQUAKE ARE BEING FELT all the way to this capital city in the form of finger-pointing about the pace and scale of rescue and relief efforts. But even a tragedy of these massive proportions will not long keep India from turning its attention outward again. And that includes returning to its unlikely suitor in the blossoming US love affair with India.

It wasn't love at first sight. During the Cold War, with a policy of "you're for us or you're against us," America viewed nonaligned India as sleeping with the enemy.

Even after the disintegration of the Soviet Union, New Delhi barely made a blip on Washington's strategic radar screen. It took five big bangs in May 1998 to wake up the White House. After countless rounds of talks, America gave up its nuclear hypocrisy of allowing itself to have nuclear weapons for its security, but not the Indians. And after decades of preaching nonviolence and nuclear disarmament, India discarded its self-righteous halo to declare itself a nuclear weapons state.

The world's oldest democracy and the world's largest democracy began an adult relationship with President Bill Clinton's visit to India last spring and Prime Minister Atal Bihari Vajpayee's reciprocal trip to the United States in the fall. In the words of Mr. Vajpayee, the United States and India are "natural partners."

The Bush administration now has an opportunity to build on this partnership.

The Indians will accept or welcome many of the positions that the new White House team is likely to take.

The Comprehensive Test Ban Treaty is dead, and New Delhi will not at the moment mourn its passing. Missile defense will be a top priority for the United States, and India may not necessarily object. Curbing proliferation of nuclear missile technology will be a primary focus, and Indians may see this in their own interest, especially as it affects China. Sanctions are likely to have a "sunset" clause providing that they automatically end or have to be renewed, and India will welcome that, having smarted under US sanctions in the past.

India will join China, Russia, Japan, and the European Union in a class by themselves for US policymakers.

Soon to be the most populous country in the world, India has the potential to help keep the peace in the vast Indian Ocean area and its periphery.

As the second most powerful military nation in Asia, India is an ideal strategic partner for America. A benevolent nuclear-armed democracy can be a counterweight to China.

India's "Look East" policy is evident, with visits by the prime minister to Vietnam and Indonesia last month and trips to Malaysia and Japan scheduled for this month. New Delhi is finally improving its ties with the military junta in Burma.

India is playing both sides in the Middle East. Israel has become its second-largest provider of military equipment, after Russia. During the first visit by an Indian foreign minister to Saudi Arabia, Jaswant Singh said the two nations must work together, recognizing that the security of the Middle East and South Asia were inseparable. Iraq, one of India's closest friends in the region until the Gulf War, has resumed high-level contacts. Turkey and India are cooperating in the struggle against terrorism coming from Afghanistan. Iran is India's most important non-Arab source of imported oil.

Despite all the attention that is paid to India's perennial rivalry with Pakistan, China is "our central strategic competitor economically, technologically, politically, and militarily," says Jasjit Singh, director of New Delhi's Institute of Defense and Analysis.

China has 2.5 million troops (compared with India's 1.2 million), more than 1,000 naval vessels, and some 4,000 combat aircraft. It occupies a large chunk of northeastern India and has built electronic listening posts along the Bay of Bengal and the Andaman Sea to keep eyes and ears on military movements by India. Beijing supplies Pakistan with advanced missile and nuclear technology.

India sees its strategic interest stretching from the Arabian Sea to the South China Sea, and is putting a premium on sea power. Wanting to bolster the growing numbers of Asians wary of the Middle Kingdom, New Delhi has conducted or is planning joint exercises with Vietnam, Japan, South Korea, Indonesia, and Singapore. It has invited the world's navies to a grand fleet review off the coast of Mumbai.

Alas, there is a great divide between India's aspirations and its capabilities, domestically and militarily. Its affluent middle class—estimated at a world-high 200 million, mostly fluent in dot-com essential English—lives uncomfortably with more than half of India's billion people who subsist on less than a dollar a day. Its armed forces are desperately in need of a top-to-bottom overhaul.

Its army is bloated with guns that don't shoot. Its air force loses too many planes to poor maintenance. Its "minimum credible nuclear deterrent" is still more a draft doctrine than a viable way to deter would-be aggressors. And the Ministry of Defense has yet to integrate its politically aloof uniformed military with its bureaucratically inert civilians.

Yet the many political parties are united in their determination for India to emerge as an Asian superpower. It has a booming high-tech sector, a jealously independent judiciary, and a feisty, free press. The country's scientists plan to launch a moon rocket. And there is mounting pressure for India to have a permanent seat on the United Nations Security Council.

A decade from now, those who scoff at India for delusions of grandeur will get a big surprise. Washington should make sure that the US-Indian honeymoon is long, happy, and mutually fruitful.

The Two Faces of India:
Preserving a Secular State in
a Religious Country

International Herald Tribune, March 25, 2003

TO VISIT WITH LAI KRISHNA ADVANI IS TO ENCOUNTER THE JEKYLL-AND-Hyde nation that is the secular democratic republic of India.

There is Advani the distinguished elder statesman, deputy and heir apparent to Prime Minister Atal Bihari Vajpayee, who tells me proudly that the United States and India are "the twin towers of democracy." He speaks of an "enduring peace" between India and Pakistan and "equal respect" between Hindus and Muslims.

Then there is Advani the ideologue, the firebrand whom many Indians blame for inciting Hindu activists to destroy a disputed ancient mosque in 1992, which ignited religious riots that killed thousands. The wave of Hindu fervor propelled his Bharatiya Janata Party (BJP) to power in 1998.

Which Advani reflects the true face of India? Actually, both.

On the one hand, India's challenge, as described by its first prime minister, Jawaharlal Nehru, has been to build "a secular state in a religious country." Indeed, the 1950 Indian constitution affirms "the right freely to profess, practice, and propagate religion."

On the other hand, the constitution made no mention of the word "secular" until 1976 during Prime Minister Indira Gandhi's brief authoritarian Emergency rule. India's founding fathers were deliberately ambiguous on religious rights—giving the Muslim minority their own Islamic-based civil code but also promising the overwhelming Hindu majority that the government would work toward a uniform civil code.

Because the constitution gives something to everyone, all sides claim to march under the banner of secularism. Muslims, Christians, Sikhs, and political parties like Sonia Gandhi's Congress Party say secularism means government intervention on behalf of persecuted minorities. Hindu nationalists and parties like the BJP decry this as "pseudo secularism" and say true secularism means government remaining neutral.

In fact, Advani, Vajpayee, and a majority of Vajpayee's cabinet belong to the controversial Rashtriya Swayamsevak Sangh (RSS), or National Volunteer Group, dedicated to ending separate rights for Muslims in favor of a "Hindu nation." Proclaimed one recent headline here: "The BJP Reigns and RSS Governs."

Some fear that the BJP will upset India's delicate religious balance by repeating its bloody electoral success last year in the state of Gujarat. Capitalizing on riots that left 2,000 Muslims dead, Gujarat's BJP chief minister, Narendra Modi, called new elections, campaigned on an anti-Muslim platform, and was re-elected in a landslide. One analyst called the gruesome strategy "Kill Muslims and win the Hindu vote." Hindu fanatics speak of making Gujarat a "laboratory" for the entire nation.

But reports of the death of Indian secularism are greatly exaggerated. Gujarat was an aberration, not a harbinger of India's future.

In India all politics is local. A western border state with Pakistan, Gujarat's balloting reflected the hysteria surrounding last year's riots and the military standoff between New Delhi and Islamabad. Modi campaigned not only against his political rivals, but against Pakistani President Pervez Musharraf—an easy choice for Indian voters.

The first attempt to test the Gujarat "laboratory," in the state of Himachal Pradesh last month, backfired miserably. With Muslims comprising only 2 percent of the population and Hindus irate over local government services, voters tossed the BJP out of office. "The verdict," conceded the defeated BJP leader, "shows that Indians are secular by nature."

Second, coalitions curb extremists. Vajpayee is constrained by the realities of a 23-party coalition government that includes parties hostile to the BJP's aggressive Hindu agenda. In fact, Hindu fundamentalists are increasingly embittered as they fear their radical agenda will never be implemented.

Finally, Muslims matter. Vajpayee may pander to the BJP's Hindu base by blaming Muslims for their own massacre at Gujarat ("wherever Muslims are, they do not want to live peacefully"). But the Congress Party is guilty of playing both sides of the "religious card," at times stoking Muslim fears, at times appealing to Hindu nationalism.

Comprising 12 percent of the population, India's 150 million Muslims are comfortably integrated into secular India's political, business, and entertainment communities and cannot be ignored. Major parties ignore them at their peril.

After a visit to the charred ruins of Gujarat last year, Vajpayee reportedly asked, "What face will I now show the world?"

Robert Louis Stevenson's classic novel holds the answer. Unable to continue swinging wildly between his good and evil side, the respectable Dr. Jekyll loses control to the diabolical Hyde, who ultimately destroys them both.

There is only one way India will realize its full potential as the world's largest democracy and gain its rightful place as a leading global power. New Delhi must preserve the delicate balance of a secular state in a religious country.

India and Pakistan:
Trade Offers Sure Path to Peace

International Herald Tribune, February 21, 2004

THE HISTORIC TALKS THIS WEEK BETWEEN INDIAN AND PAKISTANI officials in Islamabad, the first since the nuclear rivals nearly went to war in 2002, open the door to the ultimate confidence-building measure—making money, not war.

To the credit of both sides, their new "composite dialogue" will address not only the disputed Kashmir province, but "all bilateral issues," including "economic development."

Commerce between rivals does not guarantee peace, but good economics can promote good politics.

The European Union proves the link between prosperity and security. Indeed, the decision last month by the seven-nation South Asian Association for Regional Cooperation to seek a South Asia free trade area by 2006 prompted Prime Minister Atal Bihari Vajpayee of India to predict an EU-style common market and single currency for the region.

Pragmatic entrepreneurs help remind governments that being dead is bad for business. Surging trade between India and China has helped New Delhi and Beijing make progress toward resolving their decades-old border disputes. Beijing's rhetorical outbursts aside, China is unlikely to invade Taiwan, one of its biggest trading partners and largest investors.

The subcontinent has no such economic brake on military escalation. Official bilateral trade between India and Pakistan is a trickle—a mere $200 million, less than 1 percent of their global trade.

This virtual "no trade area" is unnatural. By the late 1940s, nearly 60 percent of Pakistani exports went to India and a third of Pakistani imports came from India. But Partition cut off Indian factories and mills from their supplies of raw materials in Pakistan. Punjab, the breadbasket of South Asia, was divided and devastated.

New Delhi and Islamabad finally seem to recognize that reversing this economic partition is in their own self-interest.

Krishna Rasgotra, a former Indian foreign secretary, told me that "greater economic ties will, in due course, help facilitate calm deliberation of more complex political and security-related issues." Rajesh Shah, a prominent business executive, agreed. "It is in India's interest," he said, "to encourage democratization of Pakistan and to create strong trade and economic links."

Prime Minister Zafarullah Khan Jamali of Pakistan, addressing the US Chamber of Commerce last autumn, said, "People-to-people contact and mutual business interests create a more enduring relationship between nations than is possible through governments alone."

The talks this week in Islamabad set the stage for genuine trade diplomacy. First, as South Asia's strongest economy, India should take the lead and continue reducing tariffs, [which are] among the highest in the world— especially those on goods from developing countries like Pakistan.

Second, Pakistan should reciprocate by granting India "most-favored nation" trading status—which India has already bestowed on Pakistan—as required by the World Trade Organization and as implied in the regional free trade agreement signed last month. This would include opening the Pakistani market beyond the list of 610 Indian products now permitted.

Analysts here predict that annual free trade between India and Pakistan could reach $6 billion within a year. Illegal trade via Dubai, Hong Kong, and Singapore is already estimated at $2 billion. [If merchants could] avoid expensive smuggling routes, lower transit costs would mean lower prices for consumers and higher revenues for both governments.

Islamabad need not fear being swallowed by the economic giant next door. On the contrary, under its free trade agreement with New Delhi, Sri Lanka has increased its exports to India by 137 percent. Under a free trade pact, Pakistan's textile sector, the backbone of its economy, would gain access to India's 300 million–strong middle class.

Third, India should drop its reservations over the so-called peace pipeline to Iran through Pakistan. India, one of the world's largest gas importers, needs Iran, home to the world's second-largest natural gas reserves. New Delhi's fears of dependence on a trans-Pakistan pipeline are understandable.

But the estimated $700 million in annual transit fees would give Islamabad an enormous stake in regional stability and prosperity.

Finally, India and Pakistan should rebuild the nuts and bolts of their trade infrastructure. The resumption last month of bus, air, and rail links was a start. Lifting burdensome visa restrictions would enable business leaders to travel and trade more freely. As both India's and Pakistan's largest trading partner, the United States can help by encouraging exchanges between industry chiefs and economists.

For decades, vested interests—including the millionaire generals who control much of the Pakistani economy—have acted as a constituency for conflict, holding trade hostage with the excuse that Kashmir comes first. But as one Pakistani commentator observed recently, "Kashmir is not a core issue but a corps commanders' issue."

Instead of Indian and Pakistani soldiers exchanging gunfire on the battlefield, imagine Indian and Pakistani entrepreneurs exchanging business cards in boardrooms.

Recognizing Reality:
The Consequences of Saying No to India

The Washington Times, May 8, 2006

LIKE THE EAGER PARENTS OF AN ARRANGED MARRIAGE, PRESIDENT George W. Bush and Indian prime minister Manmohan Singh have shaken hands, toasted the future, and agreed to a dowry long coveted by New Delhi—a historic civilian nuclear agreement that tacitly recognizes India as the world's sixth nuclear state.

Both leaders must now convince reluctant compatriots back home to go along with the deal, raising the question that confronts every arranged marriage: Will love follow?

Unlike nuptials of the past, when Indian brides and grooms met for the first time at the altar, the United States and India have been getting to know one another since President Clinton's landmark visit in 2000. By then, New Delhi had largely shed its Nehruvian socialist past, and today Washington sees India as the attractive partner it is—the world's largest democracy and second-fastest growing economy, and a reliable partner in the war on terrorism and reconstruction in Afghanistan.

But standing in the way of a more perfect union is India's small arsenal of nuclear weapons, which under US law and the nuclear Non-Proliferation Treaty prevents New Delhi from receiving nuclear assistance for its civilian energy program. Intended as the crowing jewel of a new US-Indian strategic partnership, the nuclear deal unveiled in March has triggered grumbling on both sides.

American critics say Bush gave away too much—giving India sensitive nuclear technology without capping New Delhi's production of fissile material for nuclear weapons or opening its entire civilian program to international inspection. It is "nuclear hypocrisy," they cry, to embrace Indian nuclear ambitions while condemning those of Iran and North Korea.

Indian critics say just the opposite—that Mr. Singh gave away too much by agreeing to separate the country's civilian and military nuclear programs, effectively limiting its fissile supplies and undermining New Delhi's nuclear deterrent. The real "nuclear hypocrisy," Indians say, is a non-proliferation treaty that arbitrarily recognized the "big five" nuclear states who had arsenals in 1968 but not India, which went nuclear later.

The new agreement perpetuates this hypocrisy, Indians complain. If Washington shares nuclear technology with Beijing, the great nuclear proliferator, why not India, with its solid record of preventing proliferation?

Imperfect though it may be, the nuclear agreement now before the US Congress is like any dowry—turning it down risks spoiling the larger relationship. Indeed, overlooked in the current debate are the dangerous consequences if Congress rejects the agreement or imposes new conditions that make it a deal-breaker for New Delhi.

Even more than about technology, Indians see the deal as about trust. Foreign Secretary Shyam Saran, the chief Indian negotiator on the agreement, tells me that it "sends the political message that India is no longer perceived as a target, but as a partner." K. Subrahmanyam, a former member of India's National Security Council, says failure would result in a "total loss of trust" that could contaminate the entire US-Indian political, economic, and military relationship, including intelligence cooperation in the war on terrorism.

Mr. Singh, whose fragile ruling coalition survives with the support of leftist and communist parties, could suffer a fatal political blow for aligning India so closely with Washington. A senior aide to the prime minister tells me that the deal's defeat would limit Mr. Singh's ability to work with Washington and would embolden anti-American voices in India, who could claim, "We told you so—never trust the Americans."

Indeed, perhaps the greatest damage of the deal's demise would be to the broader Asian power balance. Just as US officials implicitly acknowledge democratic India's potential role as counterweight to China, the deal's ruin could achieve the precise opposite.

New Delhi and Beijing pledged themselves last year to a new strategic partnership, and Moscow has pursued, without much success, greater Russian–Indian–Chinese cooperation. Failure of the US–India nuclear agreement would "breathe a fresh dose of oxygen into the rapidly dying Moscow–New Delhi–Beijing triangle," says Krishna Rasgotra, the former Indian foreign secretary.

Given the consequences of failure, blocking the agreement because of

India's limited economic, political, and military ties with Iran—as some US lawmakers have threatened—would be a historic blunder. Cooperation between Hindu India and Persian Iran, two ancient civilizations with deep cultural links, is natural and no threat to the United States.

In fact, despite Iranian threats that doing so could endanger negotiations on a new pipeline to bring Iranian natural gas to India, New Delhi has voted twice with the United States at the International Atomic Energy Agency against Iran's nuclear program.

It's hard to imagine India taking similar risks in the future if Capitol Hill votes against India's nukes today.

Three years ago, a young Indian bride named Nisha Sharma became an international celebrity when, at the altar, she called off her wedding after the groom's family suddenly demanded a larger dowry than had been agreed upon.

American lawmakers take note: you go to the altar with the dowry you have, not the dowry you might want. Trying to renegotiate this nuclear deal could poison the US-Indian relationship for years to come. And rather than love, only mistrust and missed opportunities will follow.

New Delhi's Delicate Balancing Act

International Herald Tribune, April 28, 2007

WITH HUNDREDS OF POLITICAL PARTIES, RELIGIONS, AND LANGUAGES, thousands of castes and subcastes, 3 million elected officials, 20 million government employees, and 670 million voters, "there is never a dull moment in the great Indian political circus," as one newspaper here recently put it.

Today's most dazzling act—with consequences for India's survival as a pluralistic, democratic, united nation—is the perilous high-wire act of Prime Minister Manmohan Singh as he attempts to balance the conflicting demands of a high-tech knowledge-based economy and India's low-tech farm-based impoverished masses.

Lean too far to the right, by boosting India's surging middle class without fulfilling promises of "inclusive growth" for the 600 million rural and poor majority, and Singh—and his Congress Party–led coalition—risks the kind of electoral drubbing that toppled the previous government three years ago.

But lean too far to the left—by allowing leftist and communist parties to continue blocking reform of bloated government bureaucracies, archaic labor and investment laws, and subsidies for food and fuel—and India risks missing its goal of $15 billion in annual foreign investment.

Proceed too fast, with rising inflation that recently hit a two-year high, and Indians angry over soaring food prices will exact their revenge, as they did in dealing the Congress Party stunning defeats in recent municipal and state elections.

But proceed too slowly, by failing to create enough jobs for the 10 million Indians entering the labor market every year, and the country risks a potentially destabilizing "unemployment explosion" in coming decades where perhaps 30 percent of Indians—some 200 million—are jobless.

As Singh and his coalition walk this tightrope of economic development, several dangerous distractions now threaten to knock them off balance.

The country's overcrowded and crumbling roads, railroads, ports, and airports are already blamed for slowing economic growth by perhaps two percentage points. But while people here celebrate the capital's new state-of-the-art subway and a network of expressways linking major cities, New Delhi lacks the hundreds of billions of dollars needed to resolve India's infrastructure crisis.

India's only hope will be cost-sharing partnerships with the private sector, such as new airport projects in New Delhi, Hyderabad, and Bangalore and the $5 billion infrastructure fund recently launched by Citigroup, Blackstone, and India's Infrastructure Development Finance Company.

The crown jewel of the Congress Party's poverty eradication program, a massive jobs program that guarantees every rural household 100 days' work building roads, dams, and other projects, also faces hurdles. In a country of rampant corruption, it's uncertain whether cash payments for unskilled manual labor will indeed uplift the needy or, like so many similar efforts, enrich the greedy.

Meanwhile, dozens of ethnic and tribal separatist groups across the country's remote northeast states wage decades-old rebellions against Indian rule. The bomb that greeted Singh's visit to the state of Assam this month was the latest reminder of why a region rich with oil, gas, and coal remains the poorest in India.

Most ominous, though, is the brutal Maoist insurgency, now active in half of India's 28 states, which Singh has called "the single biggest security challenge ever faced by our country." Last month, a day after police in the eastern state of West Bengal gunned down 14 people protesting the creation of special economic zones on rural lands, Maoists retaliated by murdering 55 police in one of the deadliest attacks of their 40-year insurgency.

Such is New Delhi's development dilemma. Do nothing, and the impoverished flock to the Maoists. But proceed with manufacturing-based economic zones, and displaced farmers flock to the Maoists.

Predictably, new rules announced this month making these zones smaller and granting more benefits to affected farmers have satisfied neither business groups nor rural activists, and the country is bracing for more Maoist attacks against industry and infrastructure.

And yet Indians display an exuberance for the future that, given their remarkable progress in 60 years of independence, doesn't seem so irrational. "This is a democracy—obstreperous and seemingly chaotic, but effectively functional," says Krishna Rasgotra, a former Indian foreign secretary.

"People are aware of their rights and will assert themselves. This is not a sign of India's decline or threatening doom; it is a sign of India's vitality."

And so while Western observers may lament the slow pace of Indian reform, democracy's greatest show on earth goes on, with New Delhi moving ahead the only way it can—keeping its balance and taking one careful step at a time.

India and the United States Need to Play Ball

The Huffington Post, May 1, 2014

AS A LONGTIME FAN OF THE PHILADELPHIA PHILLIES BASEBALL TEAM, I find it's not often that I cheer for the Pittsburgh Pirates, the Phillies' rival in the state of Pennsylvania. But on July 4, 2009, I couldn't help but enjoy the sight of Rinku Singh and Dinesh Patel—the first two Indians ever to play professional baseball in the United States—each take the pitcher's mound for the very first time. The two young players, both born in Lucknow, India, had never touched (or even heard of) a baseball before being discovered by an American sports agent a year earlier and selected out of 40,000 Indian athletes to train for the American major leagues.

This month, Singh and Patel's improbable story is getting the full Disney treatment in *Million Dollar Arm*, a film chronicling the search for Indians who could be trained to become Major League Baseball pitchers. It's a heartwarming account of cross-cultural success—which, given the present state of US-Indian relations, makes it a relative rarity.

In fact, observers of the chilly relationship between the world's two largest democracies have been drawing their own baseball analogies. One of India's largest English newspapers summed up an uneventful October 2013 White House meeting between President Barack Obama and Indian Prime Minister Manmohan Singh with the lukewarm headline "Singh and Obama Play 'Small Ball.'" Another reads "India Plays Hardball with United States as Diplomat Maid Row Escalates." And Subhash Agrawal, an Indian political analyst, tells me "the United States has taken its eyes off the ball" in Southeast Asia.

The results of this drift have been troubling, to say the least. The United States has filed several trade cases against India in the World Trade Organization and remains frustrated by an Indian nuclear liability act that effectively limits US investment in India's energy industry. American policymakers were incensed to see India siding with Russia—which supplies 70 percent of India's arms—over Vladimir Putin's Crimean invasion, while

Indians see that the United States has previously denied a visa to Narendra Modi, likely to be the country's next prime minister.

Then there is that "diplomat maid row," a reference to the United States' arrest, strip-search, and indictment of Indian diplomat Devyani Khobrogade for lying on a visa application and underpaying her housekeeper. India retaliated by investigating American diplomats' visas, snubbing a visiting US delegation, and—most provocatively, a year after deadly attacks on the American embassy in Benghazi—removing the security barriers around the US embassy in New Delhi.

The paradox is that before this string of real and perceived disagreements, US-India relations were on the upswing. After keeping a wary distance during the Cold War—and after the United States sanctioned India for conducting nuclear tests in 1998—President Bill Clinton and Prime Minister Atal Bihari Vajpayee inaugurated a new chapter of US-Indian relations when Clinton visited India in 2000. The United States and India drew even closer under President George W. Bush, culminating in a landmark 2006 agreement to share civilian nuclear technology. By the time Obama visited India in 2010—during which the usually reserved Singh hugged Obama around the waist—he was touting the relationship as "one of the defining partnerships of the 21st century."

But that was then. As India's growth has fallen by half, the Center for Strategic and International Studies' Scott Miller and Karl F. Inderfurth note, "Investors are less willing to overlook . . . things like poor infrastructure, power outages, corruption, and bureaucratic red tape." Meanwhile, urgent crises elsewhere have distracted US policymakers. "They're busy with Russia, Syria, the Middle East, and Iran," one senior Indian diplomat told the *New York Times*. "It is vital that they also pay attention to the India relationship soon, since the current drift could get much worse."

Exacerbating this drift is the subcontinent-sized void in the Obama administration's foreign policy—symbolized by the resignation of the US ambassador to India, Nancy Powell, in the wake of the Khobrogade incident. As Agrawal asks me incredulously, "Who is running US South Asia policy? I've never seen the United States make so many strategic mistakes." Summing up the feelings of many in Washington and New Delhi, Prabhat Shukla, director of the Vivekananda International Foundation, tells me that this once-promising partnership is now "OK, but stagnant."

But taken as a whole, talk of drift between the United States and India seems overblown. After all, bilateral trade has quintupled in the past decade, and India conducts more annual military exercises with the United States than with any other country. Over 100,000 Indian students study in American universities, while researchers in both countries are collaborating on everything from solar technology to low-cost medical devices. Despite the recent squabbles, Indians are nearly four times more likely to view the United States favorably than unfavorably, while 72 percent of Americans view India in a positive light.

"We are looking at the wood rather than the trees," Vikram Doraiswamy, India's joint secretary for the Americas, says to me. "There's nothing to set the imagination on fire, so the press is saying nothing is happening, but that's not true. We have $100 billion in trade and blue chips on both markets, joint venture on [military aircraft], and all this is not noticed. It's a management issue, I think, and we are victims of our own success. We allow problems to drive the narrative rather than the good stories."

Modi's likely ascension to prime minister—however objectionable his outspoken Hindu nationalism and alleged culpability in a 2002 massacre of over 1,000 Muslims in his home state of Gujarat—offers a golden opportunity to reset the relationship. It was Modi's Bharatiya Janata Party that reached out to President Clinton the last time they were in power, and their pro-growth agenda makes them more likely to once again seek out foreign investment and stronger international ties.

If the United States does not wish to miss a similar window, there are three things it should do.

First, President Obama should be the first foreign leader to reach out to Modi after his presumptive victory. Modi may have intensely nationalistic views and a muddy human rights record, but he also may be America's best hope to strengthen its relationship with India at a time when US policy continues to shift to Asia. As analyst Deep Pal notes, far from being an inward-looking nativist during his tenure as chief minister of Gujarat, "Modi has been progressive and proactive, building ties around the world to bring more opportunities to his state." He promises to do the same for India.

Second, the United States must find a professional ambassador to India. While Powell is a seasoned diplomat, the increasing complexity of the US-India relationship demands more than a career civil servant—it requires a strategic thinker whose counsel is heard at the highest levels of American government. Choosing a well-respected ambassador would signal American seriousness and allow the United States and India to move forward on a number of thorny issues, from sorting out energy issues to resolving lingering pharmaceutical and intellectual property disputes. A good choice might be Ashton Carter, the highly respected former US deputy secretary of defense and a longtime champion of strengthening ties with India.

Third, the business communities in both countries need to overcome their respective bureaucracies and re-engage with their counterparts. Already, US companies have invested upwards of $50 billion in Indian industries, while Indian companies invest $17 billion in the United States and employ over 80,000 Americans. A few critical improvements—India upgrading its infrastructure and modernizing its tax system, and the United States reforming its immigration system to allow more high-skilled workers—would go a long way toward improving the investment climate and bringing the United States and India closer together.

"The overall reality is that it's a healthy relationship and heading in the right direction," a senior Indian official says to me. "I don't see any hang-ups at the people-to-people level between our two countries. I hope the next government can build on the work done over the past eight or so years."

To do that, we don't need a million-dollar arm—we just need an outstretched hand.

Narendra Modi's Surprisingly Successful Selfie Diplomacy

The World Post, June 15, 2015

LAST MONTH, IN FRONT OF THE TEMPLE OF HEAVEN IN BEIJING, INDIAN prime minister Narendra Modi and Chinese premier Li Keqiang posed for Modi's smartphone and snapped a photo. "It's selfie time! Thanks, Premier Li," Modi tweeted to his 13 million Twitter followers. The photo of the two men—together representing nearly 40 percent of the world's population—led the *Wall Street Journal* to wonder, "Did Modi Just Take the Most Powerful Selfie in History?"

Most powerful or not, it certainly isn't Modi's first. In the year since he swept into office in a historic landslide, Modi has posed for similar photos with leaders all across the globe. He took one in Fiji with Prime Minister Frank Bainimarama. He took another grinning shot at the Melbourne Cricket Ground with Australian prime minister Tony Abbott. Modi's "selfie diplomacy" has become so anticipated that, in advance of President Barack Obama's most recent visit to India, the *Hindustan Times* ran a story asking, "Where's the Obama-Modi Selfie We've Been Waiting For?" (They settled for a warm hug.)

The photos serve as a kind of digital diary of a whirlwind, almost bewildering year of bilateral and multilateral foreign visits—roughly 20 trips abroad, from critical allies like the United States and Japan to long-neglected neighbors such as Sri Lanka. ("Why on Earth Is Narendra Modi Going to Mongolia?" read one recent headline.) But while the pictures may be lighthearted, Modi's message is no joke. As a retired general in the Indian army tells me, "The message is that India is looking outwards now and it's willing to pull its weight." For the United States in particular, the message is a welcome one.

When Modi took office last May, few would have predicted that the controversial former governor of the state of Gujarat would morph into a globetrotting statesman. In its campaign platform, Modi's Bharatiya Janata

Party devoted a mere one page out of 40 to foreign policy; in his August 15 Independence Day speech, Modi glossed over the issue entirely. If the rest of the world considered India at all, this subcontinent nation of 1.2 billion was typically dismissed with a hyphen: part of the India-Pakistan situation, or the India-China relationship.

Yet foreign policy has undoubtedly become Modi's primary focus—and his pragmatic methods have far exceeded expectations. "For a politician who came to office with virtually no foreign policy experience, Mr. Modi has demonstrated impressive diplomatic acumen," observes the Indian strategist Brahma Chellaney. A well-known Indian diplomat adds, "He wanted to change the image of India. He wants to show that he will get things done and the buck stops here."

Speculating on this shift, a senior Indian official jokes to me, "Maybe he thought it's easier to deal with international affairs than domestic ones." It is true that on the home front, headaches abound—from pervasive corruption to poor infrastructure. Every year, the Indian economy must generate an estimated 10 million new jobs to employ its growing population (by contrast, the US economy has created roughly 12 million jobs in the past five years). And while the International Monetary Fund predicts that India's growth will outpace China's in 2015, India continues to grapple with an anemic manufacturing sector and high levels of poverty and growing inequality.

"India has the most number of millionaires and college graduates while at the same time has the most number of poor people," an ambassador to India tells me. "It's a country of contradictions." To make matters worse, an unexpected BJP defeat in the most recent parliamentary elections has diminished the prospects of many of Modi's desired reforms.

But the reality is that Modi's emphasis on foreign policy is not about avoiding India's domestic challenges—it's about solving them. As the Observer Research Foundation's Niranjan Sahoo writes, "Geo-economics is the key." Modi is taking a page out of his playbook in Gujarat, when he traveled extensively throughout Asia to drum up foreign investment, going so far as to have business cards printed in Chinese. Modi's hardheaded approach has largely overlooked potential diplomatic sticking points—from the United States previously denying him a visa over alleged human rights abuses to a Chinese incursion into Indian territory during Chinese president Xi Jinping's visit. Yet it also has yielded some $30 billion in commitments from China, another $33 billion from Japan, and two high-profile state visits with Obama.

Modi "needs everyone on his side," the analyst Ashok Malik told the *New York Times*. "He needs a window of relative strategic calm in his backyard to build the Indian economy." For all of these reasons, Chellaney notes, "this means that India—a founding leader of the nonaligned movement—is likely to become multi-aligned."

The impacts of this shift are potentially profound. Unlike China, whose willingness to play a leadership role on the world stage has largely been confined to self-interest, India's newly assertive and multi-aligned foreign policy could make it a powerful global partner—on issues ranging from climate change to Ukraine. And no country is better poised to partner with the world's largest democracy than the world's oldest democracy.

"There's new energy between the United States and India, and the talk that the United States is ignoring us is gone now," the Indian political analyst Subhash Agrawal tells me. "The Obama trip was a success." During that trip, Obama declared that "India and the United States are not just natural partners. I believe America can be India's best partner." The slew of agreements that have followed—from civil nuclear deals to trade commitments—have only served to reinforce this notion.

Yet with a history of mistrust and shifting alliances in the region, an Indian diplomat says, "The question is, can we trust the Americans when the chips are down?"

What should America do to ensure the right answer to that question? Three things.

First, the United States must continue to deepen the economic relationship. Obama and Modi have committed to quintupling bilateral trade to $500 billion—a target both nations can and should meet. Ultimately, India should be welcomed into the Asia Pacific Economic Cooperation Forum and could conceivably be included in the Trans-Pacific Partnership currently being negotiated in Congress.

Second, Washington should provide India the military training and support it needs to discourage Chinese aggression in the region. In January 2015, both India and the United States committed to "safeguarding maritime security and ensuring freedom of navigation and over flight throughout the region, especially in the South China Sea." This commitment must be kept.

Third, the United States should strengthen people-to-people relationships between the United States and India. "India and the United States should have youth exchanges with universities," Agrawal says. "This would make India no longer a 'weird country' to Americans." Call it "yoga diplomacy," after the Indian exercises that Modi does every morning—along with millions of fit and trendy Americans.

In the meantime, we can only hope that Modi keeps up his frenetic travels. He may be fond of the egocentric selfie—but what he's really demonstrating is that we are all in this together.

AF-PAK

———•◆•———

Pakistan Ought to Concentrate on Pulling Itself Together

International Herald Tribune, July 14, 1999

THE LATEST MILITARY ADVENTURE IN KASHMIR IS YET ANOTHER variation on a familiar theme: Pakistan's obsession with India.

In 1947, after the birth of both nations, Pakistan sent Pathan tribesmen to attack Srinagar, the capital of Kashmir; the attack failed. In 1965, Pakistan infiltrated large numbers of armed militants into Kashmir and ended up losing an all-out war. The most recent incursion appears to be out of the control of Prime Minister Nawaz Sharif.

It is the work of Pakistan's military intelligence agency supporting religious zealots so bent on integrating Kashmir that they are blind to the disintegration at home.

Pakistan was an invention of Mohammed Ali Jinnah, who promised a homeland for all of the Muslims living in British India. That dream has failed, since more Muslims live in India than in Pakistan, which is little more than a collection of tribes, warring factions, and increasingly radical Islamists.

The Pashtuns, whose homeland was cut in two by the British, come and go across an artificial border with Afghanistan, trading, smuggling, and leading the Taliban militia's successful takeover of that country. In the mountains near the Khyber Pass, one cannot tell an Afghan Taliban from a Pakistani Taliban. They envision an independent Pashtunistan, incorporating Pakistan's Northwest Frontier Province with much of Afghanistan.

The Baluchis of southwest Pakistan feel closer to their ethnic brothers in neighboring Iran and Afghanistan than to the Punjab-dominated central government, which bloodily suppressed their rebellion in the early 1970s.

Sindh, Pakistan's second-most populous province, is ruled directly by Islamabad to keep order in violence-prone Karachi, the commercial center. It is being torn apart by fighting between the indigenous population and migrants (Muhajirs) from India and Bangladesh. Muhajir groups have begun killing each other.

The Sindhis, like the Pashtuns and the Baluchis, are chafing under the domination of Pakistan's most important region, Punjab. With 56 percent of the population, the Punjabis run the country, staffing the officer corps, the civil service, and just about everything else.

Meanwhile, Shiite Muslims, around 20 percent of Pakistan's population, are being targeted by radical Sunni groups inflamed by the Taliban example. Last year almost 1,000 people were killed in clashes between Sunni and Shiite militants.

Many extreme Sunni Islamists seem to hate the Shiites more than [they hate] the West or India. The existence of the Shiites is an offense against these Sunnis' vision of a unified "Muslim community of the faithful."

It is this vision that is promoted in more than 7,000 Islamic fundamentalist schools and seminaries that have spread rapidly as Pakistan's state education failed to push literacy rates above 40 percent. These schools are breeding grounds for *mujahidin*, or holy warriors who are sent to Talibanize Kashmir. Graduates also provide the manpower for radical Islamic political parties and for the Sunni Muslim gangs waging the murderous campaign against the Shiites.

Add to this mix of ethnic conflicts and religious zealotry an economy still reeling from last year's post-nuclear testing crisis. Trying to keep up with India, a country with six times its GDP and 15 times its foreign exchange, Pakistan is running on empty. It has an external debt of $30 billion (half of its GDP) and has been bailed out by the International Monetary Fund (IMF) 17 times. The lion's share of government spending goes to defense and debt service.

The international community, including China, blames Pakistan for the flare-up in Kashmir. Pakistan's famous Three *A*s—Allah, the army, and America—may soon become *AA*, with the United States likely to re-impose trade sanctions and block further IMF loans.

And, of course, there is the growing impatience of India.

Incited by militant groups and ultranationalists, many Indians now say that their nation's problem has been the failure of Hindus to stand up and fight. They insist that Islam's intolerance and claim to exclusive truth have led to the destruction of Hindu treasures and the defiling of its holy places.

They cite the centuries when Kashmir was the route of choice for conquerors who swept down from Afghanistan onto the Indian plains, massacring

Hindus or converting them to Islam. "Today Srinagar, tomorrow Delhi" was the Moghul's fearsome cry. These Indians believe that nothing has changed. Kashmir is the only Muslim-majority state in India's union. It affirms the country's nondenominational character—a single nation with a plurality of religions and cultures. Hindus and Muslims live and work side by side throughout India, contributing to every aspect of the nation's life—so much so that the father of India's "Hindu" nuclear bomb is a Muslim.

The worst thing that could happen to Pakistan would be for it to succeed in wresting Kashmir and its 4 million Muslims from India. Led by Hindu extremists, the ethnic cleansing of millions of Muslims living in India would make Bosnia and Kosovo seem like a picnic. And a further flood of refugees would destroy Pakistan.

Present and former Indian government officials, military leaders, businessmen, and journalists—Hindus, Muslims, and Sikhs—agree that this is an all-too-likely outcome. The partition of British India in 1947 created more than 11 million refugees and provoked almost a million deaths.

Pakistan should revert to Jinnah's dream of a moderate, secular Islamic state. And when casting envious glares at Kashmir, it needs to remember the adage: Be careful what you wish for—you may get it.

Afghanistan's Need for Good Neighbors: Contest for a Region

International Herald Tribune, September 1, 2004

ACCORDING TO A STORY MAKING THE ROUNDS HERE, A VISITING US official meets a former Taliban leader along the rugged border with Pakistan. The American notices that the man is admiring his glimmering Rolex and asks what he thinks. The ex-Taliban replies, "You have the watch. But we have the time."

As Afghans head to the polls next month for the first direct presidential election in their history, the guessing game has already begun across the region: How long before the impatient Americans declare democracy in Afghanistan and go home? And how can neighbors with age-old security, economic, ethnic, and religious interests in Afghanistan prepare for when that time comes?

In this sense, the current campaign for president is as much a regional as a national contest. In Afghanistan, all politics are ethnic, and political candidates, like provincial warlords (often one and the same), are proxies for neighbors and foreign powers waging historic competitions for influence.

The interim president, Hamid Karzai, Washington's favorite and a member of the Pashtun ethnic group, which represents some 40 percent of Afghans, remains the man to beat. But with 17 challengers it will be difficult for Karzai to win an outright majority in the first round of voting on October 9 and avoid a run-off.

The Tajiks, who make up 25 percent of the population, appear to be coalescing around presidential hopeful Yunus Qanooni, Karzai's former education minister. Qanooni has the support of fellow Tajik Muhammed Qasim Fahim, the country's most powerful warlord and former defense minister, and Abdullah Abdullah, the foreign minister.

Shiite militia leader and former planning minister Mohammad Mohaqiq is backed by his fellow Persian-speaking ethnic Hazara Shiites, who comprise 20 percent of the population and enjoy deep religious and cultural ties with their Shiite brethren in neighboring Iran.

And Afghanistan's ethnic Uzbeks and Turkmen, who together comprise some 10 percent of the population, are rallying behind their ruthless warlord, General Abdul Rashid Dostum, who stands accused of war crimes.

Afghan voters will determine the next president. And a new generation of Afghan leaders gives hope for the future. As Dr. Mohammed Amin Farhang says, "I am the minister of reconstruction. My predecessor was the minister of destruction."

But if past is prologue, it will be Afghanistan's neighbors who ultimately decide whether this country succeeds as a sovereign nation or reverts to a failed state. The 19th-century Great Game between the British and Russian empires for dominance of the region led outsiders to interfere in the land of the Afghans. Discussions with political, economic, and military officials here suggest that common regional security and economic interests may finally give Afghanistan's neighbors a reason to help make it, not break it.

US ambassador Zalmay Khalilzad says that Washington is determined to "avoid a renewed cycle of destructive geopolitical competition in Afghanistan." In the Declaration on Good Neighborly Relations signed two years ago, Afghanistan's six neighbors—Pakistan, Iran, Uzbekistan, Turkmenistan, Tajikistan, and China—pledged not to interfere in Afghanistan's internal affairs. Yet given their history of meddling, none have been invited to participate in NATO's International Security Assistance Force here.

With the possible exception of Pakistan (whose military intelligence service values Afghanistan for the "strategic depth" it would provide if Pakistan were attacked by India), none of Afghanistan's neighbors have an interest in its slipping back into the hands of a fundamentalist Islamist regime that might again sponsor attacks against their governments.

Likewise, the entire region has a common interest in keeping out the Afghan opium and heroin that flow through Tajikistan, Iran, and Pakistan into Russia and Western Europe. Afghanistan is once again the world's leader in opium production. Iran is the world's leader in opium interdiction.

Landlocked Afghanistan will also need friendly neighbors if it is to realize Finance Minister Ashraf Ghani's dream of the country as a "hub of regional commerce" instead of conflict. Zalmai Rassoul, the national security advisor, envisions Afghanistan as the "Dubai of Central Asia," with its central location as "a land bridge for north–south trade" making trade and tourism the future pillars of its economy.

Afghanistan as a hub of regional commerce? In fact, Iran, Tajikistan, and Uzbekistan are already providing electricity to large chunks of Afghanistan. India is helping Iran develop road and rail routes to Afghanistan and Central Asia. The Iranian port of Chabahar will be used to move goods to and from Afghanistan.

New Delhi is also considering so-called peace pipelines—natural gas pipelines from Iran and Turkmenistan across Afghanistan and Pakistan to the Indian subcontinent, which would bring Kabul and Islamabad hundreds of millions in transit fees. But Krishna Rasgotra, the former Indian foreign secretary, tells me that "the pipelines will remain a pipe dream unless there is peace between India and Pakistan."

For the past three years, the international effort to rebuild Afghanistan has been stymied by a lack of coordination among NATO allies, the United Nations, Afghan agencies, and nongovernmental organizations. Ambassador Khalilzad has created an Afghan Reconstruction Group to better organize these efforts. Provincial reconstruction teams led by NATO and its partner countries are now coordinating humanitarian and reconstruction efforts.

But nation-building in Afghanistan will mean little without region-building. Washington must forge a comprehensive approach to the region's security and economic challenges affecting Afghanistan or lose an opportunity of historic proportions.

If the United States is not inclined to invest the time, money, and patience necessary for Afghanistan to succeed, it should consider that Afghanistan's neighbors, who may not always share American interests, have a valuable commodity Washington does not—all the time in the world.

A Civilian Surge for Afghanistan

Los Angeles Times, December 28, 2009

THE OBAMA ADMINISTRATION HAS OUTLINED A THREE-PRONGED STRATEGY in Afghanistan, focusing on security, governance, and economic development. But the implementation of those elements has been woefully lopsided. Since 2002, 93 percent of the $170 billion the United States has committed to Afghanistan has gone to military operations.

As the country prepares to send 30,000 more troops to Afghanistan, we also need to focus on providing a surge in the quality of life for the Afghan people.

US Agency for International Development workers are tremendously dedicated, but there are not nearly enough of them, which means the agency is heavily dependent on private contractors. There have been some commendable achievements, such as helping reduce Afghanistan's infant mortality rate and rehabilitating nearly 1,000 miles of roads. Still, as Secretary of State Hillary Rodham Clinton lamented in March, the lack of results for the Afghan people is "heartbreaking."

The Obama administration has pledged a new, improved approach to development aid. Yet USAID has been without an administrator for 10 months, and the president's nominee, Rajiv Shah, has yet to be confirmed. It's now time, with the president's commitment in his West Point speech to "focus our assistance in areas, such as agriculture, that can make an immediate impact in the lives of the Afghan people," to heed the experience of successful social entrepreneurs who, with far fewer resources at their disposal, have achieved impressive progress on the ground.

Take Greg Mortenson, president of the nonprofit Central Asia Institute, or CAI, who over the last 16 years has built or supported 130 schools in remote Pakistani and Afghan villages. These secular schools provide education to more than 30,000 children, the vast majority of them girls. CAI's revenues in fiscal year 2007 were a fraction of what we will spend every day in Afghanistan over the next 18 months.

Or take Sakena Yacoobi, a US-educated public health professional, who returned to her homeland in the 1990s to found the Afghan Institute of

Learning, or AIL, now a network of 45 centers in seven provinces that provide comprehensive health and education services. Seventy percent of AIL's staff of more than 400 is female. With an annual budget of $1 million, AIL reaches more than 350,000 Afghan women and children.

Or Connie Duckworth, a former partner at Goldman Sachs, who was so moved by the hardships of the women she met on a visit to Afghanistan in 2002 that she created Arai—which means "hope" in Dari—a rug-making enterprise focused on female weavers that is one of Afghanistan's largest private-sector employers, with 90 percent of its jobs in underserved, rural areas.

What are some key lessons from these social entrepreneurs' success?

First, ask, don't tell: US assistance programs must be tailored to meet local needs, not our own. Over the last eight years, too many well-intentioned US programs have been driven by what America thinks is best, which is how we wasted millions trying to launch a 25,000-acre plantation on soil that was too salty for crops, and initiating cash-for-work construction of cobblestone roads that Afghans rejected because they hurt their camels' hooves. The Afghan people know what they need.

Second, invest capital outside the capital—and devise and direct those projects from the field. Mortenson is successful in part because he spends months every year living with the villagers in the communities his organization serves. That model has not yet penetrated the thinking of US government programs. As Amy Frumin, who served as a USAID worker in Panjshir province, wrote in a June 2009 report for the Center for Strategic and International Studies: "The vast majority of USAID funds are invested in programs that are designed from Kabul"—even though more than three-quarters of Afghans live outside the capital.

Third, ensure that US assistance reaches the Afghan people. This sounds obvious. Yet last year, the nongovernmental Agency Coordinating Body for Afghan Relief reported that 40 percent of official aid to Afghanistan goes back to donor countries in corporate profits and consultant salaries.

Fourth, make women the focus, not the footnote, of aid programs. It's no accident Mortenson, Yacoobi, and Duckworth all target their limited resources toward women and girls. In Afghanistan, as elsewhere, investing in women pays dividends many times over. Women are more likely to prioritize the education, nutrition, and health of their families, creating a multiplier effect that lifts entire communities.

Finally, approach development as an evolution, not a revolution. As Afghan expert Rory Stewart recently argued in a PBS interview, "Afghanistan is very poor, very fragile, very traumatized. To rebuild a country like that would take 30 or 40 years of patient, tolerant investment."

We should invest in programs that will be sustainable long-term—and be prepared to commit for the long haul.

Mortenson called his book *Three Cups of Tea* in reference to a rural village leader's advice that slowing down and building relationships over tea in the traditional way is as important as building projects. As 30,000 more US troops prepare to depart for Afghanistan, let's hope we also have the stomach for 30,000 cups of tea.

Can "Pashtunistan" End the Af-Pak War?

The Washington Times, June 2, 2010

ON THE BORDER OF PAKISTAN AND AFGHANISTAN, IN THE FOOTHILLS of the Hindu Kush mountains, tribesmen here know him as the "Afghan Warrior Poet." Like thousands of his fellow Pashtun brothers from the surrounding Northwest Frontier Province, he stood as the first line of defense against troops invading from the West. Eventually, he grew disgusted by the corruption of leaders who lived in the capital cities and rebelled. Despite their armies, these leaders could do little to reach or control him in this rugged wasteland. In the name of Allah, he made it the cause of his life to unite his fellow believers, to create their own nation, and live by their own customs.

His story could be that of any of the young Islamic tribesmen fighting on the Af-Pak border today. And yet the Afghan Warrior Poet—Khushal Khan Khattak—lived more than 400 years ago. Today, his Pashtun descendants stand on the same land against the West, grow equally disgusted by the corruption of leaders in Kabul and Islamabad, and live beyond any army's control. Pashtun tribesmen comprise the vast majority of Taliban warriors in both Pakistan and Afghanistan. As scholar Robert Kaplan has written, "The Taliban is merely the latest incarnation of Pashtun nationalism."

As America readies another 30,000 troops to deploy to Afghanistan, at a time when Washington prepares to send billions in aid and weapons to Islamabad and Kabul (whose armies have proven unwilling or unable to root out extremists), during a month in which a member of the Pakistani Taliban allegedly tried to blow up Times Square, it's time we ask: Shouldn't we just give Pashtuns the only thing they've wanted for centuries—to live and be left alone in their own country, Pashtunistan—and finish this conflict once and for all?

There is a reason why Taliban warriors pass so freely across the Af-Pak border, frustrating American troops who cannot pursue beyond it: it is an artificial line that Pashtuns have never recognized. In 1893, Britain was concerned that the Afghans' fight for independence could inspire others, so it pressed Afghanistan into signing a border-demarcation agreement. A British delegation, led by Sir Henry Mortimer Durand, haphazardly drew a line between Afghanistan and British India.

The problem is, the so-called Durand Line ran straight through ancestral Pashtun territory, literally separating brother from brother. In 1947, the British handed the former Indian half over to Pakistan. Today, 23 million Pashtuns live on the Afghan side of the border, 12 million live in Pakistan.

A local saying—"All Taliban are Pashtun, but not all Pashtuns are Taliban"—reflects the intense dislike that many Pashtuns have for the Taliban. Public opinion polls suggest that East Afghan Pashtuns are more anti-Taliban than their southern Afghan brethren. Yet the war against the West has allowed Pashtun leaders to externalize resentment rather than turn it inward.

The idea that any government will exert influence here is fantasy. Additional US troops might temporarily wound the Taliban, at a cost of many lives, but it will do nothing to change the reality of the region, particularly as the Obama administration says it will begin to withdraw troops next year.

But imagine instead if America worked through the United Nations and its NATO allies to broker an agreement between Afghanistan and Pakistan, to carve out an independent Pashtunistan framed by the Indus River to the east and the Hindu Kush mountains to the West. The territories of Afghanistan and Pakistan would be reduced, but both would be made more secure, since Pashtun leaders would have little reason to continue their destabilization of either country. Taliban members would turn inward, focusing instead on building their own nation.

As the 193rd member of the United Nations, Pashtunistan and its leaders would be held to the same rules that apply to all nations, including the Universal Declaration of Human Rights. Islamic extremists and Al Qaeda would no longer be able to "hide behind" the border of US "ally" Pakistan, allowing America to bypass Islamabad altogether. International aid and development funds could be used to incentivize Pashtun leaders to observe UN treaties and agreements, help settle more than a million Pashtun refugees uprooted by war, and develop the Pashtunistan economy.

It won't be easy. But is it any more far-fetched than believing that additional American troops will make anything more than a momentary blip in a centuries-long struggle? The reality here for centuries is that Pashtuns simply want to be left alone: "If you don't mess with them," Pakistani journalist Ahmed Rashid says, "they won't mess with you." Isn't it time we try to bring peace by building up rather than tearing down?

MIDDLE EAST

The Hunt Is On for Osama bin Laden

The Washington Times, September 16, 1998
(with Thomas G. McInerney)

THE UNITED STATES WANTS TERRORIST MASTERMIND OSAMA BIN LADEN dead—or alive. The missile attacks on Mr. bin Laden's bases in Afghanistan represent the "dead" approach, regardless of whether the goal was bin Laden himself or his command and control. Diplomacy, such as efforts to convince the Taliban—the fundamentalist Islamic movement that controls 90 percent of Afghanistan—to turn over bin Laden, represents the "alive" approach.

It is hard to see either bearing much fruit. And in the meantime, both efforts exact a high cost on US global influence and prestige.

Take the "dead" approach. It is exceedingly difficult to kill an individual through bombings—just ask Saddam Hussein or Libyan leader Moammar Gadhafi. Even if the White House would agree to repeal the executive order banning assassination of foreigners, the United States is not believed to have any assets in place to carry out such a murderous assignment. Meanwhile, world condemnation of the United States will grow in the wake of any prolonged bombing campaign, which is required if America is to be taken seriously.

The "alive" approach will probably fare even worse. A grand jury in New York has handed down an indictment against Mr. bin Laden, accusing him of terrorist acts against the United States. But there is no indication that the Taliban will turn over Mr. bin Laden to the United States—or even expel him—in exchange for diplomatic recognition or a United Nations seat. The Taliban have failed to keep promises made to European governments and UN agencies to stop the opium trade, ease restrictions on basic rights for women, or form a broad-based government in Afghanistan. If the United States pursues this strategy instead of further military action, it will look weak and Mr. bin Laden will undertake future terrorist attacks.

There is another option. A different form of pressure can be used against the Taliban to get them to turn over Mr. bin Laden to the United States or at least expel him from Afghanistan. The United States should inform the rebel Taliban leader Mullah Mohammad Omar that unless Mr. bin Laden is delivered in 30 days, America and its allies will offer assistance to the government of Burhanuddin Rabbani, recognized by the United Nations as the legitimate president of Afghanistan.

The action would be taken at the request of Afghanistan's legal government, so that no violation of international law could be alleged. And since both the government forces and the Taliban are Muslims, America's move could not be seen as anti-Islamic. The four other permanent members of the UN Security Council—Russia, France, China, and the U.K.—could be expected to approve this anti-terrorist action. And no doubt Uzbekistan, Tajikistan, Turkey, and even Iran would offer military support of their own to Afghanistan's legitimate government. Only the Taliban's main supporter, Pakistan, and its Arab financial backers would object.

It is probable that the Taliban would promptly deliver Mr. bin Laden, rather than risk military defeat. Alternatively, he would become too hot to handle and be asked to leave. But to where? Iran is one possibility, but Mr. bin Laden, an ultra-orthodox Sunni Muslim, is a religious enemy of Iranian Shiites, and Afghanistan has reportedly killed thousands of Shiite civilians as well as 14 Iranian diplomats and a journalist. Pakistan would not harbor him; the unintended consequence of its support of the Taliban is a "Talibanizing" trend in its own country, a secular Muslim nation. If Mr. bin Laden manages to find refuge in Lebanon, Syria, Sudan, or Libya, his effectiveness as the big-man of terrorism would be greatly weakened.

This strategy is not without risks. Already in this century, Britain and the Soviet Union suffered crushing military defeat in the hills and mountains of Afghanistan. But the United States and its allies need not and should not become involved on the ground. Military supplies to the legitimate government in Afghanistan, coupled with missile and air support, should be enough to turn the tables on the Taliban.

If America is serious about wanting to bring in Mr. bin Laden "dead or alive," it clearly can be done. But he won't be gotten dead or alive unless the United States is prepared to employ all of the power at its disposal.

Uncle Sam Is Stuck in the Gulf Without a Compass

International Herald Tribune, July 5, 2001

CONTRARY TO CONVENTIONAL WISDOM, DESERT STORM DID NOT APPLY the Powell doctrine about overwhelming force and a clear exit strategy. It was an example of the doctrine's failure. Ten years after the capitulation of Iraqi forces, the United States is stuck in the Persian Gulf.

America continues an open-ended military commitment over northern and southern Iraq. The 36 servicemen and -women killed and the hundreds injured in the Khobar Towers in Saudi Arabia, and the sailors lost on the destroyer *Cole*, are the most recent casualties of a US confrontation that will soon equal Vietnam in its duration—precisely what Colin Powell's doctrine was supposed to prevent.

US and British pilots who patrol the skies over Iraq carry out a decade-old policy aimed at keeping Saddam Hussein in a box. The theory was that Saddam would be grounded, unable to use his air force to launch attacks on the Kurds in the north and the Shiites in the south. Meanwhile, United Nations inspectors would make certain that Saddam did not resume work on weapons of mass destruction. And the world's toughest economic sanctions would deprive him of the revenue to rearm.

Since the end of the Gulf War, US and British pilots have flown more than 200,000 sorties. Last year they were shot at 257 times by Iraqi surface-to-air missiles and anti-aircraft fire, and commanders say that the figure for the first four months of this year is five times that.

Granted, the Iraqis do not turn on their radar, because American planes could destroy them. Instead they shoot and run, hoping that eventually they will hit a plane. The law of large numbers suggests that they are right.

There are also risks to airliners from the 60 countries violating the UN sanctions against Iraq. If an Iraqi missile downed a civilian airplane, Saddam would try to shift the blame to the United States, using such a tragedy for his own political ends.

The flights put a strain on America's relations with Turkey, a NATO ally, which faces the wrath of much of the Arab world by allowing coalition aircraft to operate from this base. US Air Force commanders must negotiate flight schedules with their Turkish counterparts weeks in advance, with no changes allowed on the agreed flight dates. So much for the element of surprise!

Highly trained pilots in expensive equipment are used as sitting ducks, flying steady and level, instead of honing skills confronting enemy aircraft, evading air defenses, delivering bombs on target. Funding that could be used to help replace an aging fighter fleet is being consumed by this operation.

Most important, the United States cannot afford to wait until an American pilot is being paraded through the streets of Baghdad.

The Bush administration is reported to be reviewing Operation Northern Watch. Some senior officers suggest decreasing the number of flights, while drawing a line in the sand that will bring immediate, heavy retaliation if Saddam crossed it.

But any sign that the United States was scaling back its commitment in the face of Baghdad's escalation would send a dangerous signal to America's friends and enemies in the region. It could push the Kurds directly into the arms of Saddam and make oil smuggling even easier.

For now, it is Saddam who calls the shots. He ousted the UN inspection teams. He continues to reap billions from smuggling, with cooperation from Syria and Jordan. He is strengthening his military capabilities, including his air defenses, with the help of China, Syria, Ukraine, Russia, and even Yugoslavia when Slobodan Milosevic was president.

The United States should change its rules of engagement so as to bring about Saddam's downfall. Coalition aircraft should go after militarily significant targets in any part of Iraq. Chief among these should be the pillars of Saddam's regime: the Republican Guard and the security services.

These are also the organizations responsible for concealing and protecting his programs for weapons of mass destruction. Factories and facilities suspected of such production should be fair game. So should the Iraq–Syria pipeline, which carries most of the sanctions-busting oil.

These would be direct blows to the regime rather than the pinpricks that Saddam is currently subjected to.

America and its Gulf War allies got the Powell doctrine half right when they ousted Iraqi forces from Kuwait. Failure to finish the job with an exit strategy has allowed Saddam to act more like the victor than the vanquished.

He will continue to dictate the terms of the "mother of all battles" until the United States uses the force necessary to destroy his regime. Or Washington must accept his presence, with all this implies for the growing danger to the Middle East and the West.

Who Needs Whom?

International Herald Tribune, April 25, 2002

THE EMERGENCY MEETING THIS THURSDAY OF PRESIDENT GEORGE W. BUSH and Crown Prince Abdullah aims to heal recently inflicted wounds to the longstanding US-Saudi partnership.

But, like all marriages of convenience, the loveless union between the United States and Saudi Arabia has always been based more on common interests (oil) than on common values.

September 11 exposed the depths of this dysfunctional relationship.

Saudi Arabia, Americans were shocked to learn, had been cheating all along. Worse, it was funding its infidelities with US dollars. As gas-guzzling Americans pumped more money than any other nation into the oil kingdom, the royal family was pumping millions into radical religious schools at home and abroad, globalizing its strict 18th-century Wahhabi brand of Islam. From these hotbeds of hate graduated Osama bin Laden and 15 of the 19 September 11 hijackers.

The US forces deployed 12 years ago to protect and stabilize Islam's holy land have achieved just the opposite, undermining public support for the very regime they were sent to protect and inspiring bin Laden's jihad against America.

Abdullah wrote to Bush last summer, "a time comes when peoples and nations part." It was time, he added, "for the United States and Saudi Arabia to look at their separate interests."

Now the Saudis say the United States needs them. But truth be told, the United States today is less, not more, dependent on Saudi oil.

The country that provides America with more oil than any other (40 percent of the crude that Americans use) is the United States—which imports twice as much oil from its Western Hemisphere neighbors as it does from the Gulf.

The United States needs oil, but not from Saudi Arabia.

In February, Russia edged out Saudi Arabia to become the world's biggest producer of crude. The largest oil field discovered in 30 years is off the coast of Kazakhstan; some analysts are calling it a second Kuwait. The Caspian basin is believed to hold the world's third-largest reserves (perhaps up to 200 billion barrels), behind only the Gulf and Siberia. South America and West Africa together are believed to hold an additional 100 billion barrels.

To be sure, with one-quarter of the world's oil reserves and an excess capacity of 3 million barrels a day, only Saudi Arabia can moderate the markets with a turn of the spigot, as it did after Iraq's recent decision to suspend exports. Nevertheless, the Saudis need the United States as much as it needs them.

In Saudi Arabia, oil is the only game, accounting for more than 90 percent of exports and 80 percent of government revenue. As oil prices have plunged in recent years, the national debt has soared. Per capita GDP has plummeted from $28,000 in 1981 to less than $7,000 today. With dwindling receipts, the House of Saud cannot afford the generous welfare state with which it bought the loyalty of its people.

This is why the "oiligarchies" of the Gulf are not responding to Saddam Hussein's call to withhold oil, as a weapon against the United States and Israel. If they don't sell it, others will.

These petro-princes remember that their boldest attempt at using oil as a weapon, the embargo of the 1970s, failed in its main mission of forcing Israel from the Palestinian territories. Even today, half or more of Iraqi oil ends up in the United States.

Nor is the Organization of Petroleum Exporting Countries the superpower it was two decades ago. Witness the cartel's pathetic attempt at cajoling Russia, not an OPEC member, into significant production cuts to prop up prices.

Americans worried about rising oil prices need not fear a Saudi Arabia scorned. It is time for the United States to walk out on Saudi oil.

Syria's Crucial Role:
Why Damascus Meddles—and Matters

International Herald Tribune, August 9, 2006

THEY WERE THE LAST AMERICANS TO MEET WITH SYRIA'S PRESIDENT, Bashar al-Assad, in the days before the latest Middle East upheaval. The delegation, from the nonpartisan Business Executives for National Security, could not have foreseen the deadly days that would follow in the Gaza Strip and Lebanon.

But in a wide-ranging, two-hour meeting with the Syrian leader in Damascus, these American executives gained a rare glimpse into the mind-set of a man and a regime that may determine whether Israel's war with Hezbollah ends with an international force in Lebanon or escalates into a regional war.

Frustrated that the Bush administration has not responded to what he claimed was Syrian willingness to cooperate on border security to thwart Al Qaeda and Iraqi insurgents, Assad warned that the lack of a Middle East peace process was emboldening Arab hard-liners, including Hezbollah, who seek confrontation.

Assad "recognizes that Washington is trying to isolate his regime," said Charles Boyd, the retired Air Force general, and president of BENS, who led the delegation. "But he argued that the United States can't solve the region's problems without some involvement with Syria."

Bleeding Israel by proxy is Syria's old strategy for trying to force Israel from the occupied Golan Heights. And though instigated in part by Hezbollah's masters in Tehran to divert attention from Iran's nuclear program, the current crisis also serves another strategic purpose—Syria's historic ambition of establishing itself as the premier Arab power.

Such dreams are rooted in history. For 400 years under the Ottoman Turks, the region known as Syria included not only modern-day Syria but also Lebanon, Israel, the Palestinian territories, Jordan, and a sliver of Turkey. Assad's father, the long-ruling strongman Hafez al-Assad, would lecture visiting dignitaries on the arbitrary division of Greater Syria by France and Britain after World War I.

After the war, there was "almost unanimous opinion for unity and independence" in the region, according to Charles Glass, the journalist and author
held hostage by Hezbollah in Beirut in 1987. "The British and French gave
them neither." Palestine and Transjordan were claimed by Britain, and Syria
by France, which promptly carved out a Greater Lebanon, combining the
pro-French Maronite Christians of Mount Lebanon with Muslim regions,
including Beirut and the Bekaa Valley.

Many Syrians still describe the Syrian-Lebanese relationship as that of
"one people in two countries." Although Syria ended its 29-year military
presence in Lebanon last year, it still refuses to establish an embassy in
Beirut. More broadly, Syrians speak of their country as "the heart of Ara-
bism"—the unyielding defender of the Arab world.

All of this exposes the folly of Washington's refusal to talk with Damascus since the Assad regime was implicated in the assassination last year of
a former Lebanese prime minister, Rafik Hariri. "The problem isn't that
people haven't talked to the Syrians," Secretary of State Condoleezza Rice
said recently. "It's that the Syrians haven't acted." In fact, Damascus has a
long history of acting—both for and against US interests.

Under Assad the father, Syria deployed troops alongside US forces in the
1991 Gulf War, helped engineer cease-fires between Hezbollah and Israel in
1993 and 1996, and "played a constructive role" during Israel's withdrawal from
Lebanon in 2000, according to then–secretary of state Madeleine Albright.

Under Assad the son, Syrian cooperation against Al Qaeda after 9/11
"saved American lives," according to William Bums, then assistant secretary
of state. After the US invasion of Iraq, Syria periodically tightened its border
with Iraq and assisted in the arrest of Saddam Hussein's half-brother.

Damascus can also be a formidable foe when its interests are threatened.
Its deadly replies to those who would bypass or marginalize it included
supporting Hezbollah in bombing the US embassy and Marine barracks in
Beirut in the early 1980s; subverting the Saudi peace plan of 2002; and con-
spiring to kill Hariri and other Lebanese critics of Syria.

In this sense, the current bravado from Damascus masks Syrian vulnera-
bilities. The regime's greatest fear is not Israel but Iraq, where Sunni jihadists could someday target Assad's secular regime, which is dominated by the
tiny Alawite sect, considered heretical by Syria's Sunni majority.

Syria's marriage of convenience with Shiite Iran also carries risks. The
partnership "is largely one of shared interests rather than shared values,"

says Jerrold Green, a Middle East expert with the American research organization RAND Corp. "The leadership in Damascus loathes and fears religious-based politics, just as Tehran embraces it."

Yes, there are costs for Washington in dealing with Damascus, including the appearance of rewarding bad behavior and allowing Assad to assert a claim of Arab leadership. And no matter what incentives Washington might offer, there's no guarantee that Assad would be willing to back away from Iran or able to rein in Hezbollah, the new hero of the Arab world.

But as history teaches, foreign powers ignore or isolate Syria at their peril. And no cease-fire—immediate or sustained—will succeed without the backing of Assad's regime. As in the old Greater Syria, all roads still lead to Damascus.

The Confederation of Abraham

The Huffington Post, July 26, 2011

IN THE CENTER OF JERUSALEM IS A SERIES OF PLATFORMS THAT WERE built over many centuries, known as the Temple Mount, on Mount Moriah. The stone peak of Mount Moriah is visible at the center of the Temple Mount.

Jews know this as "the Foundation Stone." It is the holiest site in Judaism. According to the Talmud, it is from this rock that the world was first created; that Adam and Noah offered sacrifices to God; that Abraham displayed to God his willingness to sacrifice his son Isaac; and that Solomon built the First Temple of Jerusalem. It is also upon this rock, in a chamber within the First Temple, that Jews placed the Ark of the Covenant—the chest which contained the Ten Commandments—making it the "Holy of Holies."

It is a perfect symbol of the intertwined history of this disputed land that the Foundation Stone itself is housed within an Islamic mosque—the Dome of the Rock, which was built after the Muslim conquest of Jerusalem. Muslims believe that it was from this same rock that the prophet Mohammad first ascended to heaven, where he spoke to God, receiving instructions to take back to the faithful. After Mecca and Medina, it is Islam's third holiest site.

Meanwhile, Christians revere the rock as the site of the Second Temple, which stood in Jerusalem from 516 B.C. until 70 A.D. It is the Temple where scripture says Jesus was brought as a child; where he and his disciples preached and chased away moneychangers. For a city that has been destroyed twice, and captured and recaptured 44 times, the fact that a rock sits at the center of Jerusalem's shifting sands is perhaps the original historical irony.

The basic narrative is why Jews, Muslims, and Christians claim this land as their historic homeland. While Jews ruled on and off here for nearly a millennium, Muslims—save for the Crusader period (1095–1291)—ruled the region from 638 until 1917, when the British claimed it after the defeat of the Ottoman Empire in World War I.

As the United Nations prepares to consider a proposal to recognize an independent Palestinian state, it is worth remembering that during the 1,100 years of Muslim rule, dozens of ethnic groups lived together without real borders.

As Sari Nusseibeh, the Palestinian president of Al-Quds University in Jerusalem, reminds me, "In contrast to our states-divided world, migration from one region to another did not require passports and proof of identity. The division of the past 60 years is the exception to the history, not the rule."

We know the history: In 1917, British foreign secretary Lord Balfour promised to establish a homeland for Jews in Palestine. In 1947, the UN passed Resolution 181, portioning the area into a Jewish state and a Palestinian state, which the latter rejected. In 1948, the British withdrew, Israel declared independence, and war erupted. Some 800,000 Palestinians who lost their homes in the conflict—and their 1.5 million descendants—have never been allowed to return ([having been denied] the so-called right of return).

In 1967, Egypt, receiving false reports from the Soviet Union that Israel was moving troops to the Syrian border, massed its own troops on the Israeli border. It drew a crippling counterstrike from Israel, which went on to also defeat Jordan and Syria in the so-called Six-Day War. From Egypt, Israel claimed the Gaza Strip (and Sinai Peninsula, which was returned after a peace treaty was signed); from Syria, it occupied the Golan Heights; from Jordan, it annexed East Jerusalem and occupied the land on the West Bank of the Jordan River. International law does not recognize Israel's claim to these occupied territories.

By some counts, there have been 31 separate peace plans proposed and rejected in the past 60 years. Meanwhile, Israel has built security walls around Arab areas, established hundreds of checkpoints, and built thousands of settlements in the West Bank.

The choices remain clear. Israel can agree to some form of a negotiated two-state solution, accepting an independent Palestinian state in Gaza, the West Bank, and East Jerusalem, as was offered to the Palestinians by Israeli prime ministers Ehud Barak and Ehud Olmert—and rejected. It can agree to a bi-national solution, ceding to demographics that suggest there will be more Arabs than Jews in Israel by 2050—which would essentially mean giving up the Zionist dream of a Jewish, democratic state. Or, it can continue building settlements, which even some Israelis have compared to apartheid.

In this land where Abraham is revered both as a prophet of Islam, through his firstborn son, Ishmael, and as father of the Israelites, through his second-born child, Isaac—this is clearly a situation in need of new ideas.

One idea is the creation of a confederation between Israel and a Palestine within negotiated borders. Call it the Confederation of Abraham. Over time, Israelis and Palestinians could pass across secure borders. A demilitarized Palestine with international security guarantees could build confidence and ease reconciliation. Permanent joint bodies, modeled on South Africa's Truth and Reconciliation Commission, could litigate issues of common interest, from water rights to economic development. All told, Palestinians would get their state; and in return, the 21 Arab states in the region would agree to recognize a Jewish Israel. The Confederation would be a first step to a regional common market, which would allow the international community to focus on economics, not politics.

For now, all players in the region are stuck between a rock and a hard place.

A Brilliant Fraud

The Huffington Post, September 15, 2011

IT WAS THE FIRST TIME THAT CATTLE CARS WOULD BE USED IN THE 20th century to carry people to concentration camps, a systematic annihilation of a whole population so horrific that a new word had to be invented to capture its brutality: "genocide."

In the midst of World War I, over a million Christian Armenians in Turkey were rounded up by the Ottoman Empire and slaughtered in unspeakable ways. No less a mass murderer than Adolf Hitler, in a speech to Nazi commanders before he invaded Poland, reportedly defended his order to "kill without pity or mercy all men, women, and children of the Polish race" by asking, "Who, after all, speaks today of the annihilation of the Armenians?"

Ninety years later, the Armenian Genocide has been recognized by 21 nations, 43 American states, and a United Nations commission. But Turkey still denies it ever happened. Under Turkish prime minister Recep Tayyip Erdoğan, not only is speaking of genocide in Turkey a jailable offense, but earlier this year, Erdoğan announced that Turkey was tearing down the Turkish-Armenian "Friendship Monument" that stands on the border between the two countries, calling it "monstrous."

Yet this is the same man who lectures Israeli prime minister Benjamin Netanyahu that Israel needs to apologize for the deaths of nine Turkish activists last year on board a pro-Palestinian flotilla that was attempting to break Israel's blockade of the Gaza Strip. This is also the same leader who has promised to help pass a Palestinian resolution at the UN next week welcoming the State of Palestine as a member—at the same time Ankara continues to deny basic rights to 20 million Turkish Kurds while illegally occupying northern Cyprus, in defiance of the UN.

This is far from just a gross expression of diplomatic hypocrisy or a historical reversal of a Turkish-Israeli friendship that dates back to 1949. At a time when much of the Muslim world is turning toward democracy, one of America's oldest democratic allies in the region is headed in the other direction.

Erdoğan—who is Islamist to the core, and who once famously declared that "the mosques are our barracks, the domes our helmets, the minarets our bayonets, and the faithful our soldiers"—seems to see himself as the Islamic leader of a post–Arab Spring Muslim world.

Since taking power in 2003, Erdoğan's Islamist Justice and Development Party (in Turkish: *Adalet ve Kalkmma Partis,* or AKP) has been less interested in preserving Mustafa Kemal Atatürk's 90-year-old vision of Turkey as a secular state, and more committed (as Israeli journalist Ron Ben-Yishai writes) to bringing about "a return to the Ottoman Empire's glory days."

As prime minister, Erdoğan has wielded Turkey's aspiring membership in the European Union brilliantly as a tool to suppress secular opposition, [through no method] more efficiently than with the military—which has been the constitutional guarantor of a secular Turkey for nine decades.

Using the EU's insistence that Turkey bring its military under greater civilian control, Erdoğan has castrated military leaders. In June, with more than 40 generals in jail, Turkey's top military commanders resigned simultaneously. The vacuum leaves Erdoğan free to remodel Turkey, as Caroline Glick of the Center for Security Policy puts it, "into a hybrid of Putinist autocracy and Iranian theocracy."

Meanwhile, the judiciary—the other guardian of secular power in Turkey—had its independence garroted last year with the passage of new constitutional amendments that give the AKP control over judicial appointments and power to "investigate" judges.

Burnishing his credentials as a brilliant fraud, Erdoğan praised the new constitution as a step toward EU membership—while knowing that the EU's "Christian Club," as he calls it, won't likely ever grant Turkey full membership.

In Israel, Erdoğan has the perfect foil—and in Netanyahu, the perfect fool. Incensed by Israel's 2008 bombing of Gaza, Erdoğan engaged in a heated exchange with Israeli president Shimon Peres at the World Economic Forum in Davos, shouting, "When it comes to killing, you know well how to kill," before storming offstage.

He returned home to a hero's welcome and has made trouble for the West ever since. Last year, when Turkey sided with Iran in a UN Security Council vote on Tehran sanctions, Western scholars asked, "Who lost Turkey?" Yet while Erdoğan has sought to assert Turkish leadership across the region, every initiative he's attempted—from ending the NATO mission against Libya, to imploring Syria to end its violent crackdowns, to promoting reconciliation between Hamas and Fatah—has met with failure.

With his threats against Syria being ignored by Damascus, Erdoğan was in need of a distraction to win back the street, which the UN provided last month with the Palmer Report on the 2010 flotilla raid. It found that Israel used excessive force and was morally responsible for the deaths, but ruled that the Gaza blockade is lawful and enforceable by Israel against humanitarian vessels in international waters.

The rest was predictable: Erdoğan seethed at the UN, kicked out the Israeli Ambassador to Turkey, suspended all economic and military agreements with Tel Aviv, and warned that Turkish warships would break the Israeli blockade of Gaza. But his brilliant jujitsu continued: while bashing the Palmer Report, he also enraged Iran by agreeing to host NATO anti-missile radar on Turkey's border.

So, what's next? This week, Erdoğan becomes the first Turkish prime minister to visit Cairo in 15 years. Turkey and Egypt—which together represent half of the population of the Middle East—are expected to sign an agreement leading to new political, economic, and scientific ties. Can Egypt and Turkey work to turn the Arab Spring into an Islamic Summer—and will Erdoğan lead it, in time for the 100th anniversary of the Armenian Genocide? Only one thing is certain: somewhere, Atatürk is turning over in his grave.

Blessed Are the Businessmen and Women

The Huffington Post, September 22, 2011

SIXTY-FOUR YEARS AGO TODAY, ONE OF THE MOST PRESCIENT MEMOS IN American history was placed on the desk of George C. Marshall, the United States secretary of state. It was written by Loy Henderson, the director of the State Department's Office of Near Eastern and African Affairs. Coming less than a month after a special committee of the United Nations had recommended partitioning Palestine into two states—one Jewish and one Arab—it precisely predicted the violent future that partition would bring.

"The plan is not only unworkable," the memo argued, but "if adopted, it would guarantee that the Palestine problem would be permanent and more complicated in the future." In an equally perceptive memo to President Harry Truman two months later, Henderson wrote, "The plan . . . leaves no force other than the local law enforcement organizations for preserving order in Palestine. It is quite clear there will be widespread violence in that country, on both the Arab and Jewish sides, with which the local authorities will not be able to cope."

Henderson's message was delivered to the president personally by Undersecretary of State Robert Lovett. But Truman, wildly unpopular at the time, was convinced that in order to win the Democratic nomination for president—let alone the 1948 election—he needed to support partition. As Truman himself put it, "I have to answer to hundreds of thousands who are anxious for the success of Zionism. I do not have hundreds of thousands of Arabs among my constituents."

Five days later, the United States voted for partition in the UN General Assembly and Palestine descended into violence. The following March, Truman renounced partition and called for a UN trusteeship of Palestine, bringing charges that he was weak. Two months later, Israel unilaterally declared independence, inviting Jews to return to their historic homeland, where they had lived 2,000 years before Mohammad was even born. Truman reversed himself again, making the United States the first nation to recognize Israel as an independent nation.

As UN delegates invoke Truman's name this week in preparation for tomorrow's General Assembly vote on a Palestinian Authority request that Palestine be recognized as an independent state, it's hard not to see the irony: invoking Truman means invoking the triumph of politics. Yet it is precisely the political games being played by all parties involved in the Middle East today that has made compromise of any kind impossible.

Israeli prime minister Benjamin Netanyahu can't compromise because the ultra-orthodox members of his governing coalition, led by ultra-secular Foreign Minister Avigdor Lieberman, won't even allow Israel to apologize for killing nine Turks in last year's flotilla raid, let alone negotiate a two-state solution.

Lieberman can't compromise on the building of settlements in the West Bank, which have tripled since the failed Oslo Accords in the early 1990s, because the vast majority of new settlers are the secular Russian Jews and ultra-orthodox Jews that he represents.

President Barack Obama can't compromise, or push Israel publicly in any way, without incurring the wrath of Jewish supporters in America or opportunists in the US Congress—who have been falling all over themselves the past two weeks, competing on who can propose the most extreme punishment for Palestinians should the UN vote go through (at this point, "cutting off all US funding for the Palestinian Authority" represents the least offensive measure).

Palestinian president Mahmoud Abbas can't compromise, or even publicly state that Israel has a right to exist as a Jewish state, because the leaders of Hamas will use it to rally Palestinians against him. Hamas can't compromise because its reason for being is the destruction of Israel—preaching, as Palestinian educator Sari Nusseibeh has written, that negotiating peace pales in comparison to fighting and "a guaranteed paradise in the afterlife."

Muslim leaders across the Middle East, including Saudi Arabia and the newly combative Turkey—none of whom have lifted a finger for six decades to help Palestinian refugees, and who all but ignore the people of Gaza as anything but a political tool against Israel—can't compromise if their claims for regional leadership are to be successful.

Meanwhile, Palestinian supporters at the UN tomorrow will likely vote in favor of a fictional shortcut to Palestinian statehood, leading to celebrations in Ramallah—only to dissolve next week to the reality that nothing has changed.

Through it all, an eight-year-old girl in Sderot will go to bed tonight to the sound of rocket fire, while an eight-year-old boy in Gaza stands in line for too little food, one of the 80 percent of Gazans dependent on aid agency bread to stay alive. What becomes of him when Netanyahu retires to one of his three homes, Obama writes his memoirs, and Abbas retreats to the sun of Sharm el-Sheikh?

Will he steep himself in the wisdom of people like former US president Bill Clinton, who said in 2001 that "resolving these differences—whether this year or in 10 years—will entail the same choices, with the same geography, and the same necessity to visualize a different future and let go of old hurts"? Or will he choose to simply lead a Third Intifada—leading to more funerals and more tears, while people in the region grow poorer?

Maybe the Bible had it wrong. Maybe the peacemakers are not blessed. But maybe the businessmen and -women can be.

Everyone remembers the famous handshake between Yasser Arafat and Yitzhak Rabin in front of Clinton's outstretched arms in 1993. But they didn't see what happened next: Clinton went to the Old Executive Office Building next to the White House, where he met with 600 Arab-American and Jewish-American businessmen and women. All of them were committed to making serious investments in the Middle East, to help peace take hold. It never happened because, as Clinton has recalled, "somebody set off a bomb every time we got ready to make a little progress, which provoked Israel to close the borders, which crushed the Palestinian economy."

With all the peacemakers unable to compromise, maybe it's time for business to lead.

Maybe Clinton himself should lead a Middle East version of the Clinton Global Initiative—call it the Swords to Plowshares Initiative—and persuade business leaders to make specific commitments: that if a two-state solution can be reached, a wave of new jobs, business, and investments will flood into Gaza, the West Bank, and Israel.

Maybe the cry that helped take down apartheid in South Africa—"I ain't gonna play Sun City"—can be converted instead into "I am going to play Gaza City."

Maybe if the benefits of peace were made material and not ethereal, with concrete commitments rather than vague promises, it would be the kind of disruptive development that sparks compromise.

In other words, 64 years after Loy Henderson's memo to Harry Truman, maybe the key to Middle East peace isn't where the buck stops—but where the bucks will start.

Making Yoni Netanyahu's Sacrifice Matter

The Huffington Post, June 1, 2012

FORTY-NINE YEARS AGO LAST WEEK, A 17-YEAR-OLD JONATHAN Netanyahu—having recently arrived in America from Israel with his parents and two younger brothers—wrote a remarkable letter to a friend back home. "Man does not live forever, and he should put the days of his life to the best possible use," he wrote. "I only know that I don't want to reach a certain age, look around me and suddenly discover that I've created nothing."

Sadly, Jonathan—known to his family as Yoni—would never have the chance to realize his exceptional potential. In 1976, at the age of 30, he died heroically while leading the famous rescue of 105 hijacked Jewish hostages in Entebbe, Uganda. Instead, it fell to his younger brother, Benjamin, to make meaning of his brother's sacrifice and create a meaningful legacy.

Benjamin, of course, would go on to become the two-time prime minister of Israel—serving first from 1996 to 1999, and elected to his current term in 2009. Few would argue that he has successfully built much of anything in those two terms. His first go-around was marked by corruption charges and derailment of the Israeli-Palestinian peace process. So far, his second has been defined by an improved Israeli economy but also a marked increase in the building of illegal settlements in the occupied West Bank—land which Israel captured after the 1967 war with its Arab neighbors, but which most of the world, including the United States, regards as Palestinian territory.

But with the April death of his revered 102-year-old father, Benzion—who was there at Israel's founding and served as a longtime critic of the peace process—Bibi might have the chance to create something lasting. [As he was] mourning his father's passing, an unprecedented new center-right governing coalition was born in the Knesset, Israel's parliament. Now with nearly 80 percent of the Knesset in his coalition, Bibi finds himself potentially relieved of the weight of his father's hawkish pessimism while simultaneously offered the opportunity to secure the state—the Zionist dream—his brother died protecting: Jewish, democratic, and safe. No prime minister has ever been in a better position to make peace with the Palestinians and ensure Israel's future.

As a recent *Time* cover story proclaimed, now is the time for "Bibi's Choice."

In a very real sense, however, Bibi's choice is no choice at all. Demography dictates the end of Israel's present course. According to Israel's preeminent demographer, Professor Sergio DellaPergola, the Jewish population of Israel plus the West Bank and Gaza is a mere 51 percent. In 2009, Arabs accounted for nearly a third of Israel's natural population increase—a rate far exceeding their share of the population. Present trends are not, DellaPergola starkly observes, "truly sufficient to ensure Israel's Jewish and democratic character."

And yet the peace process has yielded only impasse and mistrust. After failing in their United Nations bid for statehood last September, the Palestinians have come no closer to their goal. Bibi has refused to negotiate with the preconditions that the Palestinians demand. Though the broad outlines of a two-state solution have been tacitly understood since the 1993 Oslo Accords, neither side has been able to establish trust and take the final plunge.

At this point, the most viable solution may be, as the former head of Israel's navy and internal security Ami Ayalon says, "Instead of building trust and then agreements, we make the agreements now." Ayalon and the organization he co-founded, Blue White Future, have proposed an approach hewing to the generally accepted two-state framework that Israel could pursue unilaterally and step by step, without waiting to hammer out the details at the negotiating table.

The proposal—declaring that Israel will return to negotiations anytime; renouncing claims of sovereignty and ending settlement construction east of the security barrier; and creating a plan to help 100,000 settlers relocate within Israel's recognized borders—could be undertaken without compromising Israel's security. It would signal Israel's true willingness to accept a Palestinian state alongside its own by simply starting to make it a reality. Over 300,000 Israelis and 200,000 Palestinians have signed a petition supporting the plan and, along with reasonable security guarantees, 80 percent of the Israeli public approves of such an approach. And on Wednesday, even Israeli defense minister Ehud Barak appeared to endorse unilateral action.

Ayalon terms this approach "constructive unilateralism," but the process might better be called "mutual unilateralism," since Bibi would have a partner working in parallel, in the person of Palestinian prime minister Salam Fayyad. Since becoming prime minister in 2006, Fayyad has doggedly worked to build a Palestinian state, with some impressive successes (until Bibi took power and began undermining him by building more settlements).

Speaking to an enthusiastic reception recently in Israel, Fayyad defiantly defended his own approach to state-building, declaring, "It is unilateral! As it should be! Because . . . if we Palestinians don't build it, who's going to build it for us?"

Certainly, neither can afford to sit on the sidelines much longer. The Palestinians' UN bid for statehood cost them millions in badly needed aid. And Ayalon, a decorated war hero, is deadly serious when he tells me, "The biggest threat to Israel's future is not Iran, but the loss of Jewish identity."

For Bibi to act would take a tremendous leap of faith, to be sure. Many are the leaders of Israel who have vowed not to be the ones responsible for conceding hard-won gains. But none of these will be remembered as true leaders. And as a student of history, Benjamin Netanyahu must know that to escape the trap of the past, a new way must be tried.

The question now is whether Netanyahu can be as courageous in securing the future of Israel as his father was in imagining it and his brother was in defending it.

It was the fate of Jonathan Netanyahu, in his heroic and all-too-brief time among the living, to battle but not to build. His younger brother, informed but not inhibited by these remembrances, now has the opportunity to step out of the shadows of the past, inscribe his name forever as one of Israel's most courageous sons, and create. It is the only thing that will ultimately make Yoni Netanyahu's sacrifice matter.

It's Time for an Independent Kurdistan

The Huffington Post, November 5, 2012

HAD THE COURSE OF HISTORY TAKEN A MODEST SWERVE, THE UNITED States and Kurdistan might have celebrated their independence on the very same day. It was July 4, 1187—825 years ago—that Saladin, Islam's greatest ruler, defeated 20,000 outmatched Crusaders at the bloody Battle of Hattin. The victory ultimately delivered Jerusalem into the hands of Saladin, the crown jewel of an Islamic caliphate stretching from the shores of Tunis through Cairo, Baghdad, and Damascus.

If the Kurds' most famous son had bothered to identify himself as such, it may well have been the beginning of a Kurdish empire to rival the Ottomans or the Persians. But Saladin fought for God and not for country, leaving his hapless compatriots at the mercy of Ottoman chieftains, British cartographers, and malevolent Arab strongmen.

Today, the 25 million Kurds clustered at the contiguous corners of Turkey, Iran, Iraq, and Syria are the largest ethnic group on earth without a formal homeland. As the US abandons Iraq to its own devices and Iran rattles uranium sabers, as Turkey cracks down on its Kurds and Saladin's Damascus descends into the unrestrained slaughter of Bashar Assad's, the millennium-long dream of an independent Kurdistan could be the answer to this unfolding Middle Eastern nightmare.

As with many conflicts in the region, the Kurdish dilemma has its roots in the fall of the Ottoman Empire. Guaranteed self-determination by the Allied powers, the Kurds signed the 1920 Treaty of Sèvres, only to watch the Europeans stand passively by as the Ottoman army officer Mustafa Kemal Atatürk cobbled together a country of his own, forming what is now Turkey out of the Kurds' promised land. In the years since, the Kurds have been massacred by the Iranian Revolutionary Guards, gassed by Saddam Hussein, and forgotten by the rest of the world. In Syria, their language is banned; in Turkey, a member of parliament with the temerity to pledge an oath "to the Turkish and Kurdish peoples" was released from a decade in jail—only to be resentenced this year.

With the Assad regime now crumbling, tensions between the Kurdish minority and their many tormentors, always tragic, are becoming a major geopolitical threat. Desperate to crush the Syrian revolution in its infancy, Assad has transferred troops away from the Kurdish provinces to the north, leaving a power vacuum into which two Kurdish political parties have stepped. If Assad falls, Syria will splinter into religiously or ethnically homogenous mini-states, one of which will almost certainly be under Kurdish control. Coupled with the recent emergence of a relatively independent Kurdish region in Iraq, this would create something of a league of semi-autonomous Kurdish states between the northeast regions of Syria and Iraq.

This combustible state of affairs greatly alarms Turkey, which has waged a bloody, three-decade civil war against its 14 million Kurds, claiming 40,000 lives. Although it has supported regime change in Syria, the Turkish government has "an almost pathological fear" of a greater Kurdistan, and can be expected to strenuously resist any attempt at Kurdish unification. Turkish tanks now patrol the shared border with Syria, intent on preventing any activity from spilling over into its borders.

Should that powder keg ignite, Turkey—a NATO ally—could very well drag the United States into a cross-border shooting war with Syria, with Russia quite possibly propping up its Syrian proxy. Meanwhile Iran, boasting an infamously brutal history with its own Kurds, remains a regional wild card, spinning nuclear centrifuges as fast as possible.

The dispossessed have become dangerously destabilizing. The overlooked can no longer be overlooked. And what was once a Middle Eastern flashpoint may yet become a safety valve for spiking regional tensions.

It will not be easy, but the uncertainty and plasticity in the region today offers an opportunity to secure a Kurdish homeland and remedy the capricious map-making of the early 20th century. Iraq is threatening to split into the pre-Iraq Sunni, Shia, and Kurdish divisions of the Ottoman Empire, with the Kurds semi-independent and the Iran-allied Shiites ruling the Sunnis. Iran's economy is in free fall. Syria will soon have no central control and no choice. And while no country is eager to surrender a fifth of its population, Turkey would do well to get ahead of this issue—ending the vicious, ongoing war with the Kurdistan Workers' Party (PKK), [thereby] saving countless lives and positioning itself to reap the benefits of a long-term strategic alliance to counterbalance Iranian influence. Not to mention, membership in the European Union will forever be out of reach for a Turkey at war with itself.

For proof of what's possible, look no further than Iraqi Kurdistan, a pro-American, pro-Israel, and semi-autonomous parliamentary democracy most Americans have never heard of. Nurtured by an American no-fly zone in the aftermath of the first Gulf War, the Kurdistan Regional Government (KRG) was established under the Iraqi constitution in 2005, a stunning testament to the success of Muslim representative government. Of more than 4,800 American soldiers killed in the brutal battles for Iraq, not a single one has lost their life—and no foreigner has been kidnapped—within the borders of Iraqi Kurdistan. Boasting two international airports, a booming oil industry, and a dawning respect for the rights of women, this 15,000-square-mile territory of nearly 4 million Kurds is the one part of President George W. Bush's "Mission Accomplished" that was actually accomplished.

Building on this unanticipated success, the United States should rethink its previous opposition to an independent Greater Kurdistan and recognize that the advantages of a friendly, democratic, and strategically positioned ally far outweigh the outdated assumption that the Kurds' national liberation would result in regional conflagration. At this point, inaction is far more likely to provoke continued regional conflict. Whether that means calling for US-brokered talks with Turkey or a temporary UN peacekeeping force, for sanctions or scaled-up foreign investment, the United States should make every effort to incentivize the consolidation and emergence of a single, stable, secure Kurdish homeland.

After a thousand years of turning a thousand blind eyes, the world can't keep kicking the Kurdish can down the road. Somewhere along that blood-stained road to Damascus, the region needs to experience this epiphany—and soon. The first major protests in Syria began outside the Ummayad Mosque, Islam's fourth-holiest site and the location of Saladin's tomb. Saladin's descendants, it seems, are on the march once more. These Kurds want to be heard. Will the United States —and the world—listen?

What Putin Should Say at the United Nations

The World Post, September 28, 2015

MY FELLOW DELEGATES: FOR THE PAST YEAR, FROM THIS PODIUM AND others, we have heard variations on the same message: that the militants of the Islamic State of Iraq and the Levant are a regional threat in the Middle East; that while their methods are brutal, ISIL is simply a "jayvee team" that grew out of Al Qaeda in Iraq; that the real danger in the region is the government in Damascus; and that by training so-called moderate Syrian fighters while supporting a campaign of air strikes led by the United States and a coalition of willing partners, it will be possible to "degrade and ultimately destroy" the Islamic State while bringing stability to Syria.

I have come here today because I think it's time that we stop lying to ourselves.

ISIL has been neither degraded nor destroyed. Despite more than 5,000 air strikes over the past year, Islamic State militants now control swaths of territory in Syria and Iraq. ISIL followers have threatened to carry out attacks from Scandinavia to Southeast Asia, from Nigeria to China, from here in the United States to my home in Russia. Even the chairman of the US Joint Chiefs of Staff has admitted that the campaign is now at a stalemate.

The highly touted $500 million effort to train "moderate" Syrian fighters has resulted in just five new recruits. Not five thousand. Not five hundred. Five. Meanwhile, 4 million refugees have flooded into Turkey, Lebanon, and Jordan. And nearly 500,000 refugees have reportedly made it across the Mediterranean to Europe, where they are encountering various forms of resistance, including tear gas, barbed wire fences, and water cannons. Far from a contained regional threat, this is now a global crisis of the highest order.

The most pressing question in Syria today is not who rules in Damascus. It is whether the world can come together—as it did more than 70 years ago—to turn back the increasingly barbaric and growing presence of ISIL across the region before it is too late. The one thing we can say for sure is what another refugee, Albert Einstein, said years after fleeing the Nazi regime in 1933: "The definition of insanity is doing the same thing over and over and expecting a different result." It is insane for the West and its allies to continue down this same path. I am here today to propose a different way forward.

Let us acknowledge from the start that we will not see eye to eye on the four-year civil war in Syria. We have a fundamental disagreement on the nature of the conflict. The popular storyline in Western capitals is that a group of homegrown secular rebels rose up four years ago against a dictator in Damascus—and that dictator, with the help of Teheran and Moscow, has slaughtered tens of thousands of his own people in a viciously desperate attempt to remain in power.

But anybody on the ground in Syria—which, by choice, does not include a single Western power, since air power is all the United States and its allies have had an appetite for—will tell you that it's a false narrative. The rebels fighting the secular Alawite government in Syria today are not, and have never been, either secular or homegrown. They are, and always have been, a group of jihadi warriors funded by Sunni interests in the Middle East and elsewhere, who used the chaotic aftermath of America's withdrawal from Iraq in 2010 to launch a new front in the 1,600-year-old Sunni-Shia war. These are the people who control more than 50 percent of the territory in Syria today.

It is a false choice to believe that the rebels fighting the legitimate government of Syria are categorically distinct from the jihadists of Islamic State: ideologically, they are cut from the same cloth. That tens of thousands of innocent people have been caught in the crossfire—as happens sadly in every civil war—is both tragic and unassailable. But to place the responsibility entirely on the barrel bombs of one side is to willfully overlook the extent to which the other side has almost gleefully used innocent civilians as human shields to spread terror and sow the seeds of anarchy in towns and cities across Syria.

I say this with the knowledge that I won't likely convince those in the West who believe otherwise. I do hope, however, that those who believe that Bashar al-Assad is entirely at fault in Syria respect the fact that those of us who do not share that view believe just as strongly in our truth as you do in yours.

Let us also put aside the history that led us to this moment: of America's support for the very Islamists that became Al Qaeda as far back as 1979, when those same extremists were shooting at my brothers in Afghanistan. Let us put aside the fact that the United States impulsively overthrew Saddam Hussein in the days after 9/11—even though he had nothing to do with the attacks on the United States—and that US-led mismanagement after the invasion led to a power vacuum that persecuted Sunnis and lit the spark for what would become the Islamic State. Let's also remember that much of the initial funding for the Islamic State came from US dollars used to bribe Sunni tribesmen to rise up against Al Qaeda during the so-called US surge in 2007. It's one of the reasons why reports about ISIL were reportedly doctored by the Pentagon.

But wherever you stand on Assad, none of us want Syria to go the way of Iraq or Libya, whose current anarchy was the direct result of a NATO-led campaign to oust its longtime leaders without a second's thought for what might come next. That is where we stand today in Syria. Should the Assad government fall in the near future, the likely Islamic State takeover of Damascus would make what is already Europe's worst refugee crisis since the Second World War pale by comparison. I believe it is incumbent on all of us, therefore, to do whatever is necessary to support the government of Syria in its fight against ISIL—starting with Islamic State–held strongholds in the north of the country—while working to improve the situation so Syrian citizens don't feel a need to migrate in the first place.

That is why Russia has moved aggressively into Syria in recent weeks at the invitation of the Syrian government, and why we are moving additional tanks, fighter jets, warships, and military advisors into the territory. We are improving airport landing strips to accept additional armaments and beefing up protections around Syrian ports. We are lending our military intelligence to help counter Islamic State positions, and we are working with the Syrian army to prevent attacks on Damascus from the sky with anti-aircraft support around the capital.

We are willing to take a broader leadership role in the region alongside troops from Iran that are already working to counter the Islamic State threat today, which are also in Syria at the invitation of the Assad government. But we cannot defeat this threat alone. Our chance of success will be much greater if we are able to join forces and counter this historic threat together, just as we did 70 years ago. Airpower alone cannot resolve this crisis. Only an international coalition of air power and ground forces will be able to stop ISIL.

That is why I am proposing today that East and West join forces, under the auspices of the United Nations, to end this threat. We can discuss the right combination of air strikes, on-the-ground intelligence, and regional alliances that will put ISIL on the run once and for all. In turn, we will work with the Assad government to begin cease-fire negotiations in the four-year civil war. I understand that working hand in hand with the Russian government and the Iranian government to defeat a common threat is something that no Western nation has had much practice [with] in the past seven decades. But that is not an excuse for not trying.

I realize that the Syrian people are reluctant to have even more foreigners enter their land, and that the West, in particular, is disliked more than ever. A recent poll found that 80 percent of Syrians believe it was Western governments that created ISIL. You may not have a lot of credibility in the region, but together, we can and we should try to defeat this threat there so it doesn't spread here.

Working together to prevent global calamity is the promise we made to each other through the United Nations seven decades ago. On the 70th anniversary, let's realize that promise in practice. In the end, that's the highest tribute we can pay.

It's Time to Kick Erdoğan's Turkey Out of NATO

The World Post, February 23, 2016

IT HAS ALWAYS BEEN A MATTER OF HISTORICAL CURIOSITY THAT ONE OF the American diplomats who was deeply involved in the creation of the North Atlantic Treaty Organization was named Achilles. As the head of the State Department's Office of Western European Affairs after World War II and the eventual US vice deputy of the North Atlantic Council, Theodore Achilles played a lead role in drafting the treaty that was designed to deter an expansionist Soviet Union from engaging in an armed attack on Western Europe. With 11 European nations joining the United States as founding members in 1949, the alliance quickly grew to include two other countries— Greece and Turkey—by 1952 and today encompasses 28 members.

It's a reflection of how difficult it was to imagine that any member of the organization would betray the rest of the alliance that to this day, NATO has no formal mechanism to remove a member in bad standing or to even define what would constitute "bad standing." Yet nearly three decades after the collapse of the Soviet Union, NATO members still make the same solemn vow to one another, known as Article 5, that they made in 1949: that an attack against any member state will be considered an attack against all member states, and will draw an immediate and mutual response. For nearly seven decades, this combination of factors has been the potential Achilles' heel of NATO: that one day, its members would be called to defend the actions of a rogue member who no longer shares the values of the alliance but whose behavior puts its "allies" in danger while creating a nightmare scenario for the global order.

After 67 years, that day has arrived: Turkey, which for half a century was a stalwart ally in the Middle East while proving that a Muslim-majority nation could be both secular and democratic, has moved so far away from its NATO allies that it is widely acknowledged to be defiantly supporting the Islamic State in Syria in its war against the West. Since Islamist strongman

Recep Tayyip Erdoğan came to power in 2003, Turkey has taken a harshly authoritarian turn, embracing Islamic terrorists of every stripe while picking fights it can't finish across the region—including an escalating war with 25 million ISIS-battling Kurds and a cold war turning hot with Russia, whose plane it rashly shot down in November. With those fights coming home to roost—as bombs explode in its cities and with enemies at its borders—Turkish leaders are now demanding unconditional NATO support, with Prime Minister Ahmet Davutoglu declaring on Saturday that he expects "our US ally to support Turkey, with no ifs or buts."

But it's too little, too late. NATO shouldn't come to Turkey's defense—instead, it should begin proceedings immediately to determine if the lengthy and growing list of Turkish transgressions against the West, including its support for Islamic terrorists, have merit. And if they do—and they most certainly do—the Alliance's supreme decision-making body, the North Atlantic Council, should formally oust Turkey from NATO for good before its belligerence and continual aggression drags the international community into World War III.

This is an action that is long overdue. As I argued five years ago, "Erdoğan, who is Islamist to the core, and who once famously declared that 'the mosques are our barracks, the domes our helmets, the minarets our bayonets, and the faithful our soldiers'—seems to see himself as the Islamic leader of a post–Arab Spring Muslim world." He has spent the past 13 years dismantling every part of Turkish society that made it secular and democratic, remodeling the country (as Caroline Glick of the Center for Security Policy once wrote) "into a hybrid of Putinist autocracy and Iranian theocracy." Last fall, he even went so far as to praise the executive powers once granted to Adolf Hitler.

Under Erdoğan's leadership, our NATO ally has arrested more journalists than China, jailed thousands of students for the crime of free speech, and replaced secular schools with Islamic-focused madrassas. He has publicly flaunted his support for Hamas and the Muslim Brotherhood while accusing longtime ally Israel of "crimes against humanity," violated an arms ban to Gaza, bought an air defense system (and nearly missiles) from the Chinese in defiance of NATO, and denied America the use of its own air base to conduct strikes during the Iraqi War and later against Islamic terrorists in Syria. As Western allies fought to help repel Islamic State fighters in the town of

Kobani in western Syria two years ago, Turkish tanks sat quietly just across the border.

In fact, there is strong evidence (compiled by Columbia University) that Turkey has been "tacitly fueling the ISIS war machine." There is evidence to show that Turkey, as *New Eastern Outlook* recently put it, allowed "jihadists from around the world to swarm into Syria by crossing through Turkey's territory"; that Turkey, as journalist Ted Galen Carpenter writes, "has allowed ISIS to ship oil from northern Syria into Turkey for sale on the global market"; that Erdoğan's own son has collaborated with ISIS to sell that oil, which is "the lifeblood of the death-dealing Islamic State"; and that supply trucks have been allowed to pass freely across Turkey en route to ISIS fighters. There is also "evidence of more direct assistance," as *Forbes* puts it, "providing equipment, passports, training, medical care, and perhaps more to Islamic radicals"—and that Erdoğan's government, according to a former US ambassador, worked directly with the Al Qaeda affiliate in Syria, the Al-Nusrah Front.

While Ankara pretends to take military action against ISIS, with its obsessive view of the Kurds, it has engaged in a relentless series of artillery strikes against the Syrian Kurdish People's Protection Units (YPG) that are routing ISIS troops in northern Syria. The Kurds are the largest ethnic group on earth without a homeland—25 million Sunni Muslims who live at the combined corners where Syria, Iraq, Iran, and Turkey meet. Turkey has waged a bloody, three-decade civil war against its 14 million Kurds—known as the Kurdistan Workers' Party, or PKK—claiming more than 40,000 lives. The most recent peace process failed when Turkey again targeted the PKK, plunging the southeast of the country back into war while increasingly worrying Erdoğan that Syrian and Turkish Kurds will join forces just across Turkey's border.

The Kurds, like the Turks, are sometimes seen through the lens of who they used to be, and not who they are now. In 1997, Turkey convinced the United States to put the PKK on its list of terrorist organizations, and Erdoğan claims Syria's Kurds are guilty by association. But in fact, the YPG has worked so closely with the United States against Islamic terrorists that the *Washington Post* recently referred to its members as "US proxy forces." The Kurds—whether in Syria, Iraq, or Turkey—are, by all accounts, the fiercest and most courageous fighters on the ground in the war against the

Islamic State in both Iraq and Syria. What's more, the group represents a powerful alternative to the apocalyptic vision of Islamic jihadists, embodying what has been described as "a level of gender equality, a respect for secularism and minorities, and a modern, moderate, and ecumenical conception of Islam that are, to say the least, rare in the region."

The Turkish government has tried to lay blame for recent bombings in Ankara at the feet of the YPG in an attempt to sway the United States to oppose the Kurds. An exasperated Erdoğan railed about the loyalties of the West, accused the United States of creating a "sea of blood" in the region by supporting the Kurds, and issued an ultimatum: he demanded that the time had come for America to choose between Turkey and the Kurds.

I couldn't agree more: the time has come for the United States to choose the Kurds over Erdoğan's Turkey.

Critics argue that the Kurds are unwilling to take the fight to ISIS beyond their borders, but this actually presents the United States with an opportunity. In exchange for fighting ISIS throughout the region, an international coalition can offer the Kurds their own state. A Kurdish state would become a critical regional ally for the United States and play an invaluable role in filling the power vacuum that has emerged in the Middle East. With the help of the United States, a Kurdish state could also help to accommodate Syrian refugees that have overwhelmed immigration systems in Turkey and Europe. In the long term, it would serve as a valuable regional partner to stabilize the region, and it would set a strong example of successful democracy. In other words, Kurdistan could play the role that Turkey used to play.

It's been said that the difference between being Achilles and almost being Achilles is the difference between living and dying. NATO can do without an Achilles' heel: It's time to kick Turkey out for good.

Three New Realities in the Middle East for the Next American President

The Huffington Post, February 18, 2016

THERE WAS A TELLING MOMENT IN LAST SATURDAY NIGHT'S REPUBLICAN presidential debate that says a lot about America's misadventures in the Middle East over the past 15 years. Donald Trump, the real estate developer and current front-runner who has done everything from calling for a ban on Muslim immigrants to ridiculing the war record of senator and former prisoner of war John McCain, finally did something to cause the Republican establishment to turn on him.

Questioned about the presidency of George W. Bush, Trump said that the Bush administration "lied" its way into the Iraq War by hyping weapons of mass destruction; called the invasion itself a "disaster"; and reminded the audience that "the World Trade Center came down" on Bush's watch. It was too much for the South Carolina audience, which booed him, and the other candidates, who unloaded on him. The irony is that the breaking point for Republicans was hearing Trump say something that was true.

The first step to solving a problem is to admit that we have one. It's time to admit what we all know to be true: American policy in the Middle East over the past 15 years has made a bad situation worse. In fact, for all intents and purposes, America no longer has a Middle East policy, at least not one grounded in today's reality. If the next president hopes to make the world safer, the United States needs to embrace a foreign policy that recognizes that the Cold War is over and deals with the Middle East as it is today—not the way it used to be.

It's not just Republicans who are stuck in denial. Supporters of President Barack Obama assert that he has done what he set out to do in the Middle East, from bringing US troops home from the wars Bush started in Iraq and Afghanistan, to killing 9/11 mastermind Osama bin Laden, to striking a deal to limit Iran's nuclear capabilities. Yet Democrats seem indifferent to Obama's policy of doing nothing in the region since Egyptians forced the resignation of longtime US ally President Hosni Mubarak five years ago last week. They seem convinced that everything that has happened since has had little to do with Obama's stated policy of "leading from behind"—not the collapse of Libya, Yemen, and Iraq, nor the ruin of Syria, nor the rightward drift of Israel. Not the implosion of the Palestinian Authority; the Islamization of formerly secular ally Turkey; the horrific spread of the Islamic State; the Iranian takeover of governments in Beirut, Damascus, Baghdad, and the Yemeni capital of Sana'a; or the reassertion of Russian power in the region for the first time in decades.

But the reality, as journalist and Middle East scholar Yaroslav Trofimov has written, is that "since . . . 2011, America's ability to influence the region has been sapped by a growing conviction that a risk-averse Washington, focused on a foreign-policy pivot to Asia, just doesn't want to exercise its traditional Middle Eastern leadership role anymore." As James Jeffrey, a former US ambassador to Iraq and Turkey, told Trofimov last fall, neither allies nor adversaries believe the United States will use its muscle "to protect our friends." Because of this, "nobody is willing to take any risks."

In a perverse way, Bush's misguided adventurism and Obama's indifference have combined to make real the goal of uniting "Muslim and non-Muslims" that Obama articulated in a 2009 speech in Cairo: across the region, friends and foes alike are united in saying they don't trust America, they don't fear America, and they don't believe a single word that America has to say.

It wasn't always this way. From the end of World War II until the fall of the Berlin Wall, American policy was clear: containment. We supported major regional powers that opposed Soviet expansion—namely, Turkey, Israel, Saudi Arabia and Iran, with Egypt taking Iran's place after the Islamic Revolution of 1979—and together, we held in check those nations (Iraq, Syria) backed by Moscow. After the Soviet Union collapsed, we shifted our policy to encourage peace between Israelis and Palestinians, worked to contain Iran and Iraq, and continued to support Arab regimes that supplied the United States with oil while overlooking their human rights abuses.

With the invasion of Iraq, all of that changed. The United States shifted from a policy of containment to an ambitious—some say "delusional"—policy of direct regional transformation. America had no plan for who should rule Iraq after Saddam Hussein, a Sunni, fell. Those who took his place, all Shiite, turned the post-war period into a Sunni witch hunt, radicalizing Saddam's former Sunni soldiers into ISIS warriors. In the process, the centuries-long conflict between Sunni and Shiite Islam moved to center-stage, driven by Sunni Saudi Arabia and Shiite Iran, while the Israeli-Palestinian conflict became a sideshow. Meanwhile, Obama has, as scholar Steven Cook writes, "erred in a variety of ways, whether it has been . . . unwillingness to consider intervention in Syria when it might have made a difference, declaring phantom 'red lines,' getting roped into a Libyan intervention . . . or placing the United States in a position where it needs a nuclear agreement with Tehran more than Iran needs a nuclear agreement with Washington."

The next president needs a new playbook for the Middle East—one grounded in three new realities that are shaping the future of the region today.

First, Islamist terrorism, starting with ISIS, is the most dangerous threat the West faces today, and defeating it must be the centerpiece of our policy going forward.

In the past year, brutal Islamist attacks from Paris to Jakarta to a Russian jetliner to San Bernardino, California, have signaled a tactical change on ISIS's part, making it clear that the group's attacks are now going global. If ISIS is allowed to consolidate its gains in Syria or Iraq, the threat to US security and regional allies will increase considerably. Just as the litmus test during the Cold War was "with us or against us" in the fight against communism, the United States should work to unify all those who oppose Sunni fanatics in ISIS and other Islamist militant groups under one strategy. If that means partnering with Russia through the United Nations, supplying the Kurds in Iraq and Syria, defending Iraqi Sunnis from Shiites in Baghdad, or engaging with Iran's Revolutionary Guards to defeat ISIS fighters—we should do what it takes.

Second, the United States should accept that the region is shifting back to more natural borders and not try to maintain the artificial lines drawn by the West a century ago.

The Middle East is no longer the Middle East that exists today on maps. The artificial Sykes-Picot line drawn by Britain and France to create Iraq and Syria in 1916 is already being worn away. Iraq has largely reverted to the three provinces—one Shiite, one Sunni, one Kurd—that existed during the Ottoman Empire. An independent Kurdistan could very well become America's greatest ally in the region as Kurds continue to defeat ISIS with regularity. Sunni Muslims could run a new country that includes part of present-day Iraq and a pluralistic Sunni-majority Syria. Just as the civil war in the Balkans in the 1990s saw the region revert to more natural borders, America should let the Middle East evolve back to its natural lines and spheres of influence.

Third, some of America's longtime friends are no longer acting like friends, and we should stop treating them as friends.

It's time for America to look beyond history to see our longtime allies for what they are now. Saudi Arabia, which America no longer needs for oil, has spent billions building anti-Western madrassas across the globe to create the next generation of jihadists while funding Islamist terrorist groups from ISIS to Al Qaeda. Our once-secular NATO ally, Turkey, is being transformed under President Recep Tayyip Erdoğan into one of the most virulently Islamist, authoritarian countries in the region, aligning itself with Hamas while opposing US interests at every turn. Pakistan will soon have the world's third-largest nuclear arsenal while providing a safe haven to Islamist terrorists. Even Israel continues to build settlements at an alarming rate in Palestinian territories while openly challenging US leadership. It's time to say as clearly as possible: change your ways or the party is over—including all financial, military, and security support.

If the history of the Middle East has taught us anything, it is that nobody follows the sound of an uncertain trumpet. Somewhere between the incompetence of George W. Bush and the indifference of Barack Obama, the region stopped listening to America. It's not too late for the next president to regain America's historic leadership position in the Middle East. But it will only happen if we leave the Cold War playbook behind and see the new world for what it is—for good and bad.

Where Have You Gone, Harry Truman?

The World Post, March 3, 2016

SEVENTY YEARS AGO THIS WEEK, IN A QUIET CORNER OF IRAN, THE COLD War between the United States and the Soviet Union began in earnest over a missed deadline. For four years, American, British, and Soviet troops had been stationed in Iran, invited by the government there to help protect Persian oil fields from Hitler's army. But there was an important caveat, agreed to in a 1942 treaty: all troops had to be gone within six months of the end of World War II. As the war wound down, Washington and London successfully pressed Tehran for oil concessions, and withdrew troops on time. But Moscow, denied the oil it believed it was due, found an excuse to stay— coming to the aid of Iranian Kurdish rebels in the northern regions of Iran. That's where Soviet troops still sat when deadline day came and went on March 2, 1946, to the great displeasure of the person who mattered most— US president Harry S. Truman.

By now, Truman was convinced the Soviets were bent on global expansion and could not be trusted. He decided that Iran was the first place the West would make its stand. Appealing to the newly created United Nations to condemn Soviet aggression, Truman issued a clear warning to Moscow that continued occupation would be met with an overwhelming military response from America. Three weeks later, the Soviets backed down. While some historians argue that the real reason the Red Army withdrew is because the Kremlin managed to wring oil concessions from Iran, the fact is that when those concessions later failed to materialize, Soviet troops never went back: Moscow was afraid to cross Truman's red line.

Seven decades on, the civil war in Syria seems like a cruel bookend to the Iran Crisis of 1946. The power, clarity, and sense of purpose that defined American policy in the region for more than half a century since Truman is embodied today not by the president of the United States, but by the president of Russia—who projects confidence and force despite a teetering

Russian economy and a weakened Russian military. For all the wrong reasons, Russia seems strong, America seems weak, and US leadership across the Middle East is in full retreat.

Today, we are living Harry Truman's playbook in reverse.

Now, as then, America's president drew a red line, in Syria in 2012, threatening that if Syrian leader Bashar al-Assad used chemical weapons against his own people in that country's brutal civil war, America would respond with force. But this time, in 2013, Assad crossed that line, and America did nothing, causing what has been called "enormous, perhaps irretrievable, damage to American credibility." It signaled to dictators everywhere that America would tolerate aggression—and it was no accident that Russia invaded Ukraine and soon after annexed Crimea.

Now, as then, a Russian leader bent on expansion has used the excuse of a rebel uprising to aggressively occupy a Middle Eastern country with weapons and troops. But this time, those actions were taken not in spite of American leadership, but because of the absence of American leadership, by a US president whose policy has been described as "a study in passivity and moral confusion." In fact, Pulitzer Prize–winning journalist Seymour Hersh recently reported that the US Joint Chiefs of Staff were so unnerved by the Obama administration's policy of arming "unvetted Syrian rebels" to overthrow Assad—rebels which the Chiefs were convinced had jihadist ties—that they worked to undermine the policy by indirectly sharing US intelligence with Assad himself.

Now, as then, the world watches as Russia and America attempt to resolve a tense—and in this case, tragic—situation with a tenuous "cessation of hostilities" that may end the battle but won't end the wider war across the region. But this time, it is Moscow dictating the terms of the cease-fire, including the understanding that Russian forces will likely remain as a presence in Syria indefinitely—despite months of cold-blooded Russian attacks that have killed so many civilians that Amnesty International says they "may constitute war crimes."

If Harry Truman had acted in Iran in 1946 like Barack Obama has acted in Syria in 2016, the Soviets never would have left.

Seventy years from now, we will likely know why the Obama administration decided to step back from American leadership in Syria. Maybe it was because the president, having brought home troops from the wars

George W. Bush started in Iraq and Afghanistan, didn't want to get involved in another Middle East quagmire. Maybe he thought the conflict was less about power and more about whose pipeline got to carry Middle Eastern gas across Syria to Europe, and had no appetite to trade more American lives for oil. Maybe he didn't foresee that the confluence of Sunni Muslim disempowerment at the hands of Iran-supported Shiite governments in Baghdad and Damascus would lead to the creation of a barbaric, jihadist threat like the Islamic State or spark a global crisis as refugees fled war zones. Or maybe he and his team were simply overmatched and cast adrift by the changes wrought by the Arab Spring, which unmoored decades-old US policies and alliances, with no clear next steps.

Whatever the reason for inaction, the bragging rights now handed to Russian president Vladimir Putin are clear. He is seen as having rescued his closest ally in the region, shored up Russia's only naval base on the Mediterranean Sea, and brought stability to a regional crisis in ways the United States and its allies would not—for the first time ever. As Middle East scholar Frederic C. Hof writes, Putin is essentially in a position now to "force the United States into a de facto alliance with Assad against ISIS, thereby enabling him to tell Russians that the American worldwide regime change campaign he has vowed to defeat has been stopped cold in Syria, that the American president has been forced to eat his 'Assad should step aside' words, and that Russia has returned to great power status—thereby ending decades of humiliation." At some level, we should be grateful that Putin acted when it became clear that Obama would do nothing.

It's too late for Barack Obama to earn back the respect of both friend and foe across the region. That doesn't mean the United States shouldn't try to create a more lasting peace—partnering with NATO allies to make the case for a no-fly zone across Syria, creating a safe haven for refugees on the Turkish border, and working toward a negotiated settlement, which is Moscow's best exit strategy. But ultimately, solving this crisis and restoring American leadership will be a job left to his successor.

So what is the next president of the United States to do? Three things.

First, take the advice of the chairman of the International Institute for Strategic Studies, Francoise Heisbourg, who suggested to journalist Celestine Bohlen last week that "the next US president is going to have to demonstrate early on—in circumstances that he or she would have preferred to avoid"—that America's inattention in the Middle East the past five years "was an Obama moment, not an America moment."

Second, realize that the region is broken, and be willing to discuss new lines in the sands of what was Syria: Alawites and pro-Assad religious and ethnic groups in a radically shrunken Syria; an independent Sunnistan for Sunni Muslims that includes areas of Syria and Iraq; and an independent Kurdistan that unites Syrian, Iraqi, Turkish, and Iranian Kurds at the point where those four countries connect.

Third, recognize that defeating Islamic terrorism, starting with ISIS, is the greatest urgency the West faces, and make it the centerpiece of our new policy in the Middle East. The United States should lead the global coalition against the Islamic State and be willing to partner with any nation (including Russia and Iran) that works with us to defeat ISIS while punishing any nation (including longtime allies Turkey and Saudi Arabia) who continue to support Islamic terrorists.

Lastly, and less officially, use the levers of diplomacy to show Russia that the United States will stand up for its interests. Make Putin feel like he's in the big leagues again, by treating Russia with the respect he feels it is due. But more quietly, begin to move US troops from Germany to the doorstep of Russia in Ukraine and the Baltics, to make Putin think twice about any further aggression. End the ban on exports of gas outside of the United States, and begin to explore how American oil and gas could replace the Russian supply that Europe relies on for a third of its energy needs. And subtly remind the Kremlin how quickly the United States could cut the access of Russian banks to global markets.

That's what Harry Truman would do, because he would understand: strength is the only language Vladimir Putin understands. It's time for the United States to get fluent again.

IRAQ WAR

Saddam's Regime in Iraq Should Be the Next Tyranny to Fall

International Herald Tribune, November 28, 2001

ALBERT EINSTEIN ONCE DEFINED INSANITY AS DOING THE SAME THING over and over and expecting a different result. If he were alive today, he might have in mind US policy toward Iraq.

For more than a decade, Washington policymakers have opted to wait for the Iraqi military to overthrow Saddam Hussein, instead of providing serious support for dissidents inside and outside Iraq.

Since September 11, America's attention has properly been focused on Osama bin Laden, the Al Qaeda terror network, and their Taliban protectors. United States and Western security demanded that bin Laden and the Taliban be the first priority in any anti-terror campaign.

With the military victory on the ground nearly secure, and bin Laden's demise sure to follow, there seems little appetite in Washington or in the capitals of Europe to go after the Iraqi dictator now.

That is a mistake. Iraq is central to the war on terrorism.

It has chemical and biological weapons and is dangerously close to having a nuclear arsenal. No one is willing to bank on Saddam's reluctance to use weapons of mass destruction or make them available to a terrorist organization. Unless the West takes him on, once and for all, George W. Bush's prediction of a long war, with many more US military and civilian casualties, will probably turn out to be prophetic.

Iraq was the primary focus of American foreign and military policy during the Gulf War. Since then, the United States and its allies have been content to "contain" Iraq through economic sanctions and a flawed (and now failed) effort to identify and destroy Saddam's capacity to produce weapons of mass destruction.

If President Bush is serious about pursuing "nations that provide aid or safe haven to terrorism," then Iraq must be next on the list of captive countries to be liberated.

The Northern Alliance's march through Afghanistan demonstrates that even the most entrenched dictatorial regime will bow to a supposedly toothless insurgency when faced with massive US airpower and US logistical assistance on the ground. And Saddam has even less support within Iraq than the Taliban had in Afghanistan. Unlike the Taliban, who come from the majority Pashtuns, Sunni Muslims are a minority in Iraq, an artificial country with a majority of Shiites and Kurds. Unlike the Taliban, who had financial and military support from Pakistan, Saudi Arabia, and the United Arab Emirates, the Iraqi regime is neither supported nor trusted by neighbors.

[Yet] Washington seems wedded to the failed approach of relying on a military coup d'état.

A decade ago, as Iraqi forces fled toward Baghdad, the United States waited in vain for a coup, while the Iraqi Kurds and Shiites it had encouraged to revolt were attacked and killed.

In 1996, the CIA, supported by Saudi Arabia, organized an officer-led coup that failed. The United States allowed what was supposed to be a safe haven for opposition forces in northern Iraq to be annihilated. Little has changed. Washington is increasing its political ties with exiled Iraqi commanders, but it continues to give the cold shoulder to the opposition Iraqi National Congress. Yet only US political and military support for a popular uprising is likely to succeed anytime soon. Most Iraqis despise Saddam. Like Afghans who welcomed liberation after suffering silently under the rule of the Taliban, Iraqis would be delighted to build a post-Saddam Iraq. US policymakers, under pressure from European capitals, fear that an attack on Iraq would blow apart the fragile anti-terrorism coalition. It probably would. But holding the coalition together should be a means to achieving its anti-terrorism goals, not the goal in itself.

Ending the threat of terrorism requires the West to address the political, economic, and cultural issues that give rise to terrorism. That begins by getting US troops out of Saudi Arabia; resolving the Israeli-Palestinian issue; and encouraging more political, economic, and social freedom in the Muslim world.

With Saddam gone, US troops would have nothing to protect the Gulf states from. And Israel would be more likely to make the concessions necessary to achieve peace with the Palestinians. With Saddam's regime overthrown, 23 million men and women could begin to breathe again as free people. The economy would be invigorated with foreign investment in reconstruction and in the oil industry.

A popular uprising that led to a popular government could allow Iraq to take its place alongside that of its northern neighbor, Turkey, as a secular Muslim democracy. The existence of a more modern Iraq would be a model for Saudi Arabia, Iran, Syria, and others.

If President Bush is serious, the United States and its allies must remove Saddam Hussein.

Governance after Saddam:
Change for the Better This Time

International Herald Tribune, October 15, 2002

IN JULY 1958, THE HEYDAY OF ARAB NATIONALISM, I WAS SAILING AROUND the Greek islands when our ketch was rocked by the wake of US warships steaming to Lebanon to defend Beirut's pro-Western government. British troops poured into Jordan to bolster 18-year-old King Hussein. Hussein's Hashemite cousin, 23-year-old King Faisal II of Iraq, was not so lucky.

Revolutionary Iraqi officers murdered him and proclaimed a republic. "The military men . . . gave more thought to the overthrow of the existing regime than to what would replace it"—writes Phebe Marr in her *Modern History of Iraq*—and "herein lay the source of most of the new regime's difficulties."

What came next were more coups and, eventually, the fascist regime of Saddam Hussein.

Today, what Iraq will look like after the shooting stops depends largely on the arrangements Washington makes before the shooting starts.

Iraq can become a source of hope to frustrated Muslims across the Middle East, a free, democratic, and economically modern nation—an attractive alternative to radical Islam. But only if the United States has a clear vision of what comes after Saddam.

Washington must reach an understanding on Iraq's territorial integrity with Turkey and Iran, two neighbors that can make or break a post-Saddam Iraq. Both oppose an independent Kurdistan that would incite restive Kurds in their countries. To forestall Turkish intervention, the United States must reach agreement on the prized Kirkuk oil fields, coveted by Turkey's Iraqi brethren, the Turkomen, and by Iraqi Arabs and Kurds.

Tehran must be assured that US action against Baghdad is not target practice for round two against the "axis of evil." A common US-Iranian policy against Saddam that includes the gradual lifting of economic sanctions against Tehran would weaken the ruling mullahs whose regime the sanctions ironically perpetuate.

Washington must pressure the fractious Iraqi opposition to form a provisional government-in-exile ready to assume power after Saddam. Ahmed Chalabi, head of the opposition umbrella group, the Iraqi National Congress, tells me that "fears of sectarian violence and a splintered Iraq are overblown." Opposition leaders should replicate last year's Bonn conference that chose an interim Afghan government and averted a power vacuum in Kabul after the Taliban's downfall. A leading choice to head an Iraqi provisional government is Chalabi.

His Iraqi National Congress would dismantle the pillars of Saddam's power—the Ba'ath Party, the security services, and the Republican Guard—and create a federal, democratic government that protects Iraq's ethnic and religious groups.

The United States and its allies will have to commit enough troops not only to win the war but to keep the peace.

Stabilizing Iraq could require $16 billion and 75,000 troops in the first year alone, according to one estimate discussed at a recent Senate hearing. A new army study reports that 100,000 peacekeepers would be needed to help reconstruct the country along the German model after World War II.

Economically, the biggest hurdle to rebuilding Iraq will be the crippling $300 billion in outstanding claims that Baghdad still owes from the 1991 Gulf War. The end of UN sanctions and an increase in oil exports will not be enough. An international conference, like the Tokyo conference for Afghanistan, will be needed to create a reconstruction fund. The world coughed up a meager $4.5 billion for Afghanistan. Iraq will need hundreds of billions.

As US troops spread out across Beirut in July 1958 and Iraqi mobs dragged the bodies of their victims through the streets of Baghdad, a *New York Times* editorial cautioned: "The forces at work in the Middle East are so complicated and powerful that the utmost care and diplomacy must be exercised to keep the action now being taken to the narrowest limits and the shortest time."

Forty-four years later, the forces at work in the Middle East are even more complicated. Removing Saddam will demand the same care and diplomacy. But the great task of replacing him with a stable, free, and prosperous Iraq will be neither narrow nor short.

Choosing a Template for Iraq: Unite or Perish

International Herald Times, October 3, 2003

"MY APOLOGIES TO ATTILA," GEORGES CLEMENCEAU ONCE REMARKED, "BUT the art of arranging how men are to live is more complex than the art of massacring them."

Free from the iron fist of Saddam Hussein, Iraqis now face the age-old question that has confronted multi-ethnic societies for centuries: How to arrange a nation from competing religious and ethnic groups that have often found it easier to massacre one another? A constitutional committee of Iraqis selected by the US-appointed Governing Council is now in the early stages of trying to find an answer.

From Quebec to the Balkans to Indonesia, there is no shortage of models to guide Iraqis in what—and what not—to do. How they choose from among the menu of options will likely decide whether they succeed as a modern, pluralistic democracy (think Switzerland) or sink into an orgy of ethno-religious bloodletting (think Bosnia).

Iraq's long-oppressed Shiites, who make up 60 percent of the population, will be the dominant player in any representative government. But political stability will also hinge on whether the nation's numerous ethnic minorities, religious sects, and tribal groups feel secure.

So far, the 25-member Governing Council and cabinet posts are apportioned among 13 Shiite Arabs, five Sunni Arabs, five Sunni Kurds, one Turkmen, and one Christian. Unable to agree on a single chief executive, the council has settled for an interim presidency that rotates monthly among nine of the most powerful members.

Here in Switzerland, often suggested as a possible model for Iraq, the presidency rotates among a federal council based on a "magic formula" that shares power among leading political parties. But Iraqis should be wary. Around the world, sharing executive power along ethnic or religious lines hasn't worked.

In Cyprus, designating a Greek Cypriot president and reserving the vice presidency and seats in parliament for Turkish Cypriots failed to prevent the division of the island along ethnic lines. Lebanon's "national pact" reserved the presidency and a parliamentary majority for Maronite Christians, the prime minister for a Shiite, and the assembly speaker for a Sunni. But when Muslims became a majority, it took a 16-year civil war for the minority Christians to acquiesce to a more equitable balance of power.

More recently, Northern Ireland's celebrated power-sharing assembly of Protestants and Catholics has been suspended and new elections delayed due to continued Irish Republican Army intransigence. In Bosnia, the ineffectual federal presidency rotates among a Muslim, a Croat, and a Serb, while Bosnians live in ethnically homogenous enclaves—countries-within-a-country, separated only by NATO-led foreign troops.

Failing to ensure the political, economic, or cultural rights of a geographically based minority is the quickest way for a central government to lose hearts and minds, and ultimately control of their country. Recall Serbia's loss of Slovenia, Croatia, Bosnia, Macedonia, and most likely Kosovo and Montenegro. Remember Ethiopia's loss of Eritrea, and Indonesia's loss of East Timor.

Failure to address historic grievances contributed to the ethnic slaughter of Tutsis by Hutus in Rwanda. Russia has retained Chechnya, but only by destroying it.

So, how to strike the right balance between a government strong enough to ensure stability yet limited enough to ensure the liberties of ethnic and religious minorities?

Iraqis should look to models that do work. In Quebec, Wales, Scotland, and Spain's Basque country, ethnically based separatist movements have been dampened by increased autonomy over political, economic, and cultural matters. In Switzerland, real power lies with cantons and communes where ethnic Germans, French, and Italians largely govern themselves. (An old joke: "Do you know who the president of Switzerland is? Neither do the Swiss.") Multiple layers of government allow Belgium's Dutch-speaking Flemings in the north and French-speaking Walloons in the south to control local affairs.

Germany's 16 *länder* (states) have their own constitutions and legislatures that govern over all matters that are not the exclusive right of the federal government, such as defense, foreign affairs, and finance. The spokesman for Ahmed Chalabi, the leader of the Iraqi National Congress opposition group and this month's Governing Council president, tells me, "We believe federalism is the only solution in Iraq, and we see the German constitution as a model. The important point is that it must be administrative federalism rather than ethnic federalism."

He warns that "a Bosnia solution would end up with Iraq as a two-state entity: one Arab and one Kurdish. We support a federal system based on Iraq's current 18 provinces, where each would have power akin to the German *länder*."

To succeed, a central Iraqi government would eventually have to control and redistribute the nation's oil proceeds under a revenue-sharing scheme that would give all groups and regions a powerful economic interest to remain in a united Iraq.

Ultimately, of course, whether Iraq's disparate ethnic groups and religious sects forge a common future lies in the hearts of ordinary Iraqis. The absence of widespread acts of revenge by Shiites following the assassination of their beloved Ayatollah Mohammed Baqir al-Hakim (presumably by former Sunni Baathists loyal to Hussein) gives cautious hope that cooler heads and the spirit of compromise will prevail.

In which case, Iraqis will be able to join Clemenceau in expressing their apologies to Attila.

Tempting the Curse:
Iraq Seeks the Blessings of Oil

Asia Times, July 20, 2005

CALL IT THE CURSE OF BABYLON. IN ANTIQUITY, THE MESOPOTAMIAN KING Nebuchadnezzar ignores the warnings of the prophet Daniel that his riches will be his ruin, and fulfills the Biblical curse that his beloved Babylon "shall become heaps."

Today, it is not pride but petroleum that poses one of the greatest challenges as Iraq tries to become the first oil state in history to succeed as a prosperous democracy. In fact, the warnings were clear long before the US invasion—the oil that many see as Iraq's greatest blessing may actually be its greatest curse.

Two years later, is Iraq breaking the oil curse that has turned so many petro-states into corrupt, impoverished heaps?

THE DANGER OF DEPENDENCE

Although Iraq's immediate challenge is too little oil due to insurgent sabotage that keeps production and exports below pre-war levels, its long-term task will be to avoid the perils of too much oil. History shows that the more a country relies on a natural resource like oil, the lower its growth rate as investment and labor are sucked from other sectors like manufacturing and agriculture.

But with oil accounting for 95 percent of government revenues, Iraq will have no choice but to rely on petrodollars for its long-term recovery. As N. K. al Bayati, director-general of Iraq's oil ministry, said of Iraq's goal to pump 6 million barrels per day by 2015, "We are very optimistic. We have to be. We have no alternative."

KEEPING POLITICIANS OUT OF THE OIL BUSINESS

With plans to reconstitute an Iraq National Oil Company by the end of this year, Baghdad will need to protect oil operations from political interference.

The oil ministry's ongoing talks with Norway's Statoil, Brazil's Petrobras, and Malaysia's Petronas give hope that Baghdad can learn the secret of these successful national oil companies—separation of powers between a ministry that limits itself to policymaking and a state-owned firm that controls production.

PETRODOLLARS FOR THE PEOPLE

Iraq risks repeating the abuses of Nigeria, Angola, and Venezuela, where vast oil wealth has done little for the impoverished masses. A series of United Nations and American audits have found that about $9 billion in oil revenues that have poured into the Development Fund for Iraq cannot be accounted for by either the US-led Coalition Provisional Authority or the successor interim Iraqi government. As the watchdog group Transparency International has reported, misuse of oil funds threatens to turn Iraq into "the biggest corruption scandal in history."

A more promising model—on the minds of some Iraqi leaders, according to a source familiar with their thinking—is Alaska's Permanent Fund, which sets aside 25 percent of oil revenues to pay yearly dividends to every Alaskan.

Distributing even a small fraction of Iraq's $20 billion in annual oil revenues directly to the people would give Iraqis a desperately needed economic boost and a powerful incentive to hold their leaders accountable for management of the country's oil wealth. The government, in turn, would gain a new source of taxation—and with it, reinforce the bonds of public representation.

COMBATING CORRUPTION

To their credit, Iraqis have retained the new anti-corruption structures left behind by the US occupation, including inspector generals in every ministry and commissions on fiscal and public integrity that audit government contracts and have investigated hundreds of government employees, including two former ministers in the interim government.

The oil sector, notorious for secret contracts, poses a special challenge. Recognizing that where there is no transparency, there can be no democracy, Baghdad should seize the chance to become an example of open government, with oil companies publishing what they pay for exploration and drilling rights.

SHARING THE WEALTH

Iraq's biggest challenge remains avoiding the fate of Congo and Sudan, where competition for control of oil fueled civil wars. Luay Towfik al Swaidi, a Sunni Arab whose father and namesake served as prime minister under the Iraqi monarchy, tells me that used wisely, oil could actually bring the country's disparate groups together: "Oil can be a source of national cooperation, not confrontation—so long as all Iraqis benefit fairly from the oil wealth of Iraq."

But what is "fair"? The constitution that must be drafted by August 15 will surely include some clause that Iraq's oil belongs to all the people of all the regions. But the constitution is unlikely to resolve either a precise formula for sharing oil revenues between the regions or the final status of the disputed oil-rich city of Kirkuk.

Iraq's best hope as a unified state therefore will hinge on a precarious Lebanese-style power-sharing arrangement where leadership positions and oil revenues are allocated along sectarian lines. Already, the oil minister has three deputies—a Shiite, a Kurd, and a Sunni, each looking out for their brethren's oil interests.

Like so much in Iraq, management of the country's oil wealth so far gives cause for both hope and alarm. The ancient warning holds true—what appears to be riches can just as easily lead to ruin.

Oil remains a temptress that beckons desperate nations with the illusion of easy money. If Iraqis can resist its temptations, their oil may yet be a blessing, not a curse.

Trickle Up: Iraq Needs a Jobs Surge

International Herald Tribune, December 27, 2007

NAME THESE MIDDLE EASTERN COUNTRIES.

Country A, plagued by decades of dictatorship, war, sanctions, corruption—and lately, vicious sectarian fighting—has a per capita income less than Mongolia's, and half its workforce is unemployed or underemployed.

Country B, with the world's third-largest oil reserves, enjoys 6 percent economic growth, has a stable currency, has slashed inflation, and—thanks to billion-dollar development and telecom deals—has been called "a capital magnet" by a leading investment publication.

Country A, of course, is Iraq. Believe it or not, so is Country B.

"From a macro-economic perspective," the deputy US Treasury secretary, Robert Kimmitt, recently told reporters in Baghdad, "we see a strong foundation having been laid by the Iraqi government." Of course, any macro-progress has yet to solve Iraq's most urgent micro-problem—the grim economic fortunes of ordinary Iraqis.

But if the new counterinsurgency strategy of General David Petraeus, the top US commander in Iraq, proves anything, it's that a dramatic change in tactics can still produce results. His "bottom up" strategy of putting small US combat outposts in dangerous neighborhoods and empowering local security forces has led to a major drop in bloodshed. But these gains will prove fleeting without an equally bold "trickle up" economic strategy focused on Iraqis where they live and work.

"In the long run," Zaab Sethna, an investment fund manager in Baghdad, tells me, "Iraq's economic revival will depend not on aid programs, but on private-sector and foreign capital." Much of that investment can come from the global diaspora of 4 million Iraqis, many of them successful entrepreneurs.

"But we won't get to the long term unless there's a serious improvement in the short term," argues Rory Stewart, a former British deputy governor in southern Iraq. "Iraqis need to see an immediate and dramatic difference in their well-being."

So how might "trickle up" work in Iraq?

To start, give petrodollars to the people. Building on the success of small US aid programs in the provinces, the Iraqi government could pour oil revenues into a New Deal–style jobs corps that puts Iraqis, especially young men, to work rebuilding newly secured neighborhoods and restoring electricity.

While Shiite, Sunni, and Kurdish politicians bicker over sharing oil revenues, the Iraqi people should demand their own share: an Alaska-like oil trust that would invest a portion of Iraqi oil profits—some $40 billion this year—and pay dividends to every citizen.

Next, bypass Baghdad. Government-managed reconstruction programs have been windfalls for corrupt Iraqi ministries and militias, but a bust for impoverished Iraqis. Instead, foreign aid could go directly to Iraqi communities, as with a successful World Bank–funded program in Indonesia where 40,000 villages have managed $1 billion worth of local projects.

For major infrastructure projects, the former Iraqi finance minister Dr. Ali Allawi tells me that dedicating a major portion of oil revenues to an independent, professional development board, as Iraq had in the 1950s, would "bypass the government machinery altogether."

For unemployed workers who still collect 40 percent of their salaries while state-owned factories sit idle, the Iraqi government should redouble its efforts—with increased US aid—to restart and eventually privatize the most modern facilities, which could employ 100,000 Iraqis. Huge potential customers are often right down the road—US military bases, which have awarded major contracts to Iraqi firms over the past year, creating tens of thousands of jobs.

For the one in four Iraqis in the agricultural sector, small-scale foreign aid programs to boost crop yields won't be enough to overcome the devastation inflicted by Saddam Hussein and UN sanctions that turned Iraq into a net food importer. Instead, the Iraqi government could get out of the food business and convert its sanction-era food ration program to a cash or credit system. That would stimulate, rather than stymie, domestic farming in the fertile lands along the Tigris and Euphrates.

For the vast majority of Iraqis who work in the informal sector—laborers, masons, carpenters, electricians, and seamstresses—carefully targeted microcredit programs to expand or start businesses would be a boon for local entrepreneurs who "have shown a remarkable dynamism amid the chaos," says Keith Crane, a RAND analyst and former US economic advisor in Iraq.

Likewise, a major Iraqi commitment to address the country's massive housing shortage could unleash a construction boom like the one underway in the relatively calm Kurdish north.

The US counterinsurgency manual lists 14 "progress indicators" for measuring whether such a strategy is succeeding. Only two relate to security; four are political and humanitarian. The remaining eight? The number of local businesses, tax revenues, acres being farmed, and other measures of daily economic life.

A jobs surge, not a military surge, remains Iraq's best hope. Iraqis need to see, as the manual says, that "peace pays."

Iraq Is Not Iraq Anymore

The World Post, July 21, 2015

SO, THIS IS WHERE WE ARE IN AMERICA TODAY: THE WEALTHY SON OF A real estate developer who used five deferments to let others go to war in his place attacks, with a straight face, a United States Naval Academy graduate who spent five years in a North Vietnamese prison camp with complications from a broken leg and two broken arms suffered when his plane was shot down—and we treat it as just another political debate. During another time in our country, had somebody like Donald Trump dared to say that somebody like Senator John McCain wasn't a war hero because he "got captured"—or that he "like(s) people who weren't captured"—my guess is that more than a few fire and food inspectors would have been kept busy for reported "complications" at Trump Hotels across America.

But while many Americans will likely hear McCain's high-minded response—that Trump doesn't owe him an apology but should express sorrow to other prisoners of war and their families—I really wish more Americans would hear what the senior senator from Arizona is saying about Iraq instead. It is much more relevant to America's future than any buffoonery babbling out of the billionaire blowhard from Queens.

As McCain said flatly in a 2013 *Foreign Policy* essay written along with fellow senator Lindsay Graham, "Iraq is being lost." The question, as they said then and say now, is not "Who is to blame for it?" The question is "What do we do about it?" McCain and Graham tried to kick-start a different conversation in May, calling for a new military surge in Iraq to counter the fall of Ramadi to ISIS warriors and what they call "a failing US war strategy in Iraq."

Let's be clear: Iraq is not Iraq anymore. It's not the Iraq it was when America ousted Saddam Hussein in 2003, and it's not the more stable Iraq it was in 2011 when President Barack Obama withdrew all American troops in December of that year. Without US troops in place to keep centuries-old sectarian hatreds at bay, as Charles Krauthammer has written, we "created a vacuum for the entry of the worst of the worst." As a result, "Iraq is now a battlefield between the Sunni jihadists of the Islamic State and the Shiite jihadists of Iran's Islamic Republic. There is no viable center."

Iraq is really three different countries today. In the south, there are Shia who have little interest in taking on the battle-hardened soldiers of the Islamic State. In the center and west of this ancient land, where the Islamic State has made its greatest inroads, there are Sunnis with little love for ISIS and its campaign of terror against fellow Sunnis, but even less love for the Shiite government in Baghdad. In the north and east, the Kurds have proven to be fierce fighters when defending their land, but have little interest in engaging the Islamic State in defense of Sunni lands or in support of Shiite fighters.

Meanwhile, Baghdad has all but abandoned the idea of a combined Sunni-Shiite army in favor of an all-Shiite fighting force, called the Iraqi Security Forces (ISF). The Iraqi army distinguished itself in May by running away from Islamic State fighters in Ramadi, despite an overwhelming force advantage, leaving US-supplied weapons behind for ISIS to use while leading US secretary of defense Ash Carter to suggest the ISF "lacked the will to fight."

That leaves the Iraqi government to depend on the Popular Mobilization Forces, made up of Iran-supported Shia militia who killed Americans prior to 2010 and exist solely to advance Shiite power in Sunni lands—and who, if they were to attack ISIS in Ramadi or further in Sunni territory, would be targeted by Sunnis who would regard them as a greater evil than the Islamic State. Indeed, the once-veiled presence of Iran in Baghdad is so open now that leaders from Iran's Revolutionary Guards reportedly arrive in the open in the capital, not far from a billboard in which the image of the Ayatollah Khomeini can reportedly be seen holding a map of Iraq in his hand. In effect, as writer Peter Van Buren has observed, the United States has "passively watched the Iranians become its proxy boots on the ground against (the) Islamic State, all the while knowing Tehran's broader agenda was a Shiite Iraqi client."

It's little wonder, then, that the Obama strategy to "degrade and destroy" the Islamic State through a combination of targeted bombing and militia training has failed to measure up to the size of the challenge: it's hard to know who to train when everybody seems to want to kill everybody else. It's one of the reasons why the United States, despite 3,500 US military trainers deployed since last year, has trained fewer than 9,000 Iraqi army and

Kurdish soldiers while recruiting just 1,300 Sunni tribesman to engage in the fight—who, in particular, don't believe the United States will support them if Iran-backed Shiite forces turn their guns on them.

It's also a leading reason why no Arab countries have showed up to help, or why there have been no Arab boots on the ground, despite a great Arab coalition announced a year ago. For a United States seen to be placating Iran both on the battlefield and at the negotiating table—where it just agreed to a historic pact that limits the size of Iran's nuclear program for a decade in exchange for economic sanctions being lifted—there is little reason for Arab nations to stick their necks out in Iraq and risk drawing the direct ire of the Islamic State.

So, what is the United States willing to do?

As Senators McCain and Graham argue, the United States can launch a new military surge that brings a sufficient number of American troops back to Iraq to battle the Islamic State directly. While critics argue that 166,000 US troops over the previous decade essentially fought enemy forces to a standstill, it overlooks the fact that US troops fighting alongside Sunni tribes in the so-called Anbar Awakening of 2007 surged past Al Qaeda militias to stabilize the country and prevent it from descending into anarchy. The combination of Special Forces and tactical air teams deployed alongside Iraqi troops—as General Martin Dempsey, the chairman of the Joint Chiefs of Staff, puts it—"would make them more than capable" of beating back the Islamic State.

Still, as Obama knows, the American people have little appetite to see more of their sons and daughters die on the battlefield in Iraq, particularly for a religious war whose roots date back 1,400 years. Should the United States be successful in stabilizing Iraq again through force, keeping that peace would require an occupation force of significant enough size to prevent precisely the return to violence we've seen since 2011—an occupation force that could approach Germany and South Korea levels of commitment. Both of [these nations] still host US troops more than half a century after their respective wars ended.

If America doesn't have the stomach for such an open-ended commitment—and honestly, it's hard to imagine a successful candidacy for the White House in 2016 built around the theme "Let's Re-invade Iraq"—the options get much more limited.

But there are three things that would make a difference.

First, the United States should recognize that the Iraqi government speaks only for a third of what was Iraq. Washington should no longer channel our aid and military assistance through Baghdad, which has proven that it cannot be an honest broker. Since 2011, successive Shiite governments have refused to pay the Kurds their share of the federal treasury, while reducing the flow of US weapons and other support intended for Kurdistan to a trickle. America should continue to support the government in some nominal way.

Second, we should send military support and aid directly to the Kurds, understanding that such support is an investment in containing the Islamic State from pushing north or east. As I have argued before, the United States should finally acknowledge what everyone knows to be reality, and recognize an independent Kurdistan as America's most loyal ally in the region outside of Israel.

Third, we should work with Sunni governments in Saudi Arabia and Turkey to provide training and assistance to Sunni tribes in the center and west of the country, and commit to the safety of Sunni tribes should Iran-backed militias push into Sunni lands.

In 2008, John McCain suggested that for peace to prevail, America "could wind up with a presence in Iraq for 100 years." Many derided John McCain's idea then—but do any of us believe Iraq would be the mess it is today if the United States had maintained a reasonable troop level in 2011? That's even harder to believe than Donald Trump.

MYANMAR/THAILAND

No Tuning Out Thailand's Muslim Insurgency: Thaksin's Reality Check

International Herald Tribune, February 20, 2006

IT WAS THE SORT OF MEDIA COVERAGE MOST WORLD LEADERS CAN ONLY dream about. For five days and nights last month, television viewers across Thailand were treated to live, round-the-clock cable coverage of Prime Minister Thaksin Shinawatra's week-long visit with villagers in the impoverished northern countryside.

Thaksin said the program was a chance to showcase his model for eradicating poverty. But the stage-managed broadcast was less about reducing poverty and more about boosting the autocratic prime minister's popularity.

Moreover, Thaksin's one-man reality show exposed his own disconnect from the political and economic realities facing this nation of 65 million. On screen, the billionaire media tycoon-turned-politician handed out wads of his own cash to destitute farmers. In reality, his family's recent $1.9 billion tax-free sale of telecom stock has sparked public outrage and growing calls for his impeachment.

The starkest contrast, however, was the televised tranquility of Buddhist life in the north compared with Thailand's Muslim south, where a stubborn insurgency has killed more than more than 1,200 people. Now in its third year, the southern insurgency is one story line the prime minister, a one-time police officer, can't seem to control.

But Thaksin may now have the chance to write a new script. Next month, Thailand's National Reconciliation Commission will propose its long-awaited peace plan for the south, forcing Thaksin to face realities he has long ignored.

First, Thaksin should admit that the daily assassinations, arson attacks, and bombings that have engulfed the three southernmost provinces of Patani, Narathiwat, and Yala are not, as he has claimed, the lone acts of "psychos, bandits, criminals, and drug addicts."

Rather, the violence is the latest flare-up in a century-long struggle by the three Muslim-majority Malay provinces, which were annexed in 1902 by Thailand (then Siam) and which have resisted the Buddhist "Bangkok Empire" ever since.

Bangkok's attempts to forcibly assimilate the Malay Muslims, with their distinct culture, language, and religion, only sparked the rise of armed separatists. Not until the 1990s did the insurgency largely subside thanks to a series of reforms that gave southern Muslims a greater voice in local affairs.

Second, Thaksin should acknowledge that his heavy-handed reaction to separatist attacks has helped resurrect the insurgency. Declaring the separatist movement dead in 2002, he dismantled the local bodies that had combated military and police abuses and given Muslims a forum to air their grievances. His no-holds-barred "war on drugs" the following year left more than 2,200 people dead, many of them Malay Muslims.

When militants raided an army depot in January 2004, Thaksin declared martial law across the south. The deaths of 80 protesters while in army custody later that year turned the scene of the tragedy, Tak Bai, into a Muslim rallying cry.

After another round of separatist attacks last summer, Thaksin declared a state of emergency in the south, including giving soldiers and police immunity from prosecution. Predictably, a new wave of violence has followed, with Malay Muslims alleging arbitrary arrests and extra-judicial killings.

Third, Thaksin should recognize his bad cop/bad cop strategy as the catastrophe it is. Insurgent attacks soared from just 50 in 2001 to more than 1,000 by 2004, according to the International Crisis Group.

Most troubling, Thailand's chaotic south risks becoming a haven for Islamic jihadists. Recent attacks in Thailand, beheadings, and bigger bombs (including car bombs) highlight the deadly potential of an alliance between locals and more sophisticated foreign fighters.

Finally, Thaksin should seize the reconciliation commission's report as a chance to become the statesman Thailand needs. Until now, Thaksin has played the part of Vladimir Putin, whose iron-fisted response to Chechnyan separatists radicalized the population and brought the bloodshed to the Kremlin's doorstep.

For a better role model, Thaksin should look to Indonesian president Susilo Bambang Yudhoyono, who is credited with ending the decades-old rebellion in the tsunami-ravaged province of Aceh. Recognizing that no military solution was possible, Yudhoyono has reduced the heavy military presence in the province and will allow Aceh greater autonomy and more control of its natural resources.

In exchange, rebels have given up their demand for independence and disbanded their military wing.

The choice is Thaksin's. He can continue to be Putin and risk spreading the southern violence to Bangkok and beyond. Or he can recast himself as a Yudhoyono and make the compromises necessary to bring peace to a troubled region.

Myanmar's Neighbors Hold the Key

International Herald Tribune, March 8, 2007

IN THIS RECLUSIVE, WAR-RAVAGED NATION THAT KIPLING ONCE SAID IS "quite unlike any land you know," one fact is quite clear—Western efforts to bring Burma's brutal military dictatorship to its knees have failed.

Despite a decade of American and European trade sanctions, Burma (which the junta renamed Myanmar) reported record-high foreign investment last year of $6 billion, mostly from a single hydropower project backed by Thailand, now the largest investor.

And despite a parade of foreign envoys preaching "constructive engagement," the military that has ruled for 45 years remains defiant. Aung San Suu Kyi, the Nobel Peace laureate and democracy activist, has now spent 11 of the past 17 years under house arrest.

What's the secret to the generals' staying power?

Thank the neighbors. The junta has deftly played them off one another, notably China and India, as they compete for regional influence and natural resources, including Myanmar's natural gas reserves, the world's 10th largest.

Like the strategic Burma Road of World War II, Myanmar remains a critical link in China's security thinking. In addition to billion-dollar bilateral trade deals and major Chinese weapons sales to the junta, a new trans-Myanmar pipeline will carry Middle East oil from the Bay of Bengal to China's southern Yunnan province.

Not to be outflanked, India has made Myanmar a lynchpin of its "Look East" foreign policy and has dampened its support for Burmese democracy activists. In return, New Delhi has won the junta's military cooperation against long-running insurgencies in India's northeast border states and its blessing for a new gas pipeline to India.

Myanmar's generals have become masters at turning energy deals into protection money.

In September, Russia—also a major arms supplier to the regime—voted against formally putting Myanmar on the UN Security Council agenda. The very same day, Russia's state-owned Zarubezhneft oil company was awarded Moscow's first contract to explore Myanmar's offshore oil and gas reserves.

In January, China and Russia vetoed a US-backed Security Council resolution condemning the junta. Days later, Myanmar awarded major contracts to China's National Petroleum Corp. Indonesia, the self-styled leader of Southeast Asia with growing military ties of its own with Myanmar, abstained.

So, how to avoid the carrot of Chinese, Indian, and Russian trade canceling out the stick of US and European sanctions? Consider a key ingredient of the six-party talks on North Korea that produced last month's tentative agreement—a united international front that coordinates both sticks and carrots.

To be sure, Burma doesn't present the same galvanizing threat as North Korean nuclear weapons. But Myanmar's neighbors—especially China, India, and Thailand—increasingly worry about Myanmar's destabilizing exports: HIV/AIDS, huge quantities of heroin and opium, and refugees from the junta's latest onslaught against ethnic rebels.

New Delhi has an interest in showing that its ties with Myanmar can promote reform instead of simply tarnishing India's image as the world's largest democracy. And Beijing surely wants to avoid yet another case of disenchanted Asians targeting Chinese minorities. Meanwhile, Myanmar's fear of Chinese domination gives New Delhi some leverage.

Tying future Chinese, Indian, and Thai trade to economic and political liberalization could be the one stick to which the junta might respond.

Simultaneously, just as the Bush administration showed new flexibility toward Pyongyang—lifting financial sanctions and offering economic assistance—Washington could offer Myanmar specific incentives, such as the gradual easing of sanctions, if the junta met certain benchmarks, such as releasing political prisoners like Suu Kyi and undertaking certain reforms.

Of course, there's no guarantee that the junta would ever relinquish its rule. But "there are examples of the regime responding to specific incentives and disincentives," says Thant Myint-U, author of a new history of Burma, *The River of Lost Footsteps*.

After years of Asian and Russian trade negating Western sanctions, it's time to try something else.

"The younger generation of upcoming generals needs to know what they can gain by being more open, with the world laying out specific incentives and disincentives," said Myint-U. "No one has attempted that, so it's worth a try."

Thailand: A King's Lesson in Democracy

International Herald Tribune, March 12, 2008

THE DRAMATIC RETURN TO THAILAND OF FORMER PRIME MINISTER THAK-sin Shinawatra—after 17 months of self-imposed exile following a bloodless military coup—marks the next round in the bare-knuckled free-for-all that characterizes this country's deeply polarized politics.

There's Thaksin versus the courts—his battle against corruption charges filed by the junta and the five-year ban from politics imposed on him and his party, which regrouped under a new name and prevailed in recent elections.

There's Thaksin versus the opposition Democratic Party, which two years ago led massive protests against his autocratic rule and which—suspicious of his pledge to "never, ever" return to politics—is threatening more protests if he evades the rule of law.

There's the civilians versus the military, which—though now back in its barracks—succeeded in leaving behind a new constitution that weakens civilian rule, including that of the new prime minister, Samak Sundaravej, who countered by naming himself defense minister.

There's even Thaksin versus Samak, who—initially seen as Thaksin's puppet—recently ruled out early amnesty for Thaksin and, as Thaksin began receiving political allies at his hotel headquarters here, declared, "I am the real prime minister!"

And underlying it all is city versus country—the Bangkok bureaucracy, intelligentsia, and urban middle class that opposed Thaksin and backed the coup versus Thailand's poor and rural majority, which benefited from his populist policies of debt forgiveness and low-cost health care and which put Thaksin's proxy party back in power.

But what makes this moment especially ominous is the prospect of losing the nation's foremost political referee—King Bhumibol Adulyadej, revered as a *dhammaraja* (righteous Buddhist king) whose interventions during political crises are credited with preventing a slide into chaos.

"We keep in the middle, neutral, in peaceful coexistence with everybody," Bhumibol once said of the monarchy. "We could be crushed by both sides, but we are impartial." But with the king now 80 years old and in failing health, Thailand could, in the not-so-distant future, lose its greatest safety valve against a political meltdown.

"His Majesty's reign has, of course, helped with economic and political development," a former Thai diplomat told me, insisting on anonymity since *lèse-majesté* laws make criticism of the monarchy punishable by up to 15 years in jail. "But maybe he has been so influential that Thais never learned to help themselves mature politically."

Moreover, the king's likely heir—the 55-year-old Crown Prince Maha Vajiralongkorn—"is not prepared to guide the country through its turbulent road to the future," said the diplomat, reflecting the fears of many Thais. "He does not have a few decades to grow into his office, as his father did."

Yet the topic of life after Bhumibol remains taboo. "Many have conjectured privately that Thailand may enter a period of tension in the coming years, including royalism versus republicanism," a member of a prominent Thai family tells me, also requesting anonymity. "It's the elephant in the room that everyone conveniently ignores."

Indeed, Thai politicians and power brokers would be wise to heed the lesson their king has apparently been trying to teach them for several years: it's time to grow up and start solving your own problems without royal intervention.

Although celebrated for supporting democracy movements that overturned military regimes, most notably in 1973 and 1992, Bhumibol has cautioned Thais against relying on the monarchy as a one-stop cure-all. When massive protests urged him to oust Thaksin two years ago, he called the idea "irrational," adding, "You cannot think in haste and pass the buck to the king."

And although he has blessed many of modern Thailand's 18 coups—including the most recent one—Bhumibol is reported to have discouraged other military takeovers and had supported the progressive constitution that the recent junta voided. "Soldiers and civilians must work in harmony," he said in his annual birthday speech in December. "If there is no harmony, the country will face disaster—the country will fall. And when it falls, where are we going to live?"

Fortunately, despite *lèse-majesté* laws and bans on recent books about the monarchy, Thais appear to begin thinking about the unthinkable. Resisting pressure from the palace, several hundred Thai and international scholars recently convened a remarkable series of seminars in Bangkok on the monarchy, including criticism of the "Sufficient Economy" philosophy of economic moderation championed by the king.

"It was unprecedented," said Andrew Walker of the Australian National University, who spoke at the conference, which proved that "the sky will not fall in if we talk freely and frankly about the king's role in contemporary Thai politics."

Let's hope so. Because if Thais cannot talk openly about their monarchy, they can't begin to resolve the current challenges to what one scholar has called their "demi-democracy." And if Thai leaders, civilian and military alike, are to pass perhaps their greatest test yet, they ought to heed perhaps the greatest lesson of their monarch: the buck doesn't stop here—it stops with you.

Burma: Are Sanctions the Answer?

International Herald Tribune, February 9–10, 2008

IN THE OFTEN BLACK-AND-WHITE, GOOD-VERSUS-EVIL DEBATE OVER HOW to deal with the brutal military regime here, Ma Thanegi lives in a world of gray.

To her admirers, the feisty 61-year-old Burmese painter and writer is a voice of reason—a former assistant to opposition leader and Nobel peace laureate Aung San Suu Kyi who, after being jailed for three years herself, bravely opposed Suu Kyi's misguided call for Western economic sanctions to pressure the junta into relinquishing power.

To her critics in the democracy movement, Thanegi is a sellout who parrots government propaganda to foreign tourists and journalists. Meeting openly with me at a major hotel suggests that—with her writings on Burmese culture and cuisine, not politics—she has little to fear in the continuing crackdown on dissidents after the fall's protests led by Buddhist monks.

In reality, Thanegi seems an equal opportunity critic, which—with the world out of options for dealing with the junta—makes hers a voice worth hearing.

Expressing her hopes for "freedom of publication," she says that with a military government "it's a given that they are very controlling and rigid, not knowing anything about the running of the economy." She slams "sycophants" in both government and the opposition who have created "so much mistrust" that any real dialogue is "a pipe dream."

"I am not a traitor or a turncoat," she insists. "I wish with all my heart that I had been wrong, that the strategy laid down by Suu Kyi, whom we love so much, was the right one." But Western sanctions are "costing us jobs and hurting people, who need to eat on a daily basis."

In brief, nervous encounters, ordinary Burmese—street vendors, taxi drivers, tour guides, waiters—tell me much the same thing: "We love Suu Kyi. We hate the military. But please, get rid of the sanctions."

For Maung Zarni, it's an especially "bitter pill" to admit that sanctions have failed to moderate the regime. As a graduate student in the United

States a decade ago, his Free Burma Coalition led the grassroots campaign for sanctions and divestment, which forced corporations like PepsiCo and Texaco to leave Burma.

But we "failed to account for China and India," he says, explaining why he began opposing sanctions. "We can't isolate a regime that's trading and buying arms from the fastest-growing economies in the world."

He concedes that more foreign investment could further enrich the criminal regime he opposes. But Zarni—who first befriended Westerners as a young tourist guide in his native Mandalay—argues that "this is a small price to pay in the short term for the longer term benefit of creating jobs for farmers and workers."

"It's extremely politically incorrect to say it," he says, "but economics, perhaps even more than politics, is the key to progress." As in dictatorships-turned-democracies like Indonesia, South Korea, Taiwan, and Chile, "economic reform could lead to political reform."

Thant Myint-U also challenges anti-sanctions orthodoxy.

A historian and grandson of former United Nations secretary general U Thant, he argues that "if over the last 15 years there had been trade and investment, and not just increasing isolation from the West, there could have been real economic growth and the emergence of much better conditions for political change."

His thanks for speaking such common sense? A liberal US magazine lashed out at him for espousing a view that "justifies the junta's policies" and "forestalls democracy."

Tragically, Myanmar now represents the worst of all possible worlds. Having crushed the biggest challenge to its rule in two decades, the junta—which sees itself as the only force able to prevent the Balkanization of multi-ethnic Burma—seems in no mood to compromise, if it ever was.

In a message last week, Suu Kyi, now under house arrest for 12 of the past 18 years, urged supporters to "hope for the best, and prepare for the worst."

The regime's worst enablers—neighbors and trade partners, especially China, the junta's biggest military supplier—show no interest in applying the economic pressure that might persuade the generals to change course.

The United States and the European Union, having already sanctioned themselves out of influence over the junta, have imposed still more sanctions that will likely push the generals even closer to Beijing.

Meanwhile, 55 million Burmese—including an estimated 1 million ethnic refugees in the countryside—are trapped in a growing humanitarian catastrophe of ethnic cleansing, disease, drugs, malnutrition, and forced labor, including as child soldiers.

"The landscape that's been created is exactly the landscape that will keep things just as they are for a very long time," says Myint-U. "And branding people as 'pro-junta' for trying to suggest different ways forward only prevents the creative discussion we desperately need if we don't want to be facing the same situation 20 years from now."

After a decade of experience, it's clear: economic sanctions on Myanmar may feel right, but they have helped produce the wrong results. Encouraging Western investment, trade, and tourism may feel wrong, but maybe—just maybe—could produce better results.

That might be politically incorrect, but at least it wouldn't be politically futile.

A First Step Toward Democracy?

International Herald Tribune, February 23, 2010

WHEN BRITISH FORCES FIRST FLOATED UP THE IRRAWADDY RIVER IN 1885 to depose King Thibaw of Burma, locals were startled to see a Burmese prince, in full regalia, sitting on the deck of one of the steamers. His presence reassured locals that the British planned to seat a new king, not overthrow the kingdom. As Thant Myint-U recalls in his book *The River of Lost Footsteps*, it was only when a young student talked his way onto the ship and came face-to-face with the royal prince that the truth was discovered: The "prince" was an imposter, a former classmate of the student's. By then, it was too late—the telegraph line to the palace in Mandalay had been cut.

The question, 125 years later, is whether the Burmese military junta—which has ruled this country, now known as Myanmar, since 1962—is about to pull its own version of bait-and-switch.

For the first time since 1990—when officials arrested 2,000 people, including the opposition leader Daw Aung San Suu Kyi, after the last general election—the ruling generals have announced that parliamentary elections will take place this year. Reportedly, the generals are preparing to switch their uniforms for *longyis* and run for office—the equivalent of Fidel Castro swapping his army greens for *guayaberas* and hitting the campaign trail.

Many in the West are disposed to see the election as a fraud, since the junta's constitution reserves 25 percent of the seats for the military and bars Mrs. Aung San Suu Kyi—imprisoned for 14 of the past 20 years—from running.

Still, the question remains: Even if the election is stage-managed by the military, even if Mrs. Aung San Suu Kyi's National League for Democracy chooses not to participate, and even if Senior General Than Shwe selects the next president—if the election occurs without violence or repression, will it represent a step forward?

The answer seems to be: yes.

"I don't know if the elections will have legitimacy in the eyes of the West," said the Myanmar scholar Robert Taylor. "But they will have legitimacy in Asia, and that is all the regime is worried about."

I asked an official of the junta how the West should regard this election. "This is a first step toward democracy," he told me. "After ruling the country for 48 years, the military needs some mechanism to safeguard the interests and safety of persons. This is also an exit strategy for older leaders, because in five years, the new generation will take over—not only the military, but civilian politics. They will work to change the military role in politics."

The Burmese writer Ma Thanegi, who spent three years in prison after working as Mrs. Aung San Suu Kyi's assistant, was blunt. "Yes, elections would represent a step forward—what other choice is there?" she asked. "If the West really wants to help the people, they should accept the new government as no longer the military rule, and give it a chance."

"What America should do," a prominent businessman told me, "is shift the conversation from sanctions to engagement, from scolding to giving, and find soft steps to help bring about outcomes that will be beneficial to both Myanmar and the United States."

The Obama administration so far has sought to engage the junta, urging a dialogue between the regime, the National League for Democracy, and other opposition parties, while calling for Mrs. Aung San Suu Kyi's release. In November, Assistant Secretary of State Kurt Campbell led a US team to Yangon for the highest-level talks in 14 years.

Where should the US focus its efforts? Here are three ways:

· It should provide opportunities for students to attend US universities, to build ties to the next generation.
· It should start a program of cultural, educational, and sporting exchanges, including a new program to send teachers to Myanmar.
· It should review its current sanctions policy.

No nation in Asia—from South Korea to Taiwan to Indonesia—has made an easy transition from dictatorship to democracy. But change needs to start somewhere. As the United Nations secretary general, Ban Ki-moon, recently said, "2010 will be a very critical year for Myanmar." There may yet be light at the end of the Irrawaddy.

Counterpoint on Myanmar's Transition

Stanley A. Weiss Blog, March 17, 2011

AS DEMONSTRATORS FROM TUNIS TO CAIRO TO TRIPOLI WONDER IF THEIR revolutions will succeed, Myanmar remains an unfortunate poster child for what happens when revolutions go wrong. With a population equal in size to the United Kingdom, and a per capita income of less than two US dollars per day, Myanmar has suffered under military rule since 1962.

Peaceful demonstrations for democracy like those seen in Tunisia, Egypt, and Libya (seen, that is, everywhere but here, since coverage is censored) led to soldiers opening fire on defenseless monks and students—first in 1988 when an estimated 6,000 were killed, and again in 2007 when hundreds died and thousands were jailed in unrest that became known around the world as the Saffron Revolution.

So, it came as no surprise last November when the international community dismissed Myanmar's first general election in two decades, which saw regime-backed candidates win handily, as "neither free nor fair," in US president Barack Obama's words. As the new elected government prepares to take over this month, there are still unanswered questions about what the people in Myanmar think and what people in the West understand about Myanmar's transition. This writer reached out to contacts made in the years I've traveled to Myanmar, and three strong themes emerged from their insights.

First, the elections mattered more than the West realizes. "What has been missed in the West is that these elections took place within a much broader political transition," said Myanmarese historian Thant Myint-U, the grandson of former United Nations secretary general U Thant. "Nearly the entire junta has resigned their military commissions. Many ran in the elections, and some will wind up in the new government. A whole new generation of army officers has been promoted to the leadership. Under the new constitution, the National Assembly and various regional assemblies will be one of three political actors, along with the presidency and the army."

I received a similar reaction from a longtime political activist who was once jailed by the junta, who echoed Thant's point, saying, "When the junta started the Union Solidarity and Development Party (USDP) that won the elections, the high-level members they chose for ranking positions were from small towns—doctors, high school principals, businesspeople who were already well-known and popular in their society. When you look at the candidates who won, they won. What has escaped notice by the West is that the new president, Thein Sein, is clean and his children are clean, with no corruption scandals. It's a start."

Longtime Myanmar scholar Robert Taylor said, "While outwardly it appears that the generals have traded suits for uniforms, underlying it there is change of a more substantial nature. The army realizes that it cannot govern alone forever and wants to open up political space and opportunities for those who share its goal of economic development, political stability, and political nationalism."

"And don't forget," added Thant Myint-U, "In the election, dozens of parties competed, most entirely independent of the junta. Millions have voted for the first time in 20 years. Is this a step toward democracy? Only time will tell. But who can say, even in hindsight, what the important steps were that eventually led to democracy in, say, South Korea or Indonesia?"

Second, many Myanmarese feel embittered toward the West. "There is solid mistrust and resentment toward the West, not only among the generals but [throughout] the country as a whole," says the activist. "We're tired of being represented in your newspapers as cowering in fear and barefoot, scrabbling in the mud. It's just insulting. America now talks about China's growing influence here. We just happen to be right next to it. So, finally the American administration is looking at a map?"

A local expatriate who requested anonymity said, "It is too late for the United States here now. You were arrogant for too long to think Western input was needed. It's not. Now, a major economic corridor is forming in Myanmar, and massive investment is flowing in. Sad to say, but you've lost this generation."

Third, Western sanctions are not just useless, but they actually strengthen the regime while weakening the opposition. "What the West doesn't understand," says a transplanted British citizen, "is that the sanctions of the international community (imposed by the United States) have not only failed, but the community itself has failed to achieve the respect of the generals that would enable meaningful dialogue."

Thant Myint-U agrees: "US policy for a long time has been based on an objective that was extremely unlikely to be met—a dialogue between opposition leader Aung San Suu Kyi (who was recently released after 17 years in jail and under house arrest) and the junta leading to democratic change. Western sanctions that were put in place to force the dialogue have not bankrupted the government, nor pressured leaders toward political reform. What they have done is severely weaken the position of independent businessmen and the middle classes on whom an open society depends."

Adds the expatriate: "The regime has no reason or incentive to want sanctions lifted. They want no NGOs, no UN, and no ILO (International Labor Organization) to have to compromise with."

"Like it or not," Thant Myint-U adds, pointing to Tunisia, Egypt, and Libya, "we have to accept that we no longer live in a time when the West can determine political change halfway around the world." Unfortunately for the West, that may be the revolution that lasts.

The First Thing the United States Should Do in Myanmar

The World Post, February 23, 2012

DURING THE YEARS HE LIVED AS A CHILD IN INDONESIA, PRESIDENT Barack Obama learned the culture of Jakarta, spoke the language, and survived chicken pox, and he recalls frequently feeling "the sting of [his] teachers' bamboo switches." As a young military officer training in the United States, Indonesian President Susilo Bambang Yudhoyono, known as SBY, parachuted out of planes with Fort Benning's storied 82nd Airborne Division and attended the US Army Command and General Staff College. It is an interesting parallel between presidents that each spent formative years in the other's country.

Many have remarked that President Obama's time overseas gave him the gift of a global perspective. What's unfortunate, however, is that SBY's experience is the increasingly rare one for some Southeast Asian nations. At a time when the region is undergoing a potentially seismic shift from military to civilian leadership, well-meaning restrictions on our International Military Education and Training (IMET) program—which sent SBY and thousands like him to the United States—have prevented us from exposing a new generation of leaders to principles of civilian governance, democratic values, and human rights.

Walking these streets today reminds me of the time I spent in Indonesia a decade ago, where I saw IMET-educated officers managing Indonesia's transition from dictatorship to democracy. It's hard not to feel a new energy and sense of possibility here since Myanmar's mostly democratic elections re-opened it to the world last November. If the upcoming parliamentary elections in April proceed smoothly, the United States will likely lift economic sanctions that have been in place for two decades. The very first thing the United States should do when easing those sanctions is to bring IMET back to Myanmar and help breathe new life into a society that hasn't experienced rule of law in more than half a century.

Established in 1976 to strengthen ties between the US and foreign militaries, IMET gives promising junior officers from friendly nations the opportunity to study in the United States, modeling what a vibrant civil-military relationship looks like in a free society. In 1991, Congress expanded IMET to more overtly emphasize human rights promotion, and the program currently provides roughly $100 million in grant aid to over 7,000 students from 130 countries, from Albania to Zambia.

Myanmar is not one of them. Despite rewarding ruthless dictators like Zimbabwe's Robert Mugabe and AWOL allies such as Pakistan, the United States cut off IMET and other aid to Myanmar following the junta's brutal crackdown and refusal to honor the results of the 1990 election.

Before that, thousands of young military leaders traveled back and forth between the United States and Myanmar. Within 14 years of achieving its 1948 independence, Myanmar had sent over a thousand officers to the United States in the days before IMET. Even after the military coup of 1962 and the ruthless dictatorship of Ne Win, the United States maintained aspects of this relationship. In the decade before the US imposed sanctions, 255 Burmese officers graduated from American military training programs—more than in any other country.

This support provided a promising link between an established democracy and a country wracked by successive coups and anemic economic development. But today's generals were all trained in Burma, and consequently, as Georgetown professor David Steinberg writes, "largely insulated from the outside world."

IMET's absence cuts to the heart of Myanmar's present difficulties. In a country where the military has been called a "state within a state," the insularity of the military will continue to threaten the long-term stability and potential of the nation. Across the army, there isn't an officer under the age of 55 with any memory of what a free society looks like. Until young officers experience for themselves how civil society and rule of law operate, Myanmar will never fulfill its full potential.

There's no question that militaries that have benefitted from IMET have committed reprehensible human rights violations. In a recent review by the US Government Accountability Office, only a third of IMET training programs for relatively "unfree" participant countries emphasized respect for human rights. That is an area that the Departments of State and Defense, which jointly administer IMET, can and must strengthen.

But cutting off IMET entirely weakens the hand of reform. It is a tragic catch-22 that says, "Until your military is more professional and respectful of human rights, we will not teach your military to be more professional and respectful of human rights." Much as economic engagement very often does more to liberalize a society than absolute economic isolation [can], IMET's military-to-military engagement provides us far more leverage.

Critics focus on the horror, not the hope. A study from the Center for Civil-Military Relations found that 95 percent of IMET participants reported that they had gained an improved understanding of US systems, while 84 percent said their views of the United States had changed, largely for the better. It brings to mind the many young Indonesian officers I met while living through Indonesia's halting but determined evolution who knew there was a better way—because they had seen it in America.

As Yunus Yosfiah, a former lieutenant general and minister of information fiercely supportive of a free press, said to me at the time, "I first learned about the importance of the First Amendment in the library at Fort Leavenworth, Kansas."

I look forward to the day when Myanmar's military leaders can say the same. President Obama's latest budget includes $27.2 million in aid for Myanmar, with a focus on "strengthening civil society." The best way to accomplish that would be to re-establish IMET [there], so that officers like his Indonesian presidential counterpart can live and learn in the United States.

There will always be bad apples, of course, and a single course at Fort Bragg will not change the course of a country overnight. But it would go a long way toward showing other nations that true, lasting power comes not from a bayonet, but from a ballot.

Hacking a Path Between China's California and Myanmar's Dracula

The World Post, February 25, 2013

READING THE NEWS THAT THE CHINESE ARMY SYSTEMATICALLY HACKED into United States computer networks brought to mind another group of soldiers who engaged in an entirely different kind of hacking here seven decades ago: Merrill's Marauders. What makes them most memorable is that it was one of the few times that American and Chinese soldiers fought on the same side against a common enemy.

Seventy years ago, the Second World War raged on both fronts. Japan, which had invaded China a decade before attacking Pearl Harbor, was engaged in fierce fighting with both Chinese and Allied troops. Eager to keep China in the fight, Franklin Roosevelt and Winston Churchill formed a deep penetration unit to engage Japanese forces—while supplying the Chinese army—through China's backdoor, in Myanmar, then known as Burma.

The 3,000 soldiers who volunteered were named for their commander, Brigadier General Frank Merrill. Merrill's Marauders would go on to hack two passable supply lanes across 1,100 miles of dense hillsides and jungle terrain. The so-called Burma Road is still there, along with stories of how outmanned American and Chinese troops fought shoulder-to-shoulder in a bloody and ultimately triumphant three-month campaign to capture the region's only airfield from Japanese troops. (Interestingly, the Allied force that ultimately took Burma back from Japan included the grandfather of future US president Barack Obama.)

In a twist of history, China will soon hack its own "path" across Myanmar, not far from the Burma Road: a gas pipeline that extends nearly 500 miles from the Indian Ocean across Myanmar to Southwest China. Scheduled to be accompanied by an oil pipeline that runs parallel to it later this year—and eventually, a high-speed rail line and network of highways to carry Chinese exports—the pipeline will enable China to gain something it has never had: a western seaboard. As Thant Myint-U, a historian and advisor to the Myanmar government, says, the pipeline helps give China what it lacks: "its own California, another coast that will provide its remote interior provinces with an outlet to the sea."

But while westerners debate whether Myanmar's rebranding as China's California will mean that the United States stands no chance to compete here, there is one fact that needs to be understood: the primary reason Myanmar ended its half-century military junta, released political prisoners, held an election, and has begun to open its economy to foreigners is because Myanmar leaders want to blunt China's influence in their country.

"Nobody here wants China to own us," a high-profile businessman tells me. "China is corrupt and rotten to the core." Adds another businessman active in the local chamber, "The government told me they don't want Chinese products and have been ordered not to purchase any more Chinese products. It shows that the government is starting to feel that they have been cheated by the Chinese."

Apprehension about China has long run deep here. Schools teach about Tayok-Pyay Mink—a medieval king who abandoned his capital for fear of a Chinese invasion—as well as brave warriors who defended Myanmar from Mongol invaders in the 13th century and Manchu invaders in the 18th century. While Mandalay itself is virtually a Chinese city now—about a third of the population—it brings an anxiety on the streets. It's not dislike of China, but rather, as Thant says, "a sense of the dangers of being next to an increasingly powerful and populous nation whose internal wars and politics have spilled over to wreak havoc."

Changes in China led to an improved relationship in the mid-1980s. When Western nations dealt themselves out of Myanmar with economic sanctions in the wake of crackdowns against peaceful protesters in 1988, China pounced—offering more economic help and bigger arms sales. For the two decades that followed, China had unfettered access to Myanmar, exploiting the country's rich natural resources—including millions of tons of timber, "the bulk of which has been logged and traded illegally," as the Environmental Investigation Agency reported last year.

Myanmar turned first to India to balance the influence of China and then to other members of the Association of Southeast Asian Nations. None provided what a Western observer calls "the alternative trading partner we would love to have." As America re-engages, there is a completely different spirit here: much more freedom of speech and freedom of the press. With so many people pouring into the country, restaurants are full, traffic jams abound, and it's difficult to find a hotel room.

There is also a sound being heard in the streets not heard in decades—Burmese protests against Chinese investors. As journalist Lucy Ash writes, "Burma's steps towards democracy have made it possible . . . for people to protest things they don't like—and Chinese businesses have turned out to be at the top of the list." At one demonstration outside the Chinese embassy in Yangon recently, a banner read "This Is Our Country—Dracula China, Get Out!"

The first significant public act that signaled to the West a new day was the suspension in September 2011 of a $3.6 billion Chinese-funded dam at the headwaters of the Irrawaddy River, 90 percent of whose power was slated for China, even though only one in five Myanmar households have power.

As an encore, the government suspended operations at the Monywa copper mine, the largest in the country, a joint venture between China's Wanabao Company and the deeply loathed business arm of the Myanmar army. While Wanabao reportedly loses $2 million a day, Myanmar's government is investigating charges that the venture is ruining drinking water while unlawfully seizing local land. As proof that democracy has a ways to go, more than 100 local protesters—led by two farmers' daughters, dubbed "The Iron Ladies"—were recently attacked by police, with many suffering burns from the use of an incendiary device.

Whatever is decided, China still enjoys an enviable position as Myanmar's largest trade and investment partner. Two-way trade grew by nearly 50 percent in 2012. But if China hopes to maintain its economic lead, it will have to embrace much greater corporate responsibility, especially on environmental issues.

While America slowly lifts sanctions, the opportunity to engage on issues that Beijing has no competency in is vast—from civil society and rule of law, to university-to-university partnership, to vocational training for the vast majority of Burmese who will never go to college. The challenge of overcoming a half-century head start will be daunting. But as Merrill's Marauders once proved, Americans are skilled at creating new openings where none existed before—even if it means threading the needle between China's California and Myanmar's Dracula.

Thailand's Andrew Jackson Moment

The World Post, February 14, 2014

IT WAS THE ROWDIEST PRESIDENTIAL INAUGURATION IN AMERICAN history. On March 4, 1829, thousands of Americans flooded into the White House to revel in the election of Andrew Jackson as the seventh president of the United States. To them, Jackson was one of their own: the orphan son of backwoods farmers, a rough, frontier populist who thumbed his nose at the country's ruling elite and threw open the doors of democracy to a broader cross-section of the country than ever before.

The chaos was not universally appreciated. One observer compared the scene to "the inundation of the northern barbarians into Rome." A Supreme Court justice took one look at the shambles left behind and darkly declared it the beginning of "the reign of King Mob."

I can't help but think about Jackson here in Bangkok, where pro-government "red shirts" and anti-government "yellow shirts" are clashing, re-enacting their own version of "King Mob." After all, it was Jackson who sent an envoy to the court of Siam in 1832, establishing the first diplomatic link between the United States and what is now Thailand. Today, Thailand is undergoing its own Jacksonian moment in the form of one man: exiled former prime minister Thaksin Shinawatra.

Like Jackson, Thaksin rapidly rose to power by casting himself as a "backwoods kid" championing the rural poor. Though critics are quick to point out that Thaksin's family is one of the richest in the northern city of Chiang Mai, Thaksin touts his "rags-to-riches" rise: a police lieutenant colonel who failed at various business ventures before building (with the help of sweetheart government contracts) a telecom empire and then riding a populist wave into the prime minister's office in 2001.

Since 2006, when the military overthrew Thaksin, a bitter power struggle has divided Thai politics along geographic and class lines. The red shirts—mainly the rural poor from Thaksin's underdeveloped northern home—support Thaksin and his "power to the people" policies. Meanwhile, the royalist yellow shirts—made up of the Bangkok elite, members of the military, and middle-class professionals—hail from the south, despise Thaksin's excesses, and prefer rule by the privileged.

Tensions died down somewhat with the 2011 election of Thaksin's younger sister Yingluck, but flared up again when Yingluck attempted to ram an amnesty bill through parliament, permitting Thaksin to return to Thailand from his exile abroad. The minority Democrat Party—which hasn't won an election in 20 years—resigned in protest, demanding that an appointed "people's council" reform an electoral process they believe has been hijacked by the Shinawatras. Yingluck called new elections for February 2, which the Democrats boycotted, leaving the government mired in uncertainty.

It may seem like a lot of fuss over one man, but Thaksin is positively toxic to the Thai establishment.

While millions see Thaksin's meteoric rise as an inspiring story of self-made wealth, to Bangkok's ruling elite—many of them close to the ailing, 86-year-old King Bhumibol and the royal family—Thaksin is every bit the Jackson-like northern barbarian invading Bangkok. He is an unworthy usurper, a rich rustic who clawed his way to the top, bought his fellow yokels' votes with handouts, and used his political power to amass still greater wealth while squeezing the rest of the country.

As the political analyst and longtime Thailand resident Jeffrey Race explains, "In keeping with the [Buddhist teachings of the] Middle Way, political figures have been moderately corrupt but with sensitivity to the transience of life. No one until recently attempted to dominate either the state or the economy." Thaksin, Race notes, has amassed billions by consistently choosing "My Way" over the modest "Middle Way."

"This is not elite against poor," the strategic consultant Joe Horn says to me. "This is elite revolting against uber-elite. It all had to do with Thaksin's monopolizing power."

But the elite's problem with Thaksin is not merely personal—it's political.

For a country in which the rural poor had been marginalized for seven decades, Thaksin built his political career promising to narrow the gulf between the rich and the rest. Under Thaksin, Thailand witnessed the establishment of rural credit funds, universal healthcare, and education reforms. In four years, "Thaksinomics" cut poverty in half. While noting that many of Thaksin's policies were "fountains of self-serving corruption," Race acknowledges that the exiled prime minister was "the only recent political force to push policies bringing substantial and genuine uplift to rural areas."

Predictably, many rich and even middle-class Thai resent this focus on the poor in the provinces, whom they dismiss as uneducated "buffaloes" undeserving of an equal stake in Thai society. Many of the recent protests, for instance, have centered on a rice subsidization scheme that Yingluck implemented—popular with rural farmers but not with the Bangkok elite, who gripe that it has cost taxpayers $21 billion, helping to fuel middle-class rage.

As a financier friend tells me, they say, "'I pay my taxes, but what do I get? Why does all the money go elsewhere?' People in Bangkok are upset because even maids or waiters have the same right as they do to vote." In their eyes, the policies Thaksin set in motion are less about bettering the whole country than [about] bribing a part of it. And in a nation where the rural poor make up more than half of the electorate, those "bribes" will keep the yellow shirts out of power indefinitely. "The opposition knows they can't beat Thaksin in elections," Horn says—so they've taken to the streets, threatening the country's fragile democratic institutions.

What yellow shirts fear more than anything is that if he returns, Thaksin—who is known to be close to the heir apparent to the throne, Crown Prince Maha Vajiralongkorn—will win Maha's ear and splinter the decades-long alliance between the Bangkok elite and the crown.

This is not the way democracy should work. Ultimately, if Thailand is to experience real progress, both sides must recognize that politics isn't a zero-sum game. As Thai political scientist Thitinan Pongsudhirak writes, "Electoral winners cannot do as they please after scoring at the ballot box; they must accommodate the interests of the losers more openly and more systematically."

In other words, Thaksin and his party may be popular enough to continue winning elections, but that doesn't mean they should ride roughshod over everyone else once in power. And instead of crippling democratic institutions through massive boycotts and protests, what if the yellow shirts revived their electoral prospects by proposing their own policies to improve the lives of the average Thai citizen? As Horn puts it, "Just because the Democrats have been unable to beat Thaksin does not mean democracy can't."

Andrew Jackson—the man who ordered the genocidal Trail of Tears that decimated America's native tribes—was certainly no saint. Neither is

Thaksin, with a long list of graft and repression to his name. But Jackson's genius was unleashing the raw energies of mass participatory democracy, and helping to shape a two-party system better representing rich and poor alike.

"Thaksin's problem is, he read too many books on American democracy," a senior Thai political advisor tells me." For Thailand's sake, hopefully the lessons of Jacksonian America haven't been lost on him.

An End to Improvisation in Thailand

The World Post, May 14, 2015

FIFTY-FIVE YEARS AGO, THE KING OF SIAM MET THE KING OF SWING. WITH Cold War tensions ratcheting up, Thailand's young monarch, King Bhumibol Adulyadej, embarked on a month-long tour of the United States to highlight the strong ties between Washington and Bangkok. In California, Bhumibol and his family visited Disneyland and rubbed elbows with Elvis, Bob Hope, and Lucille Ball. In Washington, the king paraded down Pennsylvania Avenue in an open limousine, received the Legion of Merit from President Dwight D. Eisenhower, and addressed a joint session of Congress. On July 4, Governor Nelson Rockefeller hosted the king at a lavish party in New York.

But perhaps the most memorable part of Bhumibol's trip occurred the following afternoon, at the home of legendary jazz musician Benny Goodman. There, Bhumibol—a longtime lover of jazz and a talented composer and performer in his own right—participated in a two-hour jam session with Goodman, Gene Krupa, Teddy Wilson, and other jazz greats. At the end of the night, Goodman gifted Bhumibol with an appropriate scepter: a new saxophone.

Bhumibol's knack for improvisation has served him well—on stage and on the throne. Since the establishment of Thailand's wobbly democracy in 1932, the king has been a steadying presence, the one consistent theme in a country that has lived through 19 coups and 20 constitutions in just 80 years.

Yet now, as Thailand endures the second year of yet another coup, Bhumibol is approaching the 70th year of his reign—and his health is reputedly poor. In this Southeast Asian kingdom of 67 million, the question on everyone's mind is: When the music stops and the world's longest-serving monarch is gone, what—or who—will fill the void?

The obvious answer is Crown Prince Vajiralongkorn, whom the king declared, in 1972, to be his successor. But the prince—an infamous playboy—is as scorned as is father is revered.

Opponents of the prince—who, despite *lèse-majesté* laws that criminalize speaking ill of the royal family, are numerous—instead point to his well-liked sister, Princess Chakri Sirindhorn. "The saving grace would be the princess," a friend tells me, now that the law of succession has been amended to allow the king to choose any of his children.

"There are many ways around it," a Thailand expert says of the prince's claim to the throne. He adds, "It's very important who is the prime minister at the time of the succession."

In essence, who sits on the throne is merely a proxy for a larger fight.

On one side are the poor and rural Thai in the northeast, who support the populist policies of the self-made billionaire Thaksin Shinawatra, the ousted prime minister. A police officer who became a telecommunications billionaire, Thaksin built a formidable political majority by providing universal health care, education, and easy credit to Thais who felt "a rural sense of exclusion from government."

"Thaksin, despite his faults, is one of the few that progressed democracy in Thailand," a banker and member of the Bangkok elite tells me. "Thaksin brought awareness of the value of the vote."

The Shinawatras and their supporters are opposed by urban elites allied with the palace and the military, to whom Thaksin represents not the triumph of democracy but the epitome of vote buying and corruption. A Thai journalist informs me, "He said, 'If you didn't vote for me, you get nothing,' and he meant it. He denied budgets and other things for areas that didn't vote for him."

After the military exiled Thaksin from the country in 2006, Thaksin's younger sister, Yingluck Shinawatra, was elected in 2011. A scandal-plagued rice-subsidy program—and a heavy-headed effort to ram through parliament an amnesty bill permitting Thaksin's return from exile—led to widespread protests and clashes between Thailand's two factions. In May 2014 the military declared martial law and forced Yingluck from office. When 190 of 200 legislators in the military-stacked assembly later voted to impeach Yingluck for "dereliction of duty" over the rice subsidy—which the analyst David Merkel dryly notes is "akin to impeaching a US president over an ethanol subsidy, pork barrel spending, or a dairy program"—Yingluck rightly declared, "Democracy has died in Thailand today, along with the rule of law."

Portrayed as an impromptu effort to maintain order after years of turmoil, the coup is instead a power play by Bangkok's elite—a calculated move "to make sure that traditional royalists, and the military, are running the country when the king dies," as the Council on Foreign Relations' Joshua Kurlantzick puts it. Above all, these elites are terrified that Thaksin, long thought to be aligned with the prince, will return to power if Vajiralongkorn takes the throne (though palace watchers tell me that that alliance may be shaky, as "the prince will be close to anyone as long as he can use them," and the military may well be a better patron at the moment).

In April, General Prayuth Chan-ocha lifted martial law—but replaced it with a constitution that the UN calls "something even more draconian" and a spokesman for the Shinawatras' political party compared to "running away from a tiger into a crocodile." Prayuth insists that he's "not a ruthless person," even as he muses that he'd "probably just execute" troublesome journalists and send dissidents—including over 1,000 academics, activists, and political opponents—to military facilities for "attitude adjustment." Under the current regime, no political gatherings of more than five people are allowed in the "land of smiles."

Intended to promote stability, the coup instead raises painful new questions. Will Thailand, after years of halfhearted efforts at popular rule, let the death of a king be the death of democracy? Or, as a Thai investment banker says, will "the change in the monarchy . . . force the country to grow up?"

"The challenge of my time is how to change from a closed society to an open society and do it peacefully," a Thai writer tells me. "We have a constitutional court that doesn't follow the constitution and nullifies an election that had 20 million people participating. . . . We have an election commission that delays elections. We have a human rights commission that doesn't care about human rights. There's a lack of moral fortitude and no courage anymore, and we need some elites to say something."

Perhaps reformers can take heart that the inspiration they need is right in front of them. Bhumibol is beloved in large part because the Thai people see him as treating everyone equally and caring equally about problems from the skyscrapers of Bangkok to the humblest village. Without him—and regardless of who takes the throne—Thailand needs to stop improvising its future and start replicating that sentiment not just in the palace but across the institutions of government.

Most important, as a Thai businessman says to me, people must "accept the fact that Thaksin opened a Pandora's box that can't be closed." Thailand in the 21st century can no longer afford to ignore the needs and aspirations of any of its citizens.

When asked why he had a racially integrated ensemble, Bhumibol's bandmate Goodman replied, "It takes the black keys and the white keys both to make perfect harmony." These words are well worth heeding. Otherwise it is the people of Thailand who will be singing the blues.

Myanmar Is More Than Aung San Suu Kyi

The World Post, April 13, 2015

OF ALL THE GREAT FILMS ABOUT AMERICAN POLITICS, ONE THAT HAS stood the test of time is a 1972 classic about the triumph of symbolism over substance, called *The Candidate*. Starring Robert Redford, it tells the story of an inexperienced son of a beloved political leader, who is pulled into politics on the strength of his family name. Turning the general election into a popularity contest, Redford's character encourages the media to play up the father/son angle, delivers a series of pleasant but empty speeches, and ultimately wins election to the United States Senate. In the film's iconic closing scene, as screaming fans chase him on the way to his victory speech, the Senator-elect dodges the crowd, pulls his political consultant into a room, and asks blankly, "What do we do now?"

Here in the nascent democracy of Myanmar, it is hard not to think of that film when considering the latest chapter in the political career of Aung San Suu Kyi. The daughter of this nation's slain founding father, Suu Kyi was awarded the 1991 Nobel Peace Prize for her opposition to Myanmar's military junta, which kept her under house arrest for 15 of 21 years after winning and then being denied the presidency in 1990. Gaining a seat in parliament in 2012, in just the second election since this nation re-opened itself to the world, Suu Kyi has been heralded by many as Myanmar's great hope, described as the "one politician who could play the role (here) that Nelson Mandela played in South Africa."

That is not how the script has played out so far. Instead, as with Redford in *The Candidate*, Suu Kyi's pursuit of the political spotlight has been relentless—but her use of that spotlight to advocate for something other than herself has been absent. The result, a longtime Suu Kyi supporter tells me, is that "many of the people who love her have been disheartened by her." A former aide agrees, adding that "people once thought she was super-human, but many have changed their minds." For the first time, the global media is beginning to tell the same story—suggesting recently that Suu Kyi is a "tarnished saint"; that her "halo" has been "dented"; that her reputation as "the

Iron Orchid . . . seems to have wilted"; that her leadership has fallen "short of expectations"; and even that her revered father, the assassinated General Aung San, "would be horrified" by the positions taken by his daughter.

But there is one influential audience that still sees Aung San Suu Kyi as largely infallible: Western leaders. British prime minister David Cameron has called himself one of her "greatest admirers." Europe, as a well-known European ambassador tells me, "looks at the country on a daily basis and only sees The Lady," as Suu Kyi is known here, adding, "If The Lady calls (German Chancellor) Angela Merkel and says 'go left' or 'go right,' she will." Above all, the new Republican leadership in the United States Congress is "completely in love with her," says a leading Western official. The head of that fan club is Senate Majority Leader Mitch McConnell, who not only counts himself as The Lady's foremost advocate in Washington, but has a framed letter from her on his office wall and a wife who is rumored to be personal friends with Suu Kyi.

It has locals here asking a pointed question: If the upcoming general election, due in November, doesn't end with Suu Kyi as president, will the West see the election as legitimate—or will it be the trigger for new sanctions to be imposed on the people of Myanmar? Put another way: if Suu Kyi's party, the National League for Democracy (NLD), follows through on the threat it made this month to boycott the election if the military-drafted constitution doesn't change, will that invalidate all of the progress this nation has made the past four years in the eyes of the West?

Drafted by junta leaders in 2008 in a process that deliberately excluded the NLD, and approved in a national referendum riddled with voting irregularities, Myanmar's constitution forbids anybody with a foreign spouse or children from becoming president. Since The Lady's late husband was British, as are their two sons, there is little doubt that the provision was drafted exclusively to prevent Suu Kyi from becoming president.

David Cameron has promised to lobby military leaders to have the provision overturned. US president Barack Obama, in a visit here last November, said the law "doesn't make much sense." Yet Shwe Mann, the formidable speaker of Myanmar's parliament, has repeatedly asserted that such a change would require a national referendum and insists it would be impractical to hold such a referendum until May 2016. And since it takes a 75 percent plus one vote of parliament to call for such a referendum—at a time when

unelected soldiers, by law, hold 25 percent of parliamentary seats—the odds
are long.

It has left Suu Kyi with an inescapable paradox: if she doesn't personally
and publicly lobby for the constitution to change before the election, then
nobody else will, since "people are not ready to go to the barricades for her,"
as a respected Burmese venture capitalist said to me. But if she repeatedly
lobbies (as she has) for the constitution to change merely to allow her to run
for president, she risks looking like she only cares about herself—which is
exactly what's happening. As a longtime ambassador from the Middle East
puts it, her continual petitioning has led many to think, "She is self-centered
and likes to lecture. She likes to play the role of being a symbol."

Of course, it might be a different story if Suu Kyi better balanced her
constant attacks on the political authorities for a change that would benefit
her with a much more rigorous use of her Nobel-enhanced moral authority
for change that would benefit others. But as all those negative headlines indicate, that has not happened. Summing up the essential problem, journalist
Jane Perlez observed of the criticism last November that Suu Kyi "has hesi-
tated to take on many of her country's biggest issues . . . and has failed those
who expected a staunch human right advocate."

Since joining parliament, Suu Kyi has rarely spoken out against the government's ongoing violence against rebels in northern Kachin State—part
of a festering, 70-year war between Myanmar's military and its 135 ethnic
minority groups. Her complete silence on atrocities being committed against
more than 1 million Rohingya Muslims—who are being herded into squalid
camps by the Buddhist majority in western Rakhine state—has drawn outrage from human rights advocates. Yet when Human Rights Watch came
to Myanmar in January, she said she was too busy to meet with them. Last
month, she even threatened legal action against an NLD member for supporting student protests against a controversial proposal to decentralize the
education system, leading one publication to ask if she "turned her back on
Burma's student protesters."

In one high-profile case where protesters were attacked by police for
protesting a copper mine, Suu Kyi sided with elites and company officials.
She has yet to raise her voice on a constitutional issue that will likely dominate discussion in 2016, which is the movement toward a federalist system of
government that solidifies a cease-fire agreement signed this month between

the government and 16 armed ethnic groups and grants minorities some degree of autonomy—without which Myanmar will never be a real country.

The disappointment felt by many former supporters was summed up by lawmaker U Thein Nyunt, who told a journalist last year, "We've followed her leadership for two decades, but she's failed to get any results for her country. It is obvious now that she is not considering the people, but only her own power."

Like *The Candidate*, The Lady still uses the image of her father as often as possible. But maybe, deep in her heart, she believes that she'll never be in a position to make real change until she's president. Maybe being hailed as her nation's savior is more pressure than she, or many of us, could live up to. Or maybe the substance of Aung San Suu Kyi never really matched the symbol—and the West would do well to see that Myanmar is much more than The Lady.

Myanmar's 40 to 72 Percent Problem

The World Post, March 15, 2016

IF YOU WALK THE STREETS OF THIS CITY AT THE END OF THE WORKDAY, you'll hear a distinctive sound: the clicks and taps synonymous with Myanmar's traditional sport, known as *chinlone*. Sharing certain roots with soccer, chinlone dates back 1,500 years, when it was played for the country's royalty. While the objective is simple—kick the small woven ball around a six-player circle without letting it touch the ground—the game is difficult. Players leap and dive, executing complex footwork with a combination of dance and martial arts moves. Their athleticism is all the more remarkable given the competition: there is none. The groups of men and women who play nightly do so without any incentive to "win." Victory comes in the artistry of the moves and the cohesion of the players. In chinlone, collaboration is the name of the game—which is deeply ironic when you consider the source.

The harmony of the sport stands in sharp contrast to the sectarian conflicts that have torn Myanmar apart, but it also provides a model for the nation's best hope: to move forward in unity. Until recently, that wasn't remotely possible. Myanmar (formerly called Burma) emerged from British colonial rule in 1948, only to slide into nearly seven decades of civil war as the country's ethnic nationalities battled the ruling Burmese military regime and each other. The conflict is far from over, but has reached a critical inflection point. In December, Aung San Suu Kyi's National League for Democracy (NLD) won a sweeping victory in Myanmar's first openly contested election in a quarter century, wresting power from the military-backed Union Solidarity and Development Party (USDP). With new leadership, this government is promising a new direction, but it has yet to engage with the entrenched problem of ethnic nationals.

For Aung San Suu Kyi, the question is basic: Will Myanmar move forward as a nation that offers full citizenship to the ethnic nationals that occupy 60 percent of the country's land, or will it continue to enforce a brand of Asian apartheid that disenfranchises non-Burman ethnics at every turn? For Western governments and businesses swarming into this nascent market today, the message must be clear: it is time to make the empowerment of all ethnic nationals—and a federal system that recognizes their autonomy—priority number one.

The roots of the problem go back centuries. Ethnic Burman kings once ruled over Myanmar's central Irrawaddy Valley, ringed by independent kingdoms in the surrounding hills. Today, these early divisions are reflected in the ethnic and religious groups that still occupy the horseshoe of mountainous territory that rings the country's urban and political center. In addition to ethnic Burmans, who make up the country's largest single nationality, Myanmar's government recognizes 135 ethnic groups living within its borders.

They have never truly, voluntarily, been united. After centuries of turf wars, Burma was first knit together in the 19th century—under a foreign flag. Britain colonized the country, but lost it to Japanese invasion in 1942. Postwar, Burmese statesman-general Aung San negotiated for the independence of a unified Burma. In 1947, he convened Chin, Shan, and Kachin tribal leaders in the town of Panglong, laying out a blueprint for peace that established mechanisms of self-governance in the ethnic national regions while extending to their citizens the "rights and privileges which are regarded as fundamental in democratic countries." But the dream died five months later, before Panglong was enacted, with the assassination of Aung San, kicking off violence that continues to this day.

A 1962 coup by the Burman army produced "a million dead, millions more displaced, an economy in ruins, and a robust military machine designed to fight the enemy within," as Burmese-American historian Thant Myint-U has written. Demonstrations against the oppressive ruling regime in 1988 resulted in the deaths of 3,000 protesters. In 1990, Myanmar held its first free elections in 30 years, and voted overwhelmingly to elect the pro-democracy party led by Aung San's daughter. The military, in response, refused to cede power and restricted her under house arrest for 15 years.

That daughter, of course, is Aung San Suu Kyi. "The Lady," as she is called, took the reins of government from some of her former captors in January, after her party won 80 percent of contested parliamentary seats last December. Although constitutionally prohibited from holding presidential office by a clause barring anyone with a foreign spouse or child (a provision drafted specifically for Suu Kyi, whose late husband and children are

British), she has vowed to be "above" the position, ruling the country via proxy. The democratic changes begun in 2011 marked the start of the most sustained political reform in decades. The Lady's international acclaim, her party's electoral victory, and her personal family history have raised hopes that she will shepherd Myanmar in a new direction.

Lost in this narrative is the country's ongoing battle with ethnic nationals. The divisions are so deep-seated here that population numbers are hard to come by. While it's long been thought that ethnic minorities comprise about 40 percent of the country's total population, longtime Myanmar watcher and Dictator Watch founder Roland Watson recently suggested, in a speech to an Asia Democracy Alliance Seminar in the US Congress, that the number is closer to 72 percent.

A 2014 census by the United Nations, the first in 30 years, was meant to settle the matter, despite the fact that millions of ethnics reportedly couldn't be reached. But the previous government refused to release the findings, blocking what was called "sensitive data on religious and ethnic minorities" for fear, as one high-ranking official put it, that its release might "shatter the state's peace and stability." While some speculate that the caution might reflect concerns that this overwhelmingly Buddhist nation has more Muslims than previously thought, potentially stoking violence, others took this as a sign that non-Burmans might rebel if they realized they had more than 70 percent of the population while holding barely 10 percent of the seats in parliament.

The fate of ethnic minorities overall is an issue on which The Lady has been frustratingly silent, leading some to offer that her silence was a smart political calculation until she held real power and could do something, while others wondered if it reflected a more troubling dismissal of ethnic rights more common among her fellow Burman Buddhists. Regardless of the motivations behind her previous quiet, she no longer has any excuses for inaction. The true test of her leadership will be whether Myanmar's new leader can finish what her father started in 1947.

That means federalism. Talk of "democracy" is meaningless to ethnic nationals, who have been disenfranchised because of their ethnicity and told what languages they can and cannot speak, which customs they can and cannot follow, whom they can and cannot marry, and how many children they can have because of their religion. To truly have a voice, ethnic states must be governed by their own leaders—just as states are empowered under the

United States' federal system. They must have a say in the development of their resource-rich lands and a share of the profits from that development. And in order for these changes to even be a possibility, they must be brought to the table in good faith to end current hostilities with the military.

Eight of the 15 major ethnic militias have signed a cease-fire with the outgoing USDP, but the holdouts downgrade the deal's legitimacy. Suu Kyi claimed during the campaign that federalism would be her top objective. But the remaining groups won't sign until they're confident the military won't turn on them.

A US Special Forces veteran currently advising ethnic groups on the ground tells me, "This is the most dangerous time in ethnics' history, because the international community is generally behind the central government." But a high-level peace negotiator tells me that "the reason the military was against federalism is because they were concerned that if power was decentralized, groups would use their power and secede. The military now understands it is about reintegration. They've changed their stance, and the ethnic groups have changed, too—but groups outside the process haven't changed much. They need to be part of the process and the talks."

If Western nations want to promote real progress, they must act—now.

For the United States, that means reinstating International Military Education and Training (IMET) for Myanmar's military—with the stipulation that all young, ethnic officers train alongside the Burmese. This is an unparalleled opportunity to teach the next generation of leaders respect for human rights and to model for them the success of America's integrated military and federal system.

Not since the height of apartheid in South Africa have people who represent the overwhelming majority of a country's total population been so disenfranchised. The truth is, if all ethnic nationalities, whether 40 percent or 72 percent of the population, aren't soon made full citizens of Myanmar, it won't be a nation. Aung San, master of the political version of chinlone, knew that. We'll soon see if his daughter understands the same.

US POLITICS

In the Philippines, Trump Is Already President

The World Post, November 2, 2016

HE IS A SEPTUAGENARIAN RIDING A WAVE OF ANGER AT THE POLITICAL establishment. He has hurled insults at everybody from women to the disabled to the Pope. At home, he has promised to pursue his agenda through unconventional, and likely illegal, means. Abroad, he has questioned the existing international order while threatening decades-long alliances.

Rodrigo Duterte, the recently elected president of the Philippines, is just the latest addition to a growing group of authoritarian strongmen—from Turkish president Recep Tayyip Erdoğan to Venezuelan president Nicolás Maduro—who rose to power on a platform of populist bombast. But it is only Duterte who has earned the title of his continent's Donald Trump.

As we enter the final days of the United States presidential campaign during a week in which Trump is inviting Americans to imagine the first 100 days of his presidency, Duterte's recently completed first 100 days provides a helpful counterpoint—or, more to the point, a cautionary tale. Duterte shows us that a reckless candidate with a dangerous autocratic streak and a knack for offensive statements can quickly become an even more reckless president with a destructive governing style whose continuing insults make his country look foolish in a way that threatens global stability. Filipinos who voted for Duterte in the hopes that the presidency would change him are now horrified to see those hopes being fulfilled in reverse, as they realize he's not getting better—he's getting worse.

Let's start with the murders being carried out in his name, which have rightly earned the world's revulsion since Duterte took office in early July. For Duterte, known as the "Death Squad Mayor" during the 22 years in which he led Davao City on the southern Philippine island of Mindanao, the primary claim to fame was that his police force brutally executed hundreds of drug dealers and drug users—often without judge, jury, or even arrest.

Like the "wall" that Trump promises to build between Mexico and
America or the "deportation force" the real estate magnate says he'll deploy
from house to house to kick out illegal immigrants, candidate Duterte had
a singular focus: drugs. He simply promised to kill the bad guys without
being troubled by inconvenient barriers like due process. His vow during
the campaign to dump the bodies of drug dealers "into Manila Bay" was
laughed off by some as election-year tough talk from the Philippines' own
"Duterte Harry."

But as he approaches the beginning of his fourth month in office, nobody
is laughing anymore: nearly 3,000 Filipinos have been slaughtered in extra-
judicial killings that have made a mockery of the island nation's long adher-
ence to the rule of law. Nearly half of these deaths have occurred not at the
hands of the police, but by vigilantes that Duterte has encouraged. Critics,
from Amnesty International to the United Nations to the Catholic Church,
have condemned his campaign. Some have accused him of violating international law.

In response, Duterte threatened to withdraw from the UN, after which
his foreign minister clarified that would never happen. He used allies in the
legislature to shut down a Senate inquiry into the killings while squashing
dissent. And he bragged on national TV about trampling due process and
heroically killing criminals (his youngest victim was five years old).

That impulsiveness has extended to foreign policy, where Duterte has
made brash autocratic pronouncements that ignore both geopolitics and his
country's longtime relationships. On a state visit to China last month, Duterte announced both a separation from the United States—which is the country's only treaty ally, one that has supplied 75 percent of all arms imports to
the Philippines since 1950—and a tentative agreement over disputed claims
in the South China Sea. Within 24 hours, his trade minister, who wasn't
consulted on the announcement, started walking back the separation. And a
Foreign Ministry spokesman admitted that, since Duterte never discussed a
potential deal with members of his government, the news caught him completely by surprise, too.

These actions have confused allies and unsettled neighbors. The visit to
China, Duterte's first state visit as president, created a rift with Japan, his
country's largest foreign investor. His words have made Southeast Asian
neighbors, like Vietnam, uneasy. He followed that up with a trip to Japan,

where he was quoted as saying he would kick all foreign troops out of his country in "maybe two years," which came as news to those diplomats in Manila enforcing a treaty, signed by the previous president, to station American troops in the country. All of it has "baffled" US officials—still troubled that Duterte disgustingly dismissed President Barack Obama as the "son of a whore" in early September—who worry that Duterte's antics are creating further uncertainty in a time of growing regional instability as China aggressively and illegally extends its reach into the South China Sea.

It has all proven to be too much for former president Fidel Ramos, who played an important role in Duterte's ascension, but who announced yesterday that he is resigning as Duterte's envoy to China. A few days earlier, he published a scathing editorial that accused the president of "unwittingly shooting himself in the mouth" while embarrassing his fellow citizens.

Like the 71-year-old Duterte, the 70-year-old Trump has questioned the value of US alliances, cozied up to China and Russia, and created a lingering uncertainty in international politics. He has lashed out at his critics, shown little regard for institutions or norms, demonstrated little respect for or understanding of how democracy works, and casually discussed violence with his followers.

Would Trump suddenly change if elected president? Could a candidate who doesn't embody a single quality embraced by Christians suddenly convert as if on the road to Damascus?

The performance of Trump's Filipino twin would seem to argue: not a chance in hell. He's much more likely to simply become an American Duterte with a Queens accent.

I'm not a huge fan of Hillary Clinton, but I'm even less a fan of extremists in public office, on either the right or the left—both of which exist to gum up progress for everyone else. It gives me heartburn to imagine that a Clinton presidency would elevate the profiles of her critics on the far left, including senators Bernie Sanders and Elizabeth Warren. But at least Clinton is bright and clear and a lot more centrist than she's been given credit for, especially on foreign affairs. Trump, by contrast, is every bit as dangerous and small-minded as he seems, in every way.

Unlike Duterte, a President Trump would command the world's largest economy, its largest military, and its second-largest nuclear stockpile. He would be at the head of an alliance network that has functioned as the cornerstone of international order for the past seven decades. In just over 100 days, Duterte has already incited international havoc. With the power of the US presidency, Trump could do so on a much bigger scale.

"America has lost," Duterte proclaimed in his speech at Beijing's Great Hall. It hasn't—yet. But we've already seen what a person with Duterte's callousness and carelessness can do. If we were to elect that kind of person to the Oval Office, then we may just prove him right.

America: consider yourself warned.

Huntsman Is the
Only Electable Republican

The Huffington Post, December 2, 2011

WATCHING THE REPUBLICAN PRIMARY RACE IS A LOT LIKE BEING AT A carnival. There's the roller coaster of polling numbers, the kind that has Herman Cain surging to the top one week, then collapsing as Newt Gingrich rises. Then there's the candidates themselves, who sometimes seem more like sideshow acts—each trying to top the next with a more outrageous statement—than actual contenders to be the next president of the United States.

I'm not sure which statement stands out the most—Michele Bachmann's assertion that the American Civil Liberties Union runs the Central Intelligence Agency; Cain trying to name the president of "Ubeki-beki-beki-beki-stan-stan"; Gingrich claiming that a luxury cruise around the Aegean gave him experience to deal with Greece's foreign debt crisis; Rick Santorum stating that he wants to go to war with China; or Mitt Romney asserting that if Barack Obama is re-elected, "Iran will have a nuclear weapon," but if Romney is elected, "They will not have a nuclear weapon." My favorite is Bachmann (again) telling an Iowa crowd that if she is elected, she will close the US embassy in Tehran. Only one problem: the United States hasn't had an embassy in Iran since 1980, when 52 Americans were held hostage for 444 days—something you would expect Bachmann, a member of the House Select Committee on Intelligence, to know.

This spectacle has not gone unnoticed by Republican primary voters. Yet many continue to entertain the Gingriches of the race out of a refusal to believe that someone like Romney could really be their only option, even as others seem convinced that Romney's electability in a general election should earn him the nomination.

I tend to side with those who argue that someone who seems devoid of core principles isn't electable, particularly after viewing a devastating video released this week of his many flip-flops. Lest we forget, it was Mitt Romney who published an op-ed in the *New Hampshire Union Leader* suggesting the

Obama Recovery Act was the largest expenditure ever during peacetime. I know of no definition of "peacetime" that involves fighting two wars at once. It was also Romney, just a few weeks ago, who called for privatizing veteran care, then reneged days later.

When you also consider Romney's close connections to Wall Street at a time when left and right alike are ready to storm the castle, it becomes difficult, if not impossible, to imagine Romney winning states like Michigan. Ohio might have been feasible had he not full-throatedly flip-flopped to support the anti-collective bargaining referendum, which Ohio voters rejected by a nearly two-to-one margin. And with Romney suggesting we let the housing market hit bottom as a solution to the housing crisis, it's hard to imagine victory in places like Nevada, where more than one in 10 families with children have lost their homes.

That leaves the Republican Party in a quandary. If Romney isn't actually electable, who is? Gingrich may be attractive to Republican primary voters, but with his own flip-flops, off-putting marital history, and decades' worth of outrageous statements, he may be the least electable Republican in a general election since Barry Goldwater. While [he may be] occasionally brilliant, it's hard to imagine America electing a man whose most pronounced character trait is bullying. Given how Bill Clinton played him during the 1995 government shutdown, it's scary to think what the Chinese might do with him.

So, what's the answer? I believe it is staring Republicans in the face: Jon Huntsman. He's not just the most experienced candidate—he's also the most electable Republican.

Huntsman has been dismissed from the start—largely because he worked for "the enemy," as Obama's first ambassador to China. Yet Huntsman is no less a conservative than Mitt Romney. He is pro-life, pro-business, and deeply religious; he even favors Congressman Paul Ryan's budget plan. He still holds that global warming is real, a position Romney has retracted.

Unlike Romney, however, Huntsman has the chops to be president. An ambassador three times over, a wildly popular two-time governor who cut taxes while creating jobs, and a global businessman, Huntsman is the only one standing who can negotiate with the Chinese. As Joe Klein recently observed, his ideas are resolutely conservative, and his economic vision "is the closest any candidate has come to diagnosing the real problems at the heart of the Great Recession—and proposing a reasonable path forward."

He is the kind of candidate independent voters fawn over. His quirks—he rides Harleys, played in a rock band, speaks Mandarin, and dropped out of high school before earning his general equivalency degree—helped him get re-elected governor in Utah in 2008 with a 58-point margin of victory, even as Republicans fell around him. Were he to win the nomination, he would be difficult for the president to attack. After all, if President Obama thought Huntsman unqualified, would he really have appointed him to the most important ambassadorship in the world?

Given his strengths, there's no question that Huntsman could be the 45th president, and that's not something lost on the president's campaign team. In 2009, David Plouffe, Obama's 2008 campaign manager and current senior advisor, worried publicly about facing Huntsman in 2012. His appointment to the ambassadorship was a pre-emptive parry.

Of course, winning the general election and winning the Republican nomination are different things. Huntsman is the only candidate onstage for whom the latter poses a substantially stiffer challenge than the former. Yet even considering the low polling numbers he currently shows, don't rule Huntsman out.

This same time last election, John McCain was trailing badly in Iowa, New Hampshire, and South Carolina. He even took out a personal loan just to keep his campaign afloat. And yet when Mitt Romney lost the Iowa caucus to a candidate who wasn't really a national contender, the opening for McCain became clear; he won New Hampshire and, eventually, the nomination.

It is not hard to imagine the same Mitt Romney losing to the same kind of far-right candidate in Iowa a month from now, giving Huntsman the window he'll need. It may not seem like it now, but my prediction is that Romney will lose in Iowa, and Huntsman will win in New Hampshire and eventually be the Republican nominee for president.

Ike's Most Prescient Insight 50 Years Ago Went Unspoken

The Huffington Post, May 10, 2011

HE WAS A WEST POINT GRADUATE, A FOUR-STAR GENERAL, THE HERO OF the allied assault on Adolf Hitler, and the first commander of NATO. During his eight-year presidency, he quadrupled America's post–World War II military budget, increased the share of the federal budget spent on defense to more than 50 percent, ballooned America's nuclear stockpile from 1,000 to 23,000 warheads, and oversaw a sitting army that was 10 times larger than the military he first joined in 1911.

And yet during the final months of his presidency, in 1960, Dwight D. Eisenhower was excoriated by the Democratic nominee for President—and eventual winner—John F. Kennedy, for under-spending on the military while allowing a dangerous, nonexistent "missile gap" to open between the United States and the Soviet Union.

Twenty-five years ago, I brought together a group of business executives for a dinner to reflect back on Ike's legacy and the broadside he launched against the US defense establishment in his famous Farewell Address. The dinner featured talks by Eisenhower's grandchildren, David and Susan Eisenhower. It was the first high-profile event hosted by Business Executives for National Security, a nonpartisan, not-for-profit organization I started in 1982, which is dedicated to applying best-business practices to help government leaders implement solutions to the most challenging problems in national security.

This week, Susan Eisenhower will speak once again, at a BENS dinner looking back on the 50 years that have passed since President Eisenhower's Farewell Address, and his much-quoted warning that America "must guard against the acquisition of unwarranted influence, whether sought or unsought, by the military-industrial complex."

Fifty years of hindsight would certainly suggest that Eisenhower was right: the danger of a large standing army coexisting with a permanent arms industry has made its influence felt in every American conflict since, from

Vietnam to Desert Storm to Afghanistan and Iraq. Today, Ike would not likely be surprised that America spends more on its military than the next 15 largest military budgets combined.

However, the military-industrial complex phrase is nearly always quoted out of the context of the speech. Eisenhower was neither condemning nor praising the military-industrial complex. Rather, he was making a much deeper point.

The essence of his warning to the American people, to which Ike returned again and again, was the need for balance—"balance between the clearly necessary and the comfortably desirable," "balance between cost and hoped-for advantage," and perhaps most important of all, "balance between the actions of the moment and the national welfare of the future."

Political balance is threatened, Ike said in his address, when interests or factions in the country wield unchecked power—either as the result of growth over time or as the result of specific crises.

Two such factions concerned Eisenhower enough that he mentioned them explicitly in the speech.

One faction was created by an alliance between elements of the federal government and the scientific community. Science could become corrupted by a dependence on federal funding, Ike warned, and, conversely, "public policy itself could become the captive of a scientific-technological elite."

The other faction that worried him was the military-industrial complex. The United States had been "compelled to create" a huge national-defense establishment, Ike said, because it could no longer risk an emergency improvisation in defense—precisely because it would face a "hostile" and "ruthless" ideology for an "indefinite" duration.

Ike didn't advocate the destruction of the military-industrial complex, any more than he advocated the dissolution of the federal government's relations with the scientific community. Instead, he characteristically urged his fellow citizens to keep the parts of the whole in proportion: "Only an alert and knowledgeable citizenry can compel the proper meshing of the huge industrial and military machinery of defense with our peaceful methods and goals so that security and liberty may prosper together."

The task of democratic leadership, Eisenhower said, was to ensure that democracy's boisterous, contending factions served the nation, but never directed it. It is a challenge that BENS has acted upon since its creation—where knowledgeable citizens have worked to foster an innovative business-government partnership over the past two decades. It has helped save the Defense Department billions of dollars while positioning it to meet the new challenges of the 21st century: helping to guard against cyberattack, tracking terrorists' financial assets, securing the nation's ports, and preparing state and local governments to deal with catastrophic events or terrorist attacks.

[Ike's address was] far from being a quickly constructed message at the end of his presidency, as historians have long believed; a stash of drafts and notes discovered last year in boxes stored for decades at the Minnesota family vacation home of Eisenhower speechwriter Malcolm Moos suggest otherwise. As the documents show, the themes underpinning the Farewell Address evolved through 21 drafts over the course of 20 months.

Interestingly, one theme left out of the final address spoke to another issue of balance: divided government.

Dated December 21, 1960, the newly discovered draft has Ike saying that even though he was a Republican who faced Democratic control of the House and Senate for most of his term, "We did not fall into bitter, irreconcilable factions which in other nations have paralyzed the democratic process. Rather, we worked together, and the business of the nation went forward, and the fact that it did so is . . . a credit to the . . . sense of duty displayed by the Congress."

Of all the prescient words spoken by Dwight Eisenhower 50 years ago, it may be those words, left unspoken, that a bitterly divided America is most in need of today.

An Open Letter to Mitt Romney

The Huffington Post, May 8, 2012

YOU FIRST BECAME A CANDIDATE FOR PUBLIC OFFICE 18 YEARS AGO, WHEN you ran for the United States Senate in Massachusetts against the incumbent, Edward Kennedy. The Senate you aspired to join then included a number of Republicans—from Bob Dole to William Cohen to John Warner—whose foreign policy expertise had earned them the title of "statesman." They were joined by equally impressive Democrats—like Sam Nunn and David Boren—who had helped presidents of both parties shape America's foreign policy in the second half of the 20th century.

All of them are gone from Congress now. If polls are to be believed, the only remaining senator from either party who readily fits into their company—who earned the title of "statesman" more than two decades ago, and who has played the central role for the United States on arms control the past 30 years—is about to lose his seat today to a candidate that has charitably been described as a "Tea Party hothead."

The shame of it is not that six-term Indiana Senator Dick Lugar is on the ropes because his lifetime 77 percent rating from the American Conservative Union is now judged as "too liberal" for the increasingly right-leaning politics of Indiana. That is a judgment for the voters to make. The shame of it is that the challenger, State Treasurer Richard Mourdock, has been allowed to turn "statesman" into a dirty word.

He mocks Lugar for his work to build a bipartisan coalition to keep nuclear weapons out of the hands of terrorists, stating flatly that "the time for being collegial is past—it's time for confrontation." Never mind that Lugar's "collegiality" is what helped protect Americans from weapons of mass destruction for 36 years, or that Lugar actually served in the US military while Mourdock avoided service and now believes that "some branches of the US military might not be necessary in the 21st century." In the new Republican party, America's real enemy isn't Tehran or Beijing—it's the Democratic National Committee. We've finally reached a point where the Tea Party believes its own bumper stickers.

As a World War II veteran who wore a Wendell Wilkie button to school and remembers when Republicans like Dwight Eisenhower embodied American foreign policy competence, I was willing to look past it when Sarah Palin called Africa a "country" four years ago. I was willing to look past Minnesota congresswoman (and Tea Party favorite) Michele Bachmann's assertion that her first act as president would be to close the US embassy in Iran (which isn't hard, since it's been closed since 1980). I was willing to give former senator Rick Santorum a pass for implying that he wanted to go to war with China and bomb Iran; Herman Cain for appearing as though he'd never heard of Libya; and Newt Gingrich for envisioning a foreign policy that extended to a colony on the moon.

But slapping Dick Lugar for being a statesman is a step too far.

Governor, now that you are the presumptive Republican nominee, you face a choice. You can either give in to the ignorance and intolerance of Tea Party purists like Richard Mourdock, who threaten to make the Know-Nothings of the 1840s look like MENSA members by comparison. Or you can engage in a wider, more intelligent discussion of the US role in the world at this crucial moment in history, the way Republican statesmen have in the past. There is no in-between.

If there has ever been a time to look past sharp elbows and public polemics, it is now. China is a dictatorship without a dictator which owns an ever-increasing share of US debt. Russia is a democracy with a dictator undermining personal freedoms while threatening to destabilize Asia's future. India is a democracy without a real decision-maker. Europe is a union without any real unity whose debt threatens a return to depression. Iraq and Afghanistan are wars turning to conflicts, as clashes over succession begin. Meanwhile, the Arab Spring has turned cold without any real stability in Egypt, Libya, or Yemen, as Syria burns.

This is a serious time for serious leaders, not people who claim they can see Russia from their porch or whose foreign policy experience extends to eating Belgian waffles at the International House of Pancakes. Americans deserve an honest debate about our role in the world.

For two centuries, people like Dick Lugar have understood the role that discretion and subtlety play in foreign policy. When you've sat across a table actually negotiating the fate of thousands of nuclear warheads, as he has, you're less inclined to throw out sound bites for the evening news, or issue sweeping public positions that win big points with bloggers while backing you into a corner.

The Mourdock Doctrine is not about keeping America safe; it's about making America stupid. It's exactly the kind of blind machismo that stumbled America into Iraq, mired us down in Afghanistan, and believes the United States can go it alone at a time when every major issue facing our country—from organized terrorism to climate change to commodity volatility to global pandemics—can only be solved in cooperation with other nations.

It says a lot about Richard Mourdock that the one ad playing on endless loop in Indiana right now features two clips of President Barack Obama, one with him saying, "I've worked with Republican senator Dick Lugar to pass a law," and the other, "What I did was reach out to Senator Dick Lugar."

In both cases, the clip ends before any context is provided. But if you play the full video, in the first clip, the president says, "I've worked with Republican senator Dick Lugar to pass a law that will secure and destroy some of the world's deadliest, unguarded weapons." In the second, Obama says, "What I did was reach out to Senator Dick Lugar, a Republican, to help lock down loose nuclear weapons."

Governor, before people like Dick Lugar came along, American schoolchildren practiced putting their heads under desks. Don't side with the people who now want us to put our heads in the sand.

EPILOGUE

How to Write a Column
Like Stanley Weiss

I'M SOMETIMES ASKED HOW I LEARNED TO WRITE THE COLUMNS I DO after living roughly the first six decades of my life without getting near a keyboard of any kind. (I'm not talking about the people who express with exasperation, "How do you write *those* columns?"—which, truth be told, happens from time to time, but not nearly as often as it happens with my Greek American friend, the columnist Taki).

Well, here's how. The pieces I write are somewhere between op-eds and columns. I try to write informative, insightful arguments about people and places that have often gone overlooked by mainstream commentators. I aim to ground my writing in the rich historical context of the country or countries involved.

When I visit a country, I meet with diplomats, generals, government officials, think tankers, and others to hear their take on the latest developments on the ground, and I use their quotes extensively (with permission, of course) so that the most recent insights inform my pieces.

There's no magic formula for what I write, but here are a few tried-and-true ways to get on the right track.

FIRST, BE CLEAR ON THE THESIS—AND THE PRESCRIPTIONS
There's a lot of noise in the political and policy debate today, so it's important to start with a clear, even provocative thesis. Should we re-evaluate the US-Saudi strategic relationship? Does Myanmar's Aung Sang Suu Kyi need to transition from icon to politician?

And for whatever problem I'm identifying, I ask: What's the solution? Do we want to partition a country along ethnic lines? Leverage US investment to bring opposing parties to the table? Improve Indonesia's infrastructure? I want to offer ideas that are meaningful, relevant, and practical.

Some of my pieces are educational. I try to bring information to the table that might inspire you to think about an issue in a different way, or might help you better understand what's going on within a country and why it matters—i.e., "You might not have thought about the ongoing ethnic civil war in Myanmar/how insane our support for Saudi Arabia is/the roots of the Shia-Sunni divide, etc., but this is something we should be thinking about and concerned with because it's only going to get worse." One article you'll see in this anthology, from March 2000, is "Be Quiet While Indonesia's Chess Master Makes His Moves," about then–Indonesian president Abdurrahman Wahid. In the article, I explain all the major players in Indonesian politics as pieces maneuvering on a chess board. That was when everything finally clicked for me as a writer.

Other pieces are constructive. Rather than focus primarily on explanation, I use these pieces to draw attention to an important issue, and I offer no more than three ideas for how to address the situation. Since I typically write several pieces on a country or region—usually after I have visited—I often lay the groundwork with an educational column and follow up with a more prescriptive one.

SECOND, RESEARCH IT YOUR WAY!

I learned long ago that great writing is really about great research. No matter how well-informed you are about a particular country, it will be virtually impossible to write anything of value without doing the research to get the details right, dig into the historical context, and find an interesting frame for your writing.

Everyone has their own way of doing research. One of my favorite family photos is of my wife, Lisa, and daughter, Lori Christina, poking fun at my obsessions—posing in bed with newspapers strewn across it, cigars hanging out of their mouths, a wine glass in one hand and a book in the other. Nowadays, I like to keep clippings together with multicolored plastic paper clips, marked up in red pen, in piles of light blue plastic folders.

Reputable publications and newspapers give me a sense for the latest developments in the world. Specialized publications focused on different regions or countries also provide unique perspective and detail. Journals, think tanks, and academic institutions update me on the universe of possible policy prescriptions that are already out there.

Then there's the history, and for my money, this is the most enjoyable part. As you'll see, my articles are heavy on historical context. In the urgency of the moment, we often forget about the long backstory that informs so many of the challenges we face today. If I'm writing about the Kurds, I could go all the way back to Saladin and the Crusades. If it's the South China Sea, I may trace the origin of the boundaries that are being disputed. Americans don't spend much time thinking about history. That's where my pieces can help.

THIRD, JUST WRITE

Unlike a lot of columnists, I tend not to dive into the argument immediately. Instead, I try to come up with creative ways to frame an issue, especially if it's largely unfamiliar to the audience. For instance, is there a simple, appropriate analogy, such as what X country/leader can learn from Y country/leader, or what if X American city were Y foreign city? Is there a hit movie playing that happens to highlight the cultural ties between two countries? Are we approaching the anniversary of a key event (treaty, war, prescient document, etc.)?

Frequently, I find interesting or fascinating nuggets to drive the frame. For example, the late king of Thailand liked jazz, so I built the piece around the idea of Thailand's democracy as an exercise in improvisation. If I'm writing about Mexico, maybe I'll draw on my own experiences of hearing from intellectuals in Mexico City or working alongside Mexicans of all backgrounds, deep in the mountains or in old mining towns. If I'm writing about Indonesia, maybe I'll reference that country's ancient tradition of shadow puppetry.

This is why it's important to have a clear sense of what you're arguing. If you have that in mind, when you see an insightful historical anecdote or interesting nugget, you'll quickly see how it can be applied to make that point. That then becomes the lead and, quite often, something I can call back to at the conclusion.

The rest of the writing is reasonably straightforward. I first learned from writing op-eds for BENS: after your colorful hook, you articulate your thesis by the third paragraph, build a convincing argument using all of that research, and end on a memorable note that ties it all together. The major newspapers, of course, want all that done with no fuss, in a tight space. Most of my articles after BENS, though, take the time and space to elaborate in a way you can't often do in an op-ed for the *New York Times* or the *Wall Street Journal*.

I've had the pleasure of bringing perspectives from important countries and figures all over the world to the United States, and I value the chance to make a constructive contribution to the discussion on politics and international relations. In all those years, only one of my columns has gotten someone into trouble.

I once quoted Indonesian general and presidential candidate Susilo Bambang Yudhoyono (known as SBY), with his permission, as saying, "I love the United States, with all its faults. I consider it a second country." It was an innocent quote that reflected the importance of the US International Military Education and Training (IMET) Program that SBY had participated in.

Former president Megawati Sukarnoputri, who was running against SBY in the election, saw a chance to cause some damage. She started relentlessly citing the quote to suggest that SBY preferred the United States to Indonesia.

SBY ultimately won, but the next time he saw me, he had a request. "Can you do me a favor?" he asked.

"Sure, what?" I replied.

"Please don't write about me."

Index

About the Author

STANLEY A. WEISS WAS FORMERLY CHAIRMAN OF AMERICAN PREMIER, INC., a mining, refractories, chemicals, and mineral processing company. He is Founding Chairman of Business Executives for National Security (BENS), a nonpartisan organization of senior executives who use the best practices of business to strengthen the nation's security. Mr. Weiss has written widely on public policy matters. His work has appeared in the Huffington Post, *International Herald Tribune*, *The New York Times*, *The Wall Street Journal*, *The Washington Post*, and *The Washington Times*. He is the author of two books. The first, *Manganese: The Other Uses*, is the definitive work on the non-metallurgical uses of manganese. In 2017 he published the bestselling memoir *Being Dead Is Bad for Business*.

A former fellow at Harvard's Center for International Affairs, Mr. Weiss is the recipient of an honorary Doctor of Humane Letters from Point Park University in Pittsburgh, Pennsylvania. He currently serves on the Board of Directors for Premier Chemicals and is a member of the Council on Foreign Relations, the American Ditchley Foundation, the International Institute for Strategic Studies, and the Royal Institution in the UK Mr. Weiss has served on the Board of Directors of Harman International Industries; the Board of Visitors of Georgetown University School of Foreign Service; and the advisory boards of the RAND Center for Middle East Public Policy and the International Crisis Group. Mr. Weiss is married with two children. He divides his time between his residences in London and Gstaad, and his office in Washington, D.C.